Professional Acclaim for *Death Notification: A Practical Guide*

"Mr. Leash has written a sensitive, yet pragmatic book, full of how-to's in a field where that is rarely done. The examples he uses are revealing and illuminate many of the personal struggles we all encounter in similar arenas. Regardless of one's clinical style, the techniques and guidelines are applicable to all professionals performing this delicate task."
—Peg Cannon, MSW, LCSW, Director, Continuity of Care
Kaiser Foundation Hospital

"This book provides far more than the title implies. **Death Notification** *will enable staff to deliver this news based on professional knowledge rather than personal discomfort levels. Mr. Leash provides guidelines on relatives' immediate needs that have not been available, until now, in 'death and dying' literature. Staff who read this will experience less self doubt and self criticism."*
—Mark A. Robinson
CEO, Family Trauma Seminars

"Few things evoke more feelings of helplessness in a health care provider than having to inform family members of a loved one's death. Mr. Leash helps to dispel that discomfort with specific guidelines for notification of sudden death that are soundly based on theoretical principles of grief management as well as his own research and direct experience as a psychotraumatologist."
—Diane Salter, LCSW, Supervising Social Worker, Critical Care
University of California Davis Medical Center

"Before I went into law enforcement, I was a practicing funeral director for 12 years—dealing with issues of death and bereavement on a regular basis. It was with particular interest that I reviewed **Death Notification.** *Although law enforcement officers must often play the role of 'tough guy,' this wonderful book will encourage our personnel to develop compassion and sensitivity for one of the most difficult tasks they will ever face.* **Death Notification** *should be read by every officer and every officer-in-training!*
—Kevin R. Scully, Chief of Police
Burlington, Vt.

"This sensitive, insightful and extremely helpful guide to death notification, grief management, and organ donation, punctuated with *instructive anecdotes, should be read by a*ll health care providers, *especially those who regularly care for ext*
—Th
Center for Biom

D1482830

Death Notification:

a practical guide to the process

by

R. Moroni Leash, LCSW, MSHCA

Upper Access, Inc.
Hinesburg, Vermont

Cover design by Sue Storey
Illustration by Ella Brackett

Upper Access, Inc.
One Upper Access Road
P.O. Box 457
Hinesburg, Vermont 05461
802-482-2988
(Book ordering information) 1-800-356-9315

Library of Congress Cataloging-in-Publication Data

Leash, R. Moroni (Russell Moroni), 1958 -

Death notification : a practical guide to the process / by R. Moroni Leash.
    p. cm.

Includes bibliographical references and index.
ISBN 0-942679-08-3 (paperback) : $19.95

    1. Death. 2. Death—Psychological aspects. 3. Grief—Management.
I. Title.
HQ1073.L43 1993
306.9—dc20
                                           93-25314
                                             CIP

Dedication

I dedicate this work to the many professionals who extend themselves in helping others deal with the emotional trauma that death brings. It is my sincere hope that they may find themselves further strengthened by the information presented here.

I also dedicate this book to my wife, Moncen, and our young son, Ryan. The countless hours it took to research and prepare this material for publication required much time away from them. Their patience has been much appreciated.

Acknowledgments

I gratefully acknowledge the assistance of Ralph Johnson, Ph.D., of California State University, Sacramento. His suggestions and encouragement have significantly contributed to the success of this endeavor.

I also acknowledge the help of Glenda Olsen, who provided assistance with the data analysis format; Frank Nieto, Director, and Diane Salter, Critical Care Coordinator for Adult Social Services, University of California, Davis, Medical Center, Sacramento, for their enthusiasm and assistance with this work; and those members of the CSUS Thesis Committee and the UCD Human Subjects Research Committee, who examined and approved the study that was done.

I am grateful to Cliff Collins of PC Professionals, who provided substantial assistance with formulation of the graphs and tables in the text, and Bonnie Richardson who helped with the initial editing.

My heartfelt thanks also are extended to Peg Cannon, LCSW, Clinical Director of Social Services at Kaiser Foundation Hospital, Sacramento. Her allowances for the time required in the final stages of publication truly made a difference and made those last days "survivable."

No acknowledgement would be complete without mention of the publishers. Steve and Lisa Carlson have been extraordinarily patient and tolerant during the extended period required for completion of this writing. Numerous transitions came and went in my life, each requiring that time and energy be diverted from my efforts in completing this work. Their understanding and encouragement were priceless.

I also thank the more than 400 families and professionals who participated in the formal research project incorporated in this writing. While they cannot be personally identified, they have provided invaluable assistance in identifying the critical elements and guidelines of a successful notification. Consequently, their efforts will benefit many, many families for years to come.

There are many others who have contributed to either this work *or* my sanity while I have labored to complete it. They have my heartfelt thanks.

Death Notification
a practical guide to the process

Contents

Part I
The Notification Process

Within a Hospital
  • Notification by a Physician • Notification by a Nurse •
  Notification by a Psychotraumatologist • Notification complexity • Case
  Vignette 1.1

In the Field
  • Field Notifier Selection Guidelines • Law Enforcement Officers
  • Emergency Medical/Fire Department Staff • Coroners Staff •
  Military Personnel

Legal Issues in Notification

Contraindicators for Designators

Identification of the Deceased
  • Accident Co-victims • Ambulance/Transport Staff • Law
  Enforcement Staff • Contents of the Deceased's Pockets •
  Miscellaneous Papers and Cards • Other Belongings • Telephone
  Directory Assistance • Vehicle Registrations • Physical Descrip-
  tion • Fingerprints/Missing Persons Reports • Cautionary Notes

Family Contact
  • Timely Notice • Family Confirmation of Identity

Death Debriefing
  • Military Issues

Information and Crisis Management
  • Drug Abuse Deaths • Homicide • Complicating Information

Conclusions

Part II
Grief Management

Part III
Research Presentation

Appendices

About the Author

R. *Moroni Leash* is currently employed by Kaiser Foundation Hospitals in Sacramento, California, where he provides grief and crisis counseling. He served for several years as a clinical social worker, providing trauma counseling services at the University of California, Davis, Medical Center. Later, he worked as a psychiatric evaluator in the same facility. This hospital is the designated Regional Trauma Center for northern California and parts of Oregon and Nevada.

During the period in which the research for this writing was being completed, this hospital was the busiest trauma center in the United States, handling more than 3,500 major traumas each year. Consequently, Mr. Leash brings into this writing a wealth of experience and stands as one of the nation's foremost specialists in the psychological impact of traumatic bereavement.

Mr. Leash has taught numerous classes on topics related to this subject, including grief management, psychosocial issues in trauma care, management of families in crisis, critical care nursing, and family crisis management. For several years, Mr. Leash was a continuing presenter for grief management at the regional "Trauma Is Teamwork" symposium, held annually in Sacramento, California.

He has completed two master's degrees: one in health care administration from California State University, Long Beach, and another in social work from California State University, Sacramento. His bachelor's degree was in psychology, also from California State University, Sacramento.

As a practicing mental health therapist, Mr. Leash is a licensed clinical social worker (LCSW), and has a California educational counseling credential —Pupil Personnel Services (PPS)—for use in elementary and secondary educational work settings.

Mr. Leash served for two years as a missionary for the Church of Jesus Christ of Latter-Day Saints (LDS), and was assigned to the Thailand Bangkok Mission. Consequently, he speaks, reads and writes Thai fluently, as well as some Laotian and Northern Thai dialect.

Introduction

On March 21, 1984, Colleen, a 20-year-old model shot herself with a .22 caliber rifle. By midnight her mother had been notified of the shooting, which was to prove fatal, and frantically called the hospital to ask about her condition. "Her condition," she was told, ". . . is that a bullet went in one side of her head and came out the other side. What do you want me to tell you?"[1]

—*People Weekly* Magazine. March 14, 1988, p. 86

The pronouncement of such news is extremely traumatic—to the receiver as well as to the one who must deliver it. Efforts to distance oneself from a family's emotional pain can cause great anxiety, sterile professionalism, or even a sarcastic comment, as above. Why is it so difficult to manage this universal and inevitable part of life?

Well-trained professionals may be able to provide an accurate "expiration scenario," or clinical explanations for the cause of a death. But to answer the questions that inevitably follow is far more difficult. "Why *my* loved one?" "Why *now*?" "How could it have happened in *this* way?" Without readily available answers, it often seems preferable to avoid any extensive dialogue, and thus ward off the uncomfortable feelings.

As a trauma counselor for a regional trauma center, I have personally delivered hundreds of death notifications and have assisted with many more. Because of the nature of the cases handled at a trauma center, most of these deaths were sudden, unexpected losses, which were exceptionally distressing to all involved.

When called upon to deliver, or even assist with, a death notification, nearly all professionals become uncomfortable. It is easy to see why. In virtually every setting researched for this text, there existed numerous conflicting opinions regarding the "proper" notification process and an absence of any formalized policy or procedure. Further, the diversity of perspectives crossed all professional boundaries, leaving no room for any practical synthesis of opinion.

---

[1] *Used with permission of People Weekly publications.*

An extensive literature review for this work revealed only a handful of articles related to death notification. Even these were written in a cursory manner, with few guidelines to assist the professional in the process. The void of information, coupled with professional conflict, contributes to the anxiety and frustration in an inherently frustrating situation.

Not only is the *wording* of a notification statement often contested, but its *staging* is hotly debated as well. Numerous questions arise. Should notifications take place on the telephone? What if a family demands it? Should families be contacted late at night, or should notification of a death wait until morning? Should law enforcement personnel be called to deliver the news of a death? Is it more dangerous for the family to drive to the hospital with the certain knowledge of a death, or to drive uncertain of a loved one's condition?

Because there were no definite answers to these questions, it became obvious that a formal protocol was needed. This protocol had to ensure the best presentation for the family and also reduce the potential for injury to all involved, should they respond poorly to the news. To guarantee broad applicability, the protocol needed to be based upon more than the personal opinions of a small group of health-care professionals.

With this in mind, I was able to design a survey instrument, administered to over 400 people integrally involved with some aspect of the death process. These included 200 medical professionals involved in managing acute traumatic injuries and death, 100 university students studying "death and dying" curricula, and 100 families experiencing the traumatic injury or acute illness of a family member. The analysis and interpretation of these data provided the basic information necessary for the formulation of the needed guidelines. The research material is presented in Part III of this book.

This investigation was also based on detailed personal observations. As a psychotraumatologist, I not only had responsibility for delivering or assisting with notifications of death, but for providing all follow-up services as well. This gave me the rare opportunity to observe individual and family reactions to various notification strategies throughout the initial grieving process. I observed the emotional impact of the notification strategy, the quality of interactions among family members, their responses at the time of viewing the deceased, their ability to consider and meaningfully discuss organ and/or tissue donation, and their capacity to deal with additional family arrivals and telephone calls.

The research indicates that notification of sudden or impending death should include the following key elements:

1. A timely announcement of the death
2. Control of the physical environment of the notification
3. Details of the efforts to save the life

4. Clinical explanation of the causes of death
5. Selection of staff with special skills in crisis intervention and grief management to facilitate the mourning process.

Because the primary purpose of this writing is to clarify the staging and delivery of death notifications, this book will cover each of these key elements. Brief summaries of basic grief reactions and their management are given to provide a more complete view of the process. Case vignettes are also used to illustrate some of the difficulties involved in death notification. Some aspects of acute grief associated with particularly difficult losses are identified. Various management strategies designed to aid practitioners in facilitating positive family coping responses are also suggested.

When the results of this research study were first released, I presented them at the Regional Trauma Symposium for Northern California. Following this presentation, I received numerous requests for lectures and classes and heard the oft-repeated comment, "You should write a book on this subject." The comment was not flattery of my presentations. It reflected the desperate need for an authoritative reference.

Responsibility for delivering or assisting in death notification falls, at least occasionally, on the shoulders of many different categories of professionals, including those in the fields of health care, law enforcement, clergy, the military, coroners' staff, rescue work, firefighting, funeral service, and so on. While the focus is, necessarily, on initial notifications to next of kin, many of these professionals also find themselves in the position of breaking the news to others. Therefore, I have tried to make this book accessible to professionals who do not have formal training in psychology or related fields, as well as to those with specific mental health skills who face this difficult assignment.

I hope this book also will provide further impetus for including social workers and other professional counselors in the management of this critical aspect of death. To this end, some information has been provided solely for skilled practitioners, to assist them with an accurate assessment and method of handling various complex grief scenarios. As the field of psychotraumatology grows, the burden of death notification can then be shared with other professionals to assist all involved.

Any comments or suggestions from readers will be warmly welcomed. Should future editions of this book be requested, your suggestions and experiences can assist in refining it. Please send them to me in care of the publisher.

R. Moroni Leash
Sacramento, California

Part I

The Notification Process

Chapter 1

Initiating the Notification Process

The first step in the notification process is to identify the person or persons responsible for delivering the news of death. Most death notifications follow one of three specific scenarios: a death in a hospital, a death "in the field," or the death of a soldier in active military service (typically at some great distance from home). Each of these situations involves a variety of staff from which appropriate notifier selections can be made. Let us begin by looking at the designation process in a hospital setting.

Within a Hospital

In a hospital, the task of death notification traditionally falls to a physician. Where a team of physicians is involved, it is usually delegated to that professional immediately directing the life-saving efforts. In a teaching hospital, this responsibility may fall to the most senior-ranking staff member, or a person he or she designates for the task.

Occasionally, however, family members may arrive when the primary physician is unavailable. This is not uncommon in an emergency room or trauma center setting. In such situations, the initial notification is often delegated to a nurse, pending the physician's later availability. A family also may arrive unexpectedly and press toward a newly deceased patient's room when a physician is not present. In that instance, too, it may fall to an available nurse to handle the notification until the physician can be located.

While a physician or nurse should always be the primary provider of any detailed medical explanation for the cause of a death, there are often numerous other people who could be called upon to assist with other, more immediate, aspects of notification. These include counselors, social workers, and chaplains. In practice, any of these professionals could provide an initial death statement, pending additional medical details. It even may be preferable to have such individuals do so because of their special skills and training in managing the psychological trauma associated with death. Let us look at these approaches in greater detail.

Notification by a Physician

In the research presented in Part III, families were asked whom they would choose to provide death notification. Despite a variety of selections available, the unanimous first choice was the physician. (See Chapter 13, page 222.) Current literature supports this conclusion. For example, Hollingsworth (1977), a physician himself, states that the task of notification should always be assumed by the medical doctor. While he also advocates that a physician should enlist the help of others in this process—suggesting that the physician be accompanied by a primary nurse and a social worker, it is clearly his expectation that the physician will make the death statement.

There is a strong case to be made for this approach. The physician is the person ultimately responsible for the treatment of the patient. Only the physician can provide detailed medical information and explanations regarding the resuscitative efforts made and the cause of death, and then may be able to offer support and comfort as well.

Regardless of who tenders the initial death statement, contact with the physician is a vital element in the notification process and one that should not be supplanted. Families seem to accept the reality of death more quickly when it is confirmed by a physician. This results from the physician's professional demeanor and discussion, which lends authority, and hence finality, to the news of the death—a critical contribution.

This does not mean that the physician must always be the first to announce a death. But the physician must always be an active participant, available to the family.

Notification by a Nurse

In researching survivors' perceptions of unexpected death, one study (Jones, 1981) noted that many families interviewed indicated that they would have preferred to have been notified by a nurse. They expressed feelings that the nursing staff exhibited more compassion and more readily acknowledged the significance of the deceased than did the physician in charge. While the physician did appear to be more knowledgeable about why the person had died, he or she was perceived as being less concerned that a loss had occurred.

There may be several reasons for this perception. The first, and most obvious, is the availability of time. Nursing staff members usually spend more personal time with the family, both before and after the death, than does the physician. Consequently, these two professions may develop somewhat divergent perspectives regarding their patients. A nurse has more continuous contact with patients, and thus becomes more familiar with them, their visitors, and family issues. A hospital physician, on the other hand, is often required to move rapidly from patient to patient in a variety of settings, providing services through a much narrower window of contact. Unless the hospital physician also has been responsible for personal medical care for many years prior to the death, there is little opportunity to develop and maintain familiarity beyond diagnosis and treatment issues.

These understandable differences in emotional investment surface during the death notification process, and the family is able to perceive them in many ways. They are revealed in the focus of the conversation, the expressive words chosen, and the notifier's responses to the family's feelings. If the family members are familiar with the notifier and sense a genuine concern for their loved one and themselves, they will feel cared about, supported, and strengthened. For these reasons, notification by the primary nurse can be an appropriate choice.

In addition to familiarity concepts, the nursing profession itself is viewed in a caring, tender light. It is much more common for family members to speak affectionately of "our nurse" than of any other staff person (Jones, 1981). Consequently, it is important for them to see and know that this person was there at a critical time. The presence of their nurse can provide meaningful and caring support. The family can experience its greatest sense of security when all hospital staff members are involved with support and resolution of the death.

Notification by Social Worker, Chaplain, or Counselor

In the face of the substantial arguments for physician- or nurse-initiated notifications of death, there is a powerful argument to be made for designating a social worker, chaplain or counselor to deliver the *initial* news.

Medical personnel are taught how to preserve life. This concept is integrated into their thoughts and activities. Death is not acceptable, either personally or professionally. Providing a death notification can carry with it a subtle connotation of failure. Both the physician and the family feel a need for explanations. This need becomes very acute in the highly volatile atmosphere of the notification process. To have to break this news may place undue stress on the physician or nurse and on the family.

Further, "running a code[2]" is tremendously taxing, both emotionally and physically. It is unfair to bring a nurse or physician from a hectic,

---

[2] *The term* code *derives from the term "Code Blue," which is announced over a hospital's communications system when summoning medical personnel to a resuscitative event. It is used only in cases of respiratory or cardiac arrest, and is broadcast hospital wide until sufficient numbers of medical personnel have arrived to manage all needs of the situation. "Running a code" is a phrase used referring to that physician who is directing the resuscitative activities—"She's running the code."*

frustrating "code" experience, which wasn't successful, and then immediately require him or her to be calm, empathetic, and caring. It is far better for another professional to make the initial notification statement and then answer simple, straightforward questions regarding the death. Background information can be given regarding events at the onset of an injury or sudden illness (e.g., accident, or heart attack), helping family members to grasp more fully the reality of the event. In emergency situations, such information is often unavailable to health care providers, as they may have had little time to glean more than the medical information immediately required for treatment of the patient.

After the initial notification, and with the family in some state of composure, the physician or nurse can then provide a formal death pronouncement, including the more medically detailed information. In this way, the family members are better able to understand the information given them and to ask more germane questions. This staging retains all the integrity and value of a "physician/nurse notification," while attending more fully to time and emotional factors.

The brief interlude for the physician or nurses allows time to complete consultation and charting, and to finalize feelings regarding the ultimate cause of the death. Further, it is an opportunity to unwind emotionally from a traumatic experience without leaving the family members waiting for information, or being thrust into their midst unprepared. In addition, this staging limits the medical provider's exposure to the emotional stress of dealing with a family's initial grief response, particularly if it is atypical (e.g., hostile, violent, suicidal, homicidal). In this way, she or he can more easily return to managing other difficult medical issues, especially when working in a volatile emergency department setting.

While my research shows that the physician was deemed the appropriate individual to make a death notification, it also indicates that *who* notifies is the least significant variable in the notification process. Far more important were *how and when* the notifications were made. Even *where* the notification is made was deemed slightly more important. This leaves ample room for another professional to assume the initial task. (See Chapter 13, page 225.)

One noteworthy exception should be mentioned here. In spite of the fast-paced, impersonal medical systems of today, there are still primary care providers who have grown extremely close to their patients and family members. This is especially true of care-givers for the elderly, who may have chronic illnesses for which they are seen often. In such situations, the primary-care physician may be the person to whom the family will respond best. No substitute can be made for the long-standing rapport they may enjoy. Such a rapport will be of immense value at the time of a loss.

Regardless of these suggestions, within a hospital setting the difficult task of notification ultimately belongs to the physician alone. His or her recommendations and requests should be adhered to, even if they appear to conflict with accepted procedure or idealized structure. In a legal sense, the physician accepts full responsibility and liability for a death and should receive full support and cooperation in bearing this burden. And, reciprocally, while others may support the physician, as described above, if they are unavailable or reluctant to do so, it is the physician who must accept this task.

Notification by a Psychotraumatologist

With the development of hospital trauma centers, the new and important field of psychotraumatology has begun to emerge. Typically, a *psychotraumatologist* is someone with a degree in medical social work or pastoral counseling—usually at the graduate or post-graduate level—and one who has developed special expertise in dealing with the psychological impact of traumatic injury and death. Graham (1981) coined the title "psychotraumatologist" and notes that the goals of the psychotraumatologist are twofold: to alleviate the acute psychological distress that accompanies physical trauma and death, and to provide primary prevention of post-traumatic stress disorders. In facilities where there are personnel with applicable background and skills, providing them the opportunity to pursue this specialization can be very helpful indeed.

Notification Complexity

Death notification is always traumatic. Difficult family dynamics and death scenarios can make it much more complex. To understand the dynamics of the notification process, and the traumatic impact it has on all involved, consider the following case example. All names have been changed.

Case Vignette 1.1

Rachel was a 20-year-old caucasian female. For about two years, Rachel had been dating Ron, a 22-year-old caucasian male. Their relationship had always been erratic. They were informally engaged at one time, but were now considering ending their commitment. This became frustrating to Rachel, who decided to "bait" Ron back in. She elected to do this by accepting a date with someone Ron didn't know (in fact, she was only barely acquainted with him herself), to provoke Ron's jealousy. She hoped that this maneuver would rekindle their relationship.

She arranged for Ron to be aware of the date, and when it would occur. Her plan worked perfectly. When her date drove up at about 8 P.M., Ron was hiding in the bushes outside. Rachel entered the car and they started to leave. At this point, Ron came out of the bushes, furious. He flung open the car door and attempted to pummel the driver. The driver was, of course, terrified. Ron was a big man, whom he didn't know. The driver was only briefly acquainted with Rachel and didn't know she had a boyfriend. Ron tried to pull him from the car. In a desperate effort to escape the assault, the driver attempted to speed away, but Ron stepped into the moving vehicle and continued his efforts to injure the driver.

Meanwhile, Rachel was screaming, "Leave him alone! Ron, Leave him alone! Stop it, please!" The driver, now fully terrorized, tried to dislodge Ron from the vehicle by making a sharp right turn. Ron fell away from the vehicle —head-first into a fire hydrant. His skull was fractured upon impact, and he lapsed into unconsciousness.

At the hospital, it was a routine night with comparatively minor injuries coming into the emergency room. At 8:30 P.M., an ambulance arrived, designated "Code 3." It was Ron. Rachel arrived just a few minutes behind him, accompanied by her parents. She was nearly hysterical. I took her to a small private room where I informed her that Ron's condition was critical. I provided hot coffee for the three of them, assured them that I would keep them informed, and left to check on Ron's status. Ron had already undergone a "peritoneal lavage" (a minor surgical procedure to check for internal bleeding), and was being taken to have a CT scan. The trauma resident informed me that his pupils were not reactive, he was not responsive to pain, and was now exhibiting "decorticate posturing"—all indicators of a massive cerebral injury.

I returned to see how the family was doing and found Rachel's father waiting outside my office door. "I know it's bad," he said. "I think you should be aware that Rachel has a previous history of suicide attempts. In fact, she was hospitalized here before. I'm not sure how she'll respond if Ron dies."

Then, Ron's family arrived. I was paged to the emergency room lobby and found his mother, sister, and older brother waiting. They demanded to see Ron immediately. I explained that he was in the CT scanner and that they wouldn't be able to see him until the scan was completed. Ron's older brother then addressed me. He was a large man, about 30 years old, dressed in blue jeans, a worn sheep-skin jacket, and a cowboy-style hat. "If my brother dies," he said, "I'm gonna kill her! (Rachel). You mark my words! I'll kill her!" I excused myself and asked them to wait a moment while I found a quiet place where they could have some privacy.

Going quickly to my office, I escorted Rachel and her family to a waiting room on the other side of the hospital. I explained that Ron's family had arrived, that they were very upset, and that I thought it might be better for the two families to stay apart for now. No one argued with me, and the father and mother nodded knowingly. Rachel was still crying and wouldn't look at me. Her parents sat on either side of her, offering support.

I returned to the lobby and gathered Ron's family into my office. There were now more family members present; two other siblings, also older than Ron, and their spouses had arrived. I attempted to comfort the older brother. When I placed my hand on his shoulder in a comforting gesture, he spun away, saying, "Keep your hands off me!" I seated them all comfortably and asked for information about Ron's medical history.

Following this, I returned to the CT Scan viewing room, where the neurosurgeon informed me that Ron had a major bleed in the temporal lobe of his brain. It was beginning to swell badly. There would be immediate surgery—a craniotomy to remove the blood clot and any surrounding damaged brain tissue. The surgeon hoped that this would give Ron's brain sufficient room to swell and avoid brain-stem herniation. His prognosis for survival was very poor.

Meeting again with each family, I noted that their moods had not changed. Rachel was now verbalizing, "I don't know if I can live with this! Please, don't let him die!" Back with Ron's family, the older brother reiterated his earlier threat, but with less vehemence. After comforting the families for a few minutes, I headed back to the emergency room to address other issues that had been left unattended upon the families' arrivals. In the process of this, I called the hospital's staff police for consultation and to alert them to the threats being made by the patient's brother. They agreed to stand by, pending my further contact. For the next 30 minutes I completed other pressing tasks and then headed to surgery to see if there was any further news about Ron.

As I approached the surgical area, a young medical resident dressed in surgical scrubs stepped through the double doors. Recognizing me, he asked to speak with Ron's family. He looked harried, with blood on his shoe-coverings and beads of perspiration on his brow. As I walked with him, he informed me that Ron had died on the surgical table.

I told him about several of the sensitive issues with Ron's family and alerted him that the notifications would probably be traumatic. I did not yet speak about Rachel's family situation, because I did not want to overwhelm him with extraneous information. I noticed that he was hurrying, as if he wanted to complete the notifications quickly. "This is bad," he repeated several times. "This is really bad."

When we arrived at the office, I entered first, introducing the physician as he entered. He looked at the family for a moment, and then, without sitting down, abruptly stated, "Ron's dead." Ron's sister screamed. The mother started to cry. Looking at me, the physician said, "I'll be outside," and left the office. The older brother bolted out the door behind him.

Quickly sizing the situation, I sent a brother-in-law, who appeared somewhat composed, after Ron's brother to see if he was okay. Leaving the office for a moment, I placed a call to the security staff, alerting them to the fact that the brother, who had voiced homicidal threats, had left my office and that the threatened individual was in the main lobby. They agreed to post staff nearby. I returned to the office and helped calm and comfort the other family members. After a few minutes, I left the office. I was relieved that some time had passed, certain that the physician would have left, allowing me to make the notification to Rachel's family without his assistance. To my surprise, however, he was pacing outside the office. To my further surprise, he had somehow heard about "Ron's fiancée," and asked to see her and her family.

Having just struggled with an extremely difficult scenario and not wanting to repeat a similar incident, I took pains to thoroughly brief the physician about Rachel's situation, her suicide history, and her responses to date. He seemed to understand, so I relaxed somewhat. Rachel's family was in the main lobby, where there was little privacy available. I suggested to the physician that he go directly to a nearby conference room door, and await us there. Obtaining a key from security, I ushered the family in, followed by the physician.

I introduced the physician and seated the family. The physician said, "You know Ron has sustained a major head injury." There was silence. The physician grew tense. "He is dead," he stated bluntly. Rachel screamed, "Oh, please! It can't be true!" running for the door. I slipped an arm around her as she tried to pass me, and she began sobbing on my shoulder. The physician turned to me and said, "I'll be outside," and again left the room!

After calming the family, I faced the difficult task of providing a "Tarasoff warning" regarding the homicidal threats of Ron's older brother. I then provided appropriate follow-up crisis intervention with both families, followed by a final consultation with the staff police.

How could many of the complexities of these two scenarios have been avoided? A less traumatic notification would have helped both families to better cope with the loss. Insofar as was possible, appropriate notification techniques could have been reviewed with the physician, in advance of meeting the families. In this case, however, the physician seemed to have been unusually tense for reasons which were not entirely clear. I later learned that he was a new resident, on temporary assignment from another facility and entirely unaccustomed to a trauma center setting.

Under these circumstances, as suggested previously, it might have been better for someone else to have made the initial notifications in advance, and then to have invited the physician to meet with the families afterward to provide any further details and answer any questions. This could have spared both him and the families the trauma that resulted from the awkward presentations.

In the Field

Although deaths in 70 percent of the cases occur or are confirmed in a hospital, there are many instances when notification must take place elsewhere—at the scene of a death or in the home. Those who may be required to make notifications on scene or in the field include law enforcement officers, fire department staff, emergency medical staff (EMTs and paramedics), and coroners' staff.

Field Notifier Selection Guidelines

For those managing field notifications, a few basic guidelines may be helpful in preparing and selecting individuals well-situated to deliver a notification. When possible, select *at least two persons* for each presentation. This lends to a more stable environment, allowing support for both the family and the notifier. One person should be assigned primary responsibility for the notification task itself. Ideally, this should be someone who was directly involved with the events surrounding the death. It is meaningful to family members to meet with *someone who was present with their loved one and who was familiar with the ensuing traumatic events.* Families often ask for details that only someone who was intimately involved could provide. If such a person is not available, those selected to make the presentation should be well-briefed on all significant details of the loss. This is important, to facilitate family interactions and contribute to a healthy grieving process.

Select *staff members who can be given enough time to provide ample support.* It is important that the notifier not be called away too quickly after delivering the traumatic news. Further, try to select individuals who are *well-suited to communicating and empathizing* with the family. Not everyone is on equal footing in this area, and not everyone will be comfortable with such an assignment. In making this selection, bear in mind such variables as interactive patterns, demeanor, and approachability. These variables can have a great impact on the recipients of the news.

Recognize that notifier selections can change with varying circumstances. There will be times when normally appropriate individuals may be under unusual stress, or when the presenting scenario may be too close to personal circumstances (such as the death of a child the gender or age of their own). Appropriate notifier selections will ensure that the value and outcome of the experience will be enhanced for all involved.

To facilitate the notification process and to ensure greater uniformity of results, law enforcement and other first-responder programs should provide notification training for all new and existing staff. Instruction should include basic staging strategies, delivery techniques, and rudimentary assessment skills. For further support, each program's administration should also engage a consulting/liaison service to assist with difficult cases. Such a service should provide staff and family crisis intervention, and follow-up referrals for a broad variety of families and situations.

Law-Enforcement Officers

My research has shown that most families are reluctant to have law-enforcement officers sent to their homes to provide notification before their arrival at the hospital. (See Chapter 13, page 219.) This reluctance seemed to stem from a view of police officers as "enforcers," and as punitive figures of authority. Officers were seen as less sensitive to grief or needing to suppress these feelings to properly discharge their duty.

This view is supported, at least in part, by several other researchers. Spencer (1987), in a survey of police officers, noted that they often delivered the news with "dispatch and professional detachment . . . (believing that) bluntness was a way to neutralize the intensity of emotion." Helm (1989) cited a case where "one officer left a note on the door stating the family's son had hanged himself, and that the family should 'call this number for information'." Hendricks (1984), described the performance of these death notifiers as "inadequate," because special training and practice were needed but not made available. In short, there is widespread consensus that law enforcement training does not generally include sufficient preparation for death notification.

Yet there are times when law enforcement notifications may be necessary and are performed in exemplary manner. For example, a 15-year-old boy at home alone, whose parents both died in an auto accident while returning from work, needed special care in receiving the news of these deaths. To this end, local law enforcement officials were contacted and dispatched to the boy's home. In this situation, they provided an excellent service, helping the boy to contact relatives in a nearby city, and staying with him for several hours until his relatives could come and provide further support.

In contacting law enforcement for a notification, be clear about your concerns and the specific nature of assistance needed. This should help to ensure that those best suited to the task will be dispatched. In cities where ethnic tensions run high, sensitive notification by law enforcement personnel could provide a calming factor.

Emergency Medical/Fire Department Staff

Probably the best-informed of all field notifiers are the emergency staff who provide on-scene medical assistance. They are usually aware of most events that led to the death and are intimately aware of the last, or nearly last, moments of the person's life. They can tell families of any last words spoken and any physical responses immediately following a traumatic event.

Because of the nature of their work, paramedics are not usually available to provide field notifications. But they often assume the responsibility when a family member happens upon a scene, or when someone survives an accident and becomes concerned about the condition of others. In circumstances such as these, there are specific notification suggestions given in Chapter 4.

> With all the hurrying that goes on, somehow the patient becomes a thing. So when we know they're not going to be saved, I like to lean down and whisper good-bye. It's the one time I let my guard down. They're checking out, and why not make them feel better about it?   —Paramedic[3]

Coroners' Staff

In a published study of three county coroners' facilities, and from my own personal experience with other coroners' offices, the selection of a coroner's deputy to make a notification usually falls randomly to the next individual assigned a case (Charmaz, 1976). This method has the advantages of uniformity of work load and simplified accountability for task accomplishment. In smaller counties, with limited staff available for specialized tasks such as death notification, this may be the only workable arrangement.

As with other field responders, as described above, it is suggested that coroners' departments establish notification training programs for their staff and that they engage a consulting liaison service to manage the more difficult situations that arise. However, as notification situations occur more frequently for coroners' staff, in larger counties some departments may want to consider hiring part-time specialists who could be specifically employed to deliver death notifications. Not only would this relieve current staff from a time-consuming burden, it would enhance the likelihood of an appropriate experience and may maximize the responsiveness of family members to investigative questioning.

Military Personnel

In the armed services, it is common for a commanding officer, or someone of equal or higher rank than the deceased, to be selected to deliver a formal death notification. This individual is usually accompanied to the family's home by another officer. The notification is delivered with all solemnity and consideration for those involved. After delivery of the news, the officers are free to provide support and offer their personal condolences.

---

[3] _Staff, Denver General Hospital. "The Knife and Gun Club: Scenes From an Emergency Room," as printed in Life Magazine, April 1989, p. 54 (New York: Atlantic Monthly Press, publisher)._

Dale and Darleen Schelin were awakened at 5 a.m. Thursday by four grim-faced military officers who had arrived to tell them one of their nine children was killed in the *USS Iowa* explosion.

"Initially they read a statement saying he was missing and presumed dead, then they came back at 10 a.m. and confirmed he had been killed," Geoff's eldest brother, David, 37, said from his parents' home in El Toro.

"The Navy has offered to fly our parents back to Norfolk for a memorial service Monday," David said.[4]

In consultation with the Air Force Casualty Office[5] I learned that, similar to all branches of the service, notifiers are first briefed on the circumstances. A training film is shown, to ensure that the officers understand the demeanor and method of presentation. Following this, a written statement is prepared and a team is dispatched to the family's home. If information indicates that members of the family are in ill health or elderly, a nurse may be included on the team. A chaplain may be invited, as well.

As noted earlier, this presentation by two or more people enables the officers to provide greater support than could one person alone. However, few of the military personnel tendering notification have special skills or formal training in grief management. Such skills and training would be particularly valuable, especially in time of war when great numbers of highly traumatic notifications may be required. The process could be greatly improved by engaging persons with appropriate educational background and military designation—base chaplains, for example—to conduct training programs and supervise notification.

This training should include *advanced* instruction in all aspects of the notification process, including grief management, family assessment, and crisis intervention. With this background, the military could then provide specialized services and referrals to all families, particularly those who have difficulty responding appropriately to a loss.

Regardless of who is involved in the notification process, all possible preparations should be made. Bereavement can be a *life-threatening* trauma. While most survivors will eventually accept their losses, some are at extreme risk. Untoward outcomes or events include cardiovascular problems, automobile accidents, industrial or job-related accidents, suicide, even homicide. Providing specialized training, and/or engaging professionals who are specifically trained to deal with bereavement and grief issues, can reduce the potential for many of these post-traumatic events and illnesses.

---

[4] *The Sacramento Union*, Friday, April 21, 1989, p. 5, reporting on the explosion that killed 47 sailors on the battleship *USS Iowa*, on Wednesday, April 19, 1989.

[5] *Personal communication, 1991.*

Legal Issues in Notification

How a notification is delivered is important. Events of survivor demise following notification of a victim's death have been well documented. One researcher, Engle (1971), studied numerous deaths occurring during psychological stress, including the demise of a 14-year-old girl when she was told of the death of her brother. Selection of words and presenting manner are matters of critical public and legal interest. In one state case[6] it was determined that a hospital would be deemed liable for an employee's "inhumane method of telephone notification," demonstrating a public recognition of inappropriate technique.

To whom the notification is given is relevant as well. Helm (1989) recorded that, "During World War II, Western Union was sued when information regarding the death of sons in battle was delivered to the wrong parents." Helm continued, "Additionally, most homicides and much violence occurs within the family unit; a laissez faire communication of a family member's death could ignite additional violence in some domestic communications." Obviously due caution must be exercised in determining what is said, to whom, where, and when.

It then follows that legal issues may arise regarding who is designated to perform a death notification. I have been asked, "Is it legally prohibited for anyone other than a physician to make a notification of death?" The rationale for this questioning is clear. A physician bears a formal license that certifies competence to treat illness and injury and thus to provide detailed information and explanation regarding complex life-threatening scenarios. Further, he or she operates within a legally recognized physician-patient relationship. Is it acceptable to designate anyone else to undertake this sensitive task?

According to the legal staff of the American Medical Association (AMA) and the California Association of Hospitals and Health Systems (CAHHS)[7], there are no federal or state regulations (at least in the state of California) stipulating who may or may not deliver death notifications. Thus, it appears to be a matter that should be regulated by administrative and facility policies.

In formulating such policies, it is important to recognize two points. First, a notification of death does not necessarily require a sophisticated explanation of all medical events that precipitated the death. Any in-depth discussion of the technical aspects surrounding a death should come from a medical professional, ideally the physician. Other professionals may make general statements regarding the suspected cause of

---

[6] _Muniz v. United Hospitals Medical Center Presbyterian Hospital 379 A.2d 57 (1977) cited in George, G.E., "Risks of telephone notification, law and the emergency department nurse," Journal of Emergency Nursing,_ 1983; (9)3:171.

[7] _Personal communications, 1991._

death, or additional statements as directed by the physician, but no further assumptions should be made. These persons should confine themselves to preparing the family for the news, delivering the death statement, viewing the body, providing crisis intervention as needed, obtaining organ/tissue donation consent, discussing coroner laws and funeral arrangements, and providing follow-up referrals for services as needed.

The second important point is that of licensure. A physician must possess a valid license in order to practice medicine within the respective state. Similarly, all states in the United States offer licensure, or formal certification, to a variety of mental health professionals allowing them to provide psychological services. All psychiatrists and psychologists are required to be licensed in order to provide professional mental health services. Most states also recognize social workers and mental health counselors who have pursued graduate training, granting various additional licenses—Licensed Clinical Social Worker (LCSW) or Accredited Clinical Social Worker (ACSW), and licensed Marriage, Family and Child Counselor (MFCC), respectively. States provide formal certification processes to ensure that these professionals possess specific, skills for use in the provision of mental health services.

If such professionals are employed to provide for the management of the death notification issues described above, administrative staffs and boards of directors can rest assured that, should an unforeseen problem develop, they can easily demonstrate that they have engaged those with the appropriate training and credentials to carry out the process.

In considering professional domain, the broad range of activities required for death notification management and follow up traditionally fall into the purview of social services. Medical social workers have completed graduate course work with specific specializations in medically related issues. These professionals, when also licensed, possess the appropriate skills and credentials for such an assignment and may be appropriately engaged to provide these services.

Contraindicators for Designators

The key concepts discussed have been qualification and preparation for death notifiers. However, circumstances change from incident to incident, and allowances should be made for this.

For example, a recent loss may make it difficult for the death notifier to comfort a newly bereaved family. In such situations, an alternative staff member should be selected if at all possible, or other arrangements should be made. If this is not possible, the presence of an additional staff member during the notification may be helpful.

Chapter 2

Information Gathering

Once the notifier has been selected, the next most pressing activity is to gather information. Even a minimally acceptable notification requires a substantial amount of information and advance preparation. To deliver a well-prepared death notification, with successful family crisis management, requires becoming exceptionally well-informed.

Emergency responders, hospital emergency room staff, law enforcement personnel, and coroners' staff are those most likely to encounter death situations where there is limited information available. Assuming a worst-scene scenario—an unidentified body—appropriate notifiers need information in four specific areas: identification of the deceased, family contact, debriefing, and crisis management. Let us look at each of these tasks in greater detail.

Identification of the Deceased

The longer it takes to identify a John Doe, the more likely it is that he will remain unidentified altogether. Of those who remain unidentified, most are ". . . transients or nomads, occasionally teen-age runaways, prostitutes or kidnap victims. Often, in California, they are undocumented migrants who carry false identification or none at all. In two-thirds of the cases nationwide, they are victims of foul play."[8]

All medical and forensic facilities hold a community obligation to make every effort to identify any person brought to them, to notify families promptly when possible, and to investigate any foul play while fresh and vital information is still available. Consider the following:

There are 1,500 new unidentified bodies every year (held in coroners' morgues across the nation)," according to Marcella Fierro, ex-head of the National Association of Medical Examiners.

---

[8] Castaneda, Carol J., "Nameless bodies burden, baffle law enforcers," *USA TODAY*, Friday, April 24, 1992, p. 10a. Used with permission.

> (While) there are no good numbers on how many nameless bodies have turned up in years past, or on how many people have been buried unidentified . . . current figures give some indication.
>
> There are 1,949 unidentified bodies in California morgues—and counting. Of the 720 unidentified cases they get each year, California authorities are quickly able to identify a third of the bodies through a central registry that compares lists of unidentified bodies with lists of missing persons.
>
> In Texas, authorities are trying to identify 600 bodies dating to the early 1970s. In Oregon, 21 bodies, no names, and one twist: an unidentified living person. In an apparent suicide attempt, a man—brown eyes, brown hair, full beard, no birth marks, tattoos or identification—walked in front of a semi-truck near Eugene. He survived, but no one, not even he, can say who he is.[9]

The designated notifier is usually responsible for seeking out and finalizing identification. Most John and Jane Does can be identified. Those involved in motor vehicle accidents, auto-pedestrian accidents, drownings, or recreational mishaps may not be carrying identification, but they have usually been in company with others who know them and can assist with their identification. When friends or family are not present, identification material is often still available at the death, injury, or crime scene, although it may not have accompanied the victim to your facility. This can occur in one of three ways.

First, when emergency responders encounter an accident victim who is not yet dead, they will often remove the victim's clothing in the treatment process, cutting it away to find injury sites or to wrap and inflate "shock pants" for the treatment of blood loss. In so doing, the victim's clothing and identification may be unintentionally left at the accident scene.

Second, information from the scene of a death may be delayed if it has been intentionally retained there to facilitate the completion of law enforcement interviews and records. In either case, law enforcement officials responding to the scene usually retain these materials throughout the investigation process, and will make them available to you later at your request.

Finally, there are opportunistic individuals who, happening upon an accident, may literally steal from the dead or dying. In such situations, formal identification materials may be absent and more investigative measures may be required. These are discussed below.

A timely identification of the deceased often requires creative thinking and examination of every possible clue. Even honest identification errors can cause tremendous distress to a family and can be professionally

---

[9] Ibid. Copyright 1992, *USA TODAY*. Used with permission.

embarrassing. By studying all details that can be found or made available, you will be much more likely to determine their validity and avoid any mistakes in the family contact and notification process. Potential resources for decedent identification include the following:

• **Accident Co-victims.** When a victim is brought in, or if you respond to the scene, you must determine who was involved in the death incident and their relationships to each other. In situations where family or friends were involved in the same accident, you may be able to speak with them and obtain the identity of the deceased.

Caution should be used in this questioning to avoid an untimely or stressful notification. In response to a direct question about the deceased's condition, you might respond by saying, "Someone is with him now. I'll check for you soon," or, "I'm unable to talk with him right now. Perhaps you could help me." Then continue with your inquiry.

Ask general questions about the entire event, then follow up with specific queries. Always speak in a casual manner, such as, "So your brother was driving? Then he's the fellow in the tee-shirt with the 'Corona Beer' logo on it, right?" This is much less likely to arouse suspicion than blunt or pointed questioning such as, "Describe your brother for me, please."

• **Ambulance/Transport Staff.** If someone who knew the deceased was at the scene, or if the victim was speaking before death occurred, ambulance staff may have some information. Emergency response staff may have placed identification materials in their vehicle, and can provide them if asked. At the very least, ambulance or transport staff can usually tell you which law enforcement service investigated the scene, e.g., police, sheriff or highway patrol, and give details about accident co-victims and where they were taken. This information can help you to contact these potential resources for family contact information.

• **Law Enforcement Staff.** Law enforcement officers are specifically trained to thoroughly investigate injury and death scenes. In doing so, they interview many bystanders, often obtaining details and information a notifier may need. If a person was transported to a hospital, an officer will usually attend or send someone to document the injured person's condition. If no identification was found with the deceased, officers should be asked about it immediately upon their arrival. They may be able to locate it or speak with others on-scene before they are dispatched to other calls.

If no officer comes to the facility, or an officer has left before you had opportunity to inquire, you can call the dispatch office to relay an information request to the appropriate individual. The officer will often be able to pursue other avenues of inquiry, such as running a "make" on a vehicle to obtain an owner identification. Even if the deceased is not the owner, the person you locate may be able to assist you in obtaining an identification.

In one case, a motorcycle was traced through three friends, each having sold it to another, until the desired words were heard: "Oh, yeah, I sold the bike to Frank only yesterday. In fact, he's still paying for it. How's he doing anyway?" Of course, in a situation such as this, notification to the friend must be delayed until immediate family has been contacted. A deft deferral such as, "He's been injured badly," followed by, "How can I reach his family?" is most appropriate.

● **Contents of the Deceased's Pockets.** If no formal identification is found, there may be clues in other items found with the deceased person. Look for pay stubs, rent receipts, business cards, or other such information sources. Take particular note of various phone numbers scribbled on scraps of paper. Many times, these telephone numbers will lead to friends or business acquaintances who may be able to assist you with identification. Photocopying the items most likely to lead to family can expedite the information-gathering process. Then the original items can be locked up with the deceased's belongings, or readily released to investigating officers, if required.

● **Miscellaneous Papers and Cards.** Miscellaneous papers and cards can be invaluable. For example, video rental cards are often ready information sources. The rental facilities will often provide a home phone number. Telephone calling-cards (which include the person's home phone number on the face), pay stubs with a work phone number, business cards, or fishing and hunting licenses are all excellent leads to follow.

As mentioned earlier, care should be used in speaking with friends or acquaintances of the deceased. Although you should give general information to enlist their assistance (e.g., "He was hurt in a car accident and is at the hospital") you should avoid telling them of the death directly, as the family may then receive an inappropriate or inaccurate notification from the friend. Further, with some, the release of such information might create additional problems, such as revealing a victim's home to be unoccupied. If the victim lived alone, this could lead to theft or vandalism.

● **Other Belongings.** Although it is less common, identification is occasionally made by means of labeled clothing, inscribed ring bands, identification bracelets, "dog tags," name-bearing or initialed key fobs, or other articles. Carefully examine all available items, and record pertinent information for later reference. Be creative. An eye-glasses case, for example, may lead to an optometrist who can identify or contact the family for you.

● **Telephone Directory Assistance.** Often there are no usable telephone numbers and little more than a victim name and partial address available to assist you with location of next of kin. In such cases, a telephone directory or an information operator may help you to locate the family. In some instances, asking for the telephone company's shift supervisor can expedite inquiries. If the victim has an unusual last name, or lived in a small town, call all last-name listings in an area. This should be done regardless of the hour. Most people are understanding of these attempts, and many times family members are located in this way.

In addition, telephone companies publish restricted directories of telephone numbers that are cross-referenced with city and street names. If one is not currently available for you, consult the company that serves your area for information on how to purchase one for your professional use. If an exact address match is not given, call neighbors of the deceased and enlist their help in locating the family. Often they will go willingly to a nearby address and see if anyone is home. If no one is there, they may be willing to leave a note with a telephone number for the family to call upon their return.

● **Vehicle Registration.** Sometimes, former addresses or vehicle registration information can be obtained from investigating law enforcement staff. A former address may provide a lead for location of family members, if followed through with phone directory searches, as described above.

● **Physical Description.** If no photo identification is immediately evident, always record a thorough physical description. Be specific in your notes. Include estimated height and weight, hair and eye color, scars, tattoos, clothing worn at the time of death (if it was cut off on scene, ask transporting staff for a clothing description), contents of pockets, and any other identifying information.

Occasionally, identification is made when family members begin calling local hospitals looking for a missing person. If a description can be obtained that matches your known information, identification may begin by telephone.

● **Fingerprinting/Missing Persons Reports.** Two identification avenues of last resort include fingerprinting a deceased or fatally injured victim, and submitting a missing person report. While missing person reports are time-consuming to file, and not always successful, they are recommended if other means of identification have been exhausted.

Fingerprint identification is widely used by coroners' offices, and is available to other facilities upon request. Because it may take several days to obtain fingerprints and run a comparison check, this is usually a method used when all other avenues have been exhausted.

In cases of unidentified comatose patients, this process should not be delayed longer than seven to ten days, as the hands rapidly begin to lose their flexibility, making clear fingerprints difficult to obtain.

• **Cautionary Notes.** To avoid mistakes, use caution with any identification obtained from materials that do not include a photo identification or positive fingerprint match. When you are not certain of the identity, always make this clear to those involved early on in the contact process.

Check any photo identification carefully against the victim, since death can make a resemblance difficult to confirm. In addition, some individuals may be carrying false, borrowed, or alias-only identification. One individual I saw had *four* different driver's licenses on his person, each with his photo and different names! In questionable cases, be sure to check for discrepancies noted in the identification description, such as eye and hair color, height, weight, or age. If still in doubt, seek law enforcement confirmation.

Family Contact

During the identification process, you will usually come across information that will help you to locate the next-of-kin. Sometimes it will let you know with whom you will be speaking when you call, such as a wallet-sized directory with a "mom and dad" or "home" entry. More often, however, it will consist of various "leads."

Timely Notice

As notifier, you should begin to accumulate potential family contact information as soon as an individual arrives under your care. To facilitate this, it may be necessary to set up a John/Jane Doe referral system so that valuable information-gathering time is not lost.

Actual contact efforts should be postponed only until sufficient relevant background information has been obtained to enable the notification process to proceed in an orderly manner. My research indicates that almost all families wish to be contacted immediately, regardless of the time of day (See Chapter 13, page 214).

Inordinate delays can cause political and public relations repercussions. Some families, angered by what they perceive as poor efforts to contact them quickly, will write letters of complaint to administrative staff, and may even solicit additional letters from friends, relatives, employers, or public officials. To avoid these occurrences, act quickly, document all work done, and describe your efforts to the family, if necessary. Detailed suggestions for staging the notification are discussed in Chapter 3.

Family Confirmation of Identity

Care should be taken, when arranging the viewing of a John Doe, to establish firm visual confirmation of the deceased's identification. Some people, even family members, are reluctant to make an adequate visual examination of the body for definite identification. In their fear and trepidation, they may enter the room, glance toward the body briefly from a distance, and try to draw an instantaneous conclusion. This is often insufficient. People look different in death. Their features may be distorted by injuries. Large quantities of fluids given in an effort to save life can cause extreme edema and facial puffiness. Also, seeing someone lying down, perhaps only in profile, may give a false impression. I have actually had several experiences where family members either inaccurately denied or identified a body before being assisted nearer the bedside for a closer look.

A reasonably thorough examination is necessary to ensure accurate confirmation. To avoid these difficulties, try placing the body fairly close to the door where it will be easily seen upon entering. Undrape the face beforehand so as to not to shock or confuse the viewers with the appearance of "an unveiling," and accompany them to the victim's side. (See accepted viewing procedures, outlined in Chapter 5.)

Death Debriefing

Unlike illness, fatal accidents and violent injuries often occur outside the home without the family's knowledge. Notifications of such incidents invariably catch those involved completely by surprise. Consequently, families have no concrete sequence of events to give a sense of reality to the death. This can greatly complicate the grief process.

In such circumstances, loved ones often have a heightened need for details surrounding the death. They may ask again and again about the events that led up to the fatal moment, who was present or called in, and what was done to treat the victim. Through this process, families seek to establish a context through which they can accept their loss.

A skilled notifier will be able to supply sufficient information to assist a family in building this loss context. Thus, in accumulating background information, be sensitive to these needs. Make every effort to obtain any information, including seemingly insignificant details, that might be important to the family. The process of providing this contextual information is known as "debriefing," and will be discussed further in Chapter 5.

Military Issues

Details surrounding military deaths are often vague, due to the tumultuous circumstances under which they occur. Time, distance, and the lack of first-hand narrators all serve to complicate the debriefing process for the family. Occasionally, the body may not even be available to assist the family in fully mourning the loss. If the person has been in the service for some time or was serving in a high-security position, there may have been no recent family contact. These factors create exceptionally difficult grief experiences.

Because of "dog tags" and enlistment records, accumulating essential notification information should not be difficult. Beyond that, make additional effort to become familiar with any details that might aid the family in resolving grief. These could include not only details regarding the events surrounding the death, but also specific information about the person, his service record, friends, and recent activities. This may enable you to make the notification more personal, and will help family members know that you genuinely care about their loss.

Further, in cases where less-than-favorable circumstances were involved, thorough information may also assist you in avoiding troublesome and disconcerting problems that are better left unmentioned at the time of the notification.

Information and Crisis Management

When people are told that someone they love has died, they are immediately placed in a compromised state. They will experience a significant loss of control over aspects of their own lives and be thrust into new realms of functioning. This constitutes an extreme and potentially devastating individual and family crisis. Having initiated this sequence of events, you have become directly involved and bear some responsibility for the outcome. Your professional response to these reactions constitutes "crisis management."

In attempting to assist during a crisis, your ignorance of significant preexisting family problems can hinder or even subvert the process. Conversely, knowledge of these key issues can help you facilitate a healthy outcome and can assist you in monitoring progress. To this end, seek to acquaint yourself with all information that may assist you in the crisis-management process.

There are several ways to learn about pertinent individual and family dynamics. By far, the most successful is personal observation. From the time of your first contact with the family until you part, attune yourself to the interactions of everyone involved, including those with other staff. Closely monitor all types of communication, including body language, verbal tone, and visual clues. In this way, you can often recognize and circumvent potential problems early on.

Additional sources of information pertinent to grief management include comments volunteered by family members and others. These comments will have varying degrees of validity, depending on the nature of the information given, its specificity, and the reliability of the source. Generally speaking, the more specific the information the more reliable it is.

Some comments or allegations, such as reported thoughts of suicide or homicide, are so serious that they must never be ignored. They require further investigation and, if substantiated, immediate intervention.

Other allegations may be attended to as circumstances permit. For example, if you are told that the deceased's husband is alcoholic, the survivor may not be willing to discuss the problem openly, and you are in no position to press him. But because his drinking problem is likely to worsen with the death of his spouse, you should at least attempt to discuss your concern and offer referral information for further assistance.

The more meaningful time you are able to spend with those involved, both prior to and following the death, the greater the possibility that you will learn of important and sensitive issues. In working with families, you should be aware that personal and family development is a process, and no one has perfected it. Your goal is *not* to initiate family therapy, or to "fix" every problem that may arise. Your goal in information-gathering is to become sufficiently well-informed to be able to assist the family in recovering from its loss and moving on with productive lives. If survivors choose to address unrelated issues, you can make appropriate referrals.

Drug Abuse Deaths
The emotional and informational needs of family relatives in response to a death from drug abuse are especially acute. They may be unaware of the drug use or the extent of the abuse. Consequently, they are entirely unprepared for the news of the death and its cause. In other instances, they may have known of the drug use and done nothing about it. They may have indirectly, or even directly, "enabled" the user through financial subsidies or drug purchases. In these situations, family members will often experience tremendous guilt, feeling responsible for the death. These episodes can be very difficult to manage and require a full grasp of details in order to meet the family's needs.

Homicide
Families exposed to death by deliberate violence are also presented with difficult emotional obstacles and may need substantial information and crisis intervention to resolve their feelings. Survivors of innocent victims of violence endure not only a great sense of loss, but also a profound sense of helplessness. Their grief can be extreme and can raise many questions. Families of victims who were engaged in activities that resulted in their violent deaths may bear an additional weight of shame at the death circumstances.

Where contributory situations such as a drug deal "gone bad" are involved, families may have many questions and will need special attention. It may be helpful for them to speak with the investigating law enforcement officers, who may be able to provide additional information and support. However, it is important to note that, in some situations, other family members may also be involved in drug sales. This can complicate their grief, often precluding it, in their haste to remain uninvolved in any investigation or questioning. It can also portend further violence if the killing were gang or drug "turf" related. Be observant, carefully question others who may have been involved, and use caution when necessary.

In any event, when a homicide has occurred, you must cooperate with the law enforcement investigating staff. Do not deliver a notification or contact family members until permission is obtained.

Complicating Information

Regardless of the circumstances behind the death, families often express a genuine need to reconstruct all the events surrounding it. When dealing with violent injuries, discussion can be difficult, especially if the injuries are extensive. But if the events and injuries are carefully described, only to the degree requested, you can assist family members toward a resolution of the loss.

It is important to be honest and thorough in disclosing to survivors details of a death. Use discretion to move at the pace they initiate, holding back difficult information until they have absorbed the initial news of death and the general sequence of events. The key is to volunteer only basic information and then add detail as requested.

In some circumstances, you may decide to withhold all particularly difficult or graphic information. For example, a middle-aged man was shot to death in his car one evening. He was in the company of a prostitute. The presence of the prostitute was, in proportion, an extraneous detail, as officers reported that the shooting occurred solely as a result of an argument with a man on a street corner and did not involve the prostitute in any way. When the victim's wife arrived, I elected not to disclose to her his company with the prostitute. The wife genuinely mourned her husband's loss, and it seemed unfitting that I should complicate her grief with such information.

Similarly, particularly graphic injury details routinely are omitted or "smoothed over," unless family members press for them. You should, nevertheless, become well-briefed to meet any level of inquiry, should the family delve deeply into the details of the death.

Conclusions

All death scenarios have unique dynamics of their own. Only a well-informed notifier can meet the diverse bereavement needs of survivors. You must, therefore, ensure that you are aware of all significant aspects of each death. Obtain this information in advance of the family's arrival so that you won't be caught by surprise or reveal certain details at an inopportune time. Yet information must be gathered quickly, to avoid delay in notification.

Take care to separate facts from suppositions or possibilities. A driver who has "been drinking" is not necessarily legally "drunk." Use terminology such as "alleged," "reportedly," or "appears to be" when the information is of a sensitive nature.

Confidentiality must always be maintained. Death circumstances with related diagnoses of AIDS, psychological disorders, and drug abuse are particularly sensitive issues; they should be communicated only after consideration by risk management or medical/legal staff.

Coroner-investigated deaths are generally a matter of public record. Therefore, autopsy results are available to anybody interested enough to pay for a copy. But caution should be used in the release of information of a death prior to such an autopsy.

In cases of homicide, do *not* contact family members or notify anyone of the death without specific permission from investigating law enforcement staff. Retaliatory actions, destruction of evidence, and other legal complexities may otherwise result. In sensitive situations, consult your supervisor or departmental policy and procedure manual for specific instructions.

Chapter 3

Notification Staging and Delivery

Once you have obtained enough information to make a well-planned notification, you must then contact available family members and move them into an adequate setting for the notification to take place. In principle, this sounds easy. In practice, there may be many complications. In this chapter I address some of the obstacles you may encounter and various techniques to use in overcoming them. I shall also examine some common pitfalls to avoid in this process. Although some case situations are included, you will undoubtedly encounter many unusual experiences. Therefore, I have arranged the information into broad, general categories that should be applicable to most circumstances.

Initial Family Contacts

Professional literature often assumes that the family is already present at the hospital when a death occurs, having somehow been made aware of the event, or having witnessed its onset. This is certainly the ideal. But situations of sudden illness or accident without family knowledge can add a significant degree of complexity to the process. The notifier's first obstacle is locating the family, as discussed in Chapter 2. Once you learn where the family is, the next decision is which of possibly several family members to ask for, when to contact them, and how.

Timing the Notification

According to the research, families desire to be contacted about a death immediately, regardless of how late at night it is. (See Chapter 13, page 214.) In most circumstances, I am in complete agreement with this consensus. My experience has been that families are better able to accommodate ensuing events, however trying they may be, when they feel that they are integrally involved in the entire process. Delaying a notification may engender undue concern or hostility in a family. It may also further compromise the survivors' ability to cope with the death. In some cases, they may even feel that information has been withheld for some covert reason (e.g., questionable cause of death, inappropriate medical care, etc.). Immediate family contact minimizes these concerns.

Telephone Contacts

There are three methods for family contact when a patient is pronounced dead in a hospital without the presence of next-of-kin. You can travel personally to the home or business and speak with the family face-to-face; send a representative in your stead; or call the family on the telephone. Most initial family contacts are made by phone. Telephoning ensures prompt contact, cost-effective use of facility resources, and better quality control in the release of information.

While the telephone is extremely useful for making the initial contact with family members, it is a poor instrument for actual notification of death. Telephone notifications do occur, but *it is wise to avoid them if at all possible.* Nearly every family member, however, when informed that a loved one is at a hospital or some other unexpected location, will intuitively ask what happened. You must therefore plan to direct the conversation, to avoid telling more than is appropriate for the circumstance, especially if family dynamics and emotional stability are yet unknown.

For example, consider a situation in which the victim had been in a fatal automobile accident and was brought to the hospital for an attempt at resuscitation. In an effort to avoid a telephone notification, the conversation might proceed as follows:

> "Hello. This is Moroni Leash. I am calling from the Medical Center. I would like to speak with the family (or person's name, if known) of Fred Jones. Is this a family member?"
> "Yes, I am his wife. What has happened? Is Fred okay?"
> "Fred was in a car accident today and was brought here. We would like you to come in, too, if you could, please."
> "How is he doing? Is he okay?"
> "Well, he has been here only a short time, and I haven't had a chance to speak with Fred's physician yet. When you get here, I'll locate his primary doctor and we can tell you more then."
>
> *Quickly continue,* "Do you know how to get to the hospital?"
>
> Finally, you might say something like, "You could be here a while, so why don't you call someone to come down with you. Is there anyone who could come with you now?"

This approach will usually bypass any pressure to notify over the telephone. It is successful because the dialogue requires an immediate verbal response and prompt action toward a clear goal. This meets the family's need to be involved in resolving the demands of the moment and substitutes activity for further dialogue about the patient's medical status.

Make sure to give the family member your exact address and easy-to-follow directions, including both the route to the facility and where to go upon arrival. Also remember to give your full name and where to contact you when the person arrives.

In emotionally charged circumstances, it is very important to be clear and precise. Don't leave any ambiguity in the directions you give. While en route to the hospital, families inevitably speculate about potential scenarios and outcomes. This always heightens their fears. If they also must search for you upon their arrival, they may feel additional anxiety that will complicate the entire process. It can be very difficult to give an appropriate notification when frustrated and worried family members rush up to you in a hallway asking about their loved one's condition.

Although telephone notification is to be avoided, other statements may be appropriate to facilitate prompt family responses. For example, in situations where a family seems reluctant to come in, statements such as, "I'm told he isn't doing well," or "I'm told he has been badly injured— could you come in right now?" may be helpful. Be careful, however, in choosing your words. Volunteering too much information can necessitate a notification, not because family members insist upon it, but because their anxiety threshold is breached.

While my research indicates that there is some potential for families to become angry with you for not having volunteered the news of the death, in practice this reaction rarely occurs. (See Chapter 13, pages 215 and 220.) Indeed, in the hundreds of notifications I have made, I have never had a family become angry about this. Should it occur, it may be helpful to later share with them some of the concerns regarding telephone notification:

1. The primary concern is protection of the surviving family members. People will be more likely to travel to the hospital safely when they have some level of hope. Further, psychological and emotional distress can be reduced in a controlled atmosphere, and medical attention is available should a preexisting condition afflict a recipient of the news. Other personnel are also available to comfort and support people.

2. In cases of telephone notification, families often waste substantial time contacting other family members, delaying their own departure to the hospital. They may not arrive, for example, until after the coroner's staff has removed the body from the room. County coroners' offices rarely have sufficient facilities for viewing, and thus prohibit anything beyond immediate identification. This deprives the family of the benefits of an early viewing. (The benefits of viewing the body are discussed in Chapter 5.)

3. Interacting with families at a hospital, or in a similar setting, greatly facilitates many other matters, such as obtaining an autopsy consent, returning the personal belongings of the deceased, receiving authorization for organ and tissue donation, and allowing the family ample time to talk with the pronouncing physician.

4. When families hear the news of death in a formal setting, they are more likely to be psychologically prepared to accept the reality of the death. Otherwise, it is difficult for many family members to avoid the feeling that "this is all a dream."

Telephone Notifications "On Demand"

In my research, when families were asked to respond to the statement, "I should not be told about the death of my family member until I arrive at the hospital," 57.6 percent selected the responses "Disagree" or "Strongly Disagree." (See Chapter 13, page 215.) While this does not mean that telephone notifications are preferable to presentations in person, it does indicate that the supposed reluctance to receive a notification by telephone may be more in our minds than in the family's.

If family members are adamant about receiving a notification over the telephone, bear in mind that it is their right to know. However, you should first validate their request by saying something like, "Do you really want to talk about this over the telephone?" If they respond affirmatively, obtain one final assurance by asking, "Are you sure?" If they continue to insist, proceed slowly, following the guidelines noted in the Sequential Notification Technique described on the next pages.

As you talk with the family, pause often and listen for clues indicating whether or not they actually want the full story at this time. If there is any reluctance, discontinue the explanation process, and mention that you will meet the family members at the hospital as soon as they arrive. While it may seem irregular, I have had many families interrupt a notification during the brief description of injuries, saying something like, "Okay, we'll be right there," rather than accepting the full notification on the telephone.

Always bear in mind that you cannot be aware of numerous potentially complicating family dynamics. While you may know that John Doe died in an alcohol-related automobile accident, you may not be aware of his drinking history. You don't know that his "work buddy" regularly encouraged him to drink at the local bar after hours, and that John's father has sworn to kill the fellow should his son be hurt due to drinking and driving. If you can get the father to the hospital, or any family member who knows of the outstanding dynamics, you can much more effectively defuse a potentially dangerous situation.

There are situations when a patient is not deceased but is traumatically injured. Robinson (1982) developed a checklist and valuable suggestions for managing telephone contacts in these cases. The checklist covers information that may be given as well as information that may be needed from the family. You will find the checklist in Appendix A. You also may wish to refer to Mark Robinson's article, "Telephone Notification of Relatives of Emergency and Critical Care Patients." (See bibliography.)

Selection of Physical Surroundings

Before the family arrives you should give some thought to the appropriate surroundings for notification. In observing interactions at various hospitals, I have seen notifications of death or other dire news delivered in almost every conceivable location, including parking lots, hallways, and lobby or waiting areas.

It is never a good idea to notify someone of a death in a public area. It is much better to escort the immediate family—not everyone present, but immediate family first—to a private room. It may be helpful to have a neutral, uninformed staff person provide the escort, so as to defer any preliminary dialogue. Thus, if questions are raised the escort can honestly say, "I don't know, but someone is coming to talk with you here." The room should be a place where the family can remain for some time, uninterrupted by other staff or visitors. It should have at least one telephone available for later calls to friends and relatives. Ask the group to be seated for the discussion, so that distractions are minimized. Also, no one is likely to faint or fall and get hurt when notification occurs. In such a setting, family members can grieve in privacy, feeling free to express their emotions and provide personal support to each other as needed.

Notification Technique

When the family is in a reasonable setting, the notification should take place quickly. There are definite guidelines and suggestions that can aid you with this task, but no text can take you through every specific situation. Those who are the most successful in providing thoughtful, well-balanced notifications of death do so by careful evaluation and observation. They personalize each dialogue and time the delivery to meet the immediate needs. Presented here is an outline that can be used with most death situations. This format consistently yields positive results. One author has called it the "progressive approach" (Collins, 1989). Here it is called the "Sequential Notification Technique" (Robinson, 1981).

The Sequential Notification Technique

The value of this approach is that it does not involve a prolonged dialogue, but provides sufficient structure to prepare the family for the ultimate statement of death. No two notifications are exactly alike. But by using the guidelines provided, and tailoring the notification to meet the current circumstances, you can give families the best chance for a healthy emotional response.

After gathering the necessary information and bringing the family to a suitable location, the notifier should then:

1. Ask the family members what they already know about the situation.
2. Bridging from what they know, give a *brief* description of additional events that led up to the patient's arrival at the hospital.
3. Give information regarding the resuscitative efforts made on behalf of the patient at the hospital.
4. Conclude with the victim's response to the treatment, the statement of death, and a brief explanation of the cause of death.

Although Collins (1989) suggests that a description of injuries be given after step two, I prefer to share that information later, allowing the family to first accommodate the news of the loss. Plan each step of the notification to allow for its mental and emotional impact. *Never* start the notification process with the statement of death. Never begin with the statement, "I have bad news for you," or "I'm sorry, but—;" such an initiation throws the family members into panic, ultimately amounting to an abrupt notification.

When addressing the survivors, sit reasonably close and speak directly to them. Be willing to make gentle, comforting, physical contact, unless their responses indicate that they prefer otherwise. Speak slowly, and coordinate your statements with their emotional responses. By so doing, you allow them to control the flow of the conversation, preparing themselves as you proceed together.

Accidental Death
Here is an example of an effective face-to-face notification taken from an actual case history.

"Hello, Mrs. Smith. My name is Moroni, and I'm with Emergency Social Services. I wanted to talk with you about your husband, John. Please, have a seat. Tell me, what do you know about John's accident so far?"

"No one has told me anything! Please, tell me how he is!"

"Well, it appears that John was coming home from work this evening and ran out of gas on the freeway. He apparently left his car, taking a gas can, and started walking down the nearest off-ramp. It seems someone didn't see him, and he was struck by a passing automobile" (Pause.)

"Was he hurt badly?"

"Yes, he was injured very severely. He was flown by helicopter from the accident scene to the hospital. He came here under CPR, and we worked with him for about 40 minutes. After a time it became clear that he had injuries he couldn't survive." (Pause.)

"(Tears.) Is he dead?"

"Yes ma'am. His heart just wouldn't start again. He had lost too much blood. He died about 6:10 p.m. I know that this is difficult for you. I wish we could have done more. There was just no way he could have survived. Please accept my condolences at your loss."

"Was he in pain . . . ? I mean, did he ever feel anything?"

"No ma'am. It happened so quickly, I don't think he even had time to be startled, much less to feel pain."

"Did he ever wake up?"

"No, it appears that he was unconscious from the moment he was struck."

Natural Death

The next scenario is an oft-repeated one, that occurs several times each week in a trauma center, with only minor variations.

"Hello, Mrs. Jones. My name Moroni Leash. I am a Social Worker here at the hospital. What could you tell me about what happened to Mr. Jones today?"

"Well, Fred and I were at home when he started having pain in his left arm. It bothered him more and more, even after he took his medicine. He went to the bedroom to lie down and rest, and when I checked on him 15 or 20 minutes later, I noticed he wasn't breathing and I couldn't wake him up. I called for an ambulance right then. Please tell me how he's doing!"

"Well, Mrs. Jones, Fred came in under CPR, and we continued that for some time, about 30-40 or more minutes. There are certain medicines and procedures that can sometimes restart a heart that has stopped beating. We did everything we could, but it became obvious that we wouldn't be able to revive him."

"Is he . . . dead, then?"

"Yes, Mrs. Jones, he died a couple of minutes ago."

The actual death statement should be fairly brief, with only essential explanatory details included. Too many technical details may confuse the family members, causing them to misunderstand or interrupt an otherwise well-planned delivery.

Resuscitation in Progress

Often family members will arrive at a hospital while resuscitative efforts are still in progress. All notification guidelines continue to apply. Appropriate selection of a waiting area should be made promptly. It is important that resuscitative staff be made aware of family arrival, if medical history details will be needed by attending physicians.

Collins (1989), a critical care nurse, suggests that updates should be given the family every 15 minutes to "alleviate anxiety and convey to the family that everything possible is being done for their loved one." I wholeheartedly agree with this suggestion. It occasionally may be helpful to give updates at 5-to-10-minute intervals when efforts are close to being discontinued, to better foreshadow the impending loss. Statements such as, "They have tried a number of medications that may help restart the heart, but aren't having any success yet," are appropriate. These comments play a vital role in preparing family members for the impending news of death.

While families wait during resuscitative efforts, it is helpful to initiate the notification process by discussing events leading up to the point of their arrival. This further enables the family to begin to grasp the gravity and meaning of the situation and makes it much more real. It also may be helpful to provide a telephone, especially if someone is at the hospital alone, so that hc or she can begin to make support contacts immediately. This is especially true in cases where resuscitative efforts are expected to continue for 30 minutes or more.

However, when resuscitative efforts have ceased, and the death notification is to be tendered, you may need to interrupt while someone is on the phone. This can often be accomplished with a statement such as, "I have some more information for you. Would you mind calling them back, and giving me a few minutes now?" This is typically quite effective and allows appropriate notification staging to take place.

I have specifically mentioned this here because I have seen blunt death statements tendered while family survivors were still holding with someone on the telephone. When acute grief reactions ensue, the telephone is invariably dropped or screamed into, leaving you to attend to two separate situations—one of which is totally beyond your control. In short, help the person to get off the telephone before delivering the notification of death.

Emotional Support

Chapter 7 provides a variety of responses commonly seen following notification. You should familiarize yourself with these to be prepared for the myriad of reactions you may encounter. Regardless of the initial response, the family will need you to be empathetic and supportive. As indicated in the notification approaches described earlier, sitting close to grieving persons, being willing to listen to them, and giving empathetic responses are important keys to support. Further, to touch, hug and even cry with those in grief provides tremendous and meaningful support. Family members will sense your genuine caring and will feel strengthened by it.

Collins (1989) provides two additional suggestions for providing emotional support with which I agree. First, never reinforce denial. Denial is usually very temporary, and survivors simply need additional time to come to a realization of their loss. To facilitate this realization, you should always speak about the deceased in appropriate terms, such as "How old *was* he?" and "It sounds as though he *was* a wonderful person." Such reflections are not only good verbal ventilation for the family, but will support and actualize the death.

Second, restrain and sedate only as necessary. Violent reactions and highly emotional outbursts are not uncommon when receiving the news of a death. Occasionally, people may truly become dangerous to themselves or others, but usually they need only to physically express their pain momentarily, and, if allowed to do so, will quickly calm down. Call for security assistance only if it is actually required.

Often I have been approached by concerned family members requesting sedative medications to "calm her down" or to "help him sleep." On this issue, Collins writes:

> I explain to the family the effects of sedation—that it produces numbness and blocks the pain. However, feeling pain and crying is part of the emotional response to grief.

And very necessary responses they are. Such expressions are absolutely essential to healthy and complete grief resolution. If medications are introduced, two problems result.

First, they prolong the grief process. There is a threshold of emotional energy that eventually must be vented. Honest emotional releases are cumulative and gradually serve to satisfy this requirement. Delaying emotional advancement to this threshold serves no real value.

Second, grief experienced in a medication-induced mental state may not serve to propel the individual toward this threshold at all. In such an altered state, it is likely that emotional energy is expended for naught. While there are extreme or medically related reasons for which sedation may prove helpful, these are exceptional and certainly not the rule. The only deviation from this guideline may be a sleep aid.

Screening Information for Release

In your discussions with families regarding death, try to provide *only* the information for which you feel the family is emotionally prepared. For example, the initial death statement should never include a description of the condition of the body. While you may enumerate the injuries sustained, descriptive information should be provided only after the survivors have reasonably recovered from the shock of the death and after they have confirmed their desire to view the body. For those not viewing the body, such information may only disturb them further.

In my research, participants were asked to respond to two statements: "I should be told only that information which I specifically request," and "The caller should voluntarily give all available information about the death without requiring that I specifically request it." It was interesting to note that most participants disagreed with *both* statements! (See Chapter 13, pages 216 and 217.) Families want the notifier to use professional judgement and to filter, or perhaps slowly release, the available information.

One participant, when asked about the apparent conflict in her answers, responded, "Well, if, for example, my brother died in an auto accident, I would generally want to know all about his death. But I might not want to know that he was also drunk, and killed someone else in the accident. At least, not right away."

Extrapolation of Techniques

The death notification guidelines given here should be applied to all other critical events you encounter. The delivery of any emotionally challenging news—be it blindness, loss of hearing, paralysis, dismemberment, or disfigurement—should follow similar steps. Simply put, statements of difficult news need to be carefully staged and delivered in concert with the needs, underlying circumstances, and level of preparation of the family. By so doing, you can maximize healthy responses and protect all involved.

Chapter 4

Special Issues in Notification

Some notification issues can be particularly difficult to manage. These include long-distance notification, anticipatory notification, death-telling to children, and on-scene notification. Brief guidelines and suggestions for these complex situations are provided here.

Long-distance Notification

Travel Time

One especially gray notification area is deciding when distance precludes a face-to-face or on-site notification (e.g., when it would take the family two, three, or more hours to reach your facility).

Because telephone notification can be especially stressful and professionals can exercise little control over ensuing events, long-distance notification should be avoided. Sometimes, however, a telephone notification is necessary. My research indicates that if a family lives more than one hour from the hospital, telephone notification should be considered.

In the research, most families surveyed wanted to be given the news by phone if they had to take more than 15 minutes to drive to the hospital. (See Chapter 13, page 221.) Selections of one and two hours were the next most common choices. In discussion with those selecting two hours, most indicated that they simply did not want to be told such news on the telephone. It is important, therefore, to recognize and respond to a myriad of subtle clues when deciding whether to defer or provide a telephone notification.

Telephone Contacts

In situations of extreme distance, telephone notification is usually un-avoidable. Occasionally, you may be able to locate a family friend who can assist with a personal notification. More often, however, you will have to contact the survivors yourself.

One possible alternative is to contact local law enforcement officials and ask them to go to the home. In most situations, however, I prefer to avoid this strategy unless I know that a local officer is well-trained in notification. The research indicates that, given a choice, most people prefer not to be notified by police officers. (See Chapter 13, page 219.)

In delivering notification by telephone, there are five key points to remember:

1. Never rush the statement of death. Follow the verbal format of the Sequential Notification Technique described in Chapter 3.

2. Don't force a notification. If the family member seems hesitant or unable to cope with difficult information, offer to speak with someone else in the home or to call another family member, friend, or clergy.

3. *After* the notification, find out if the person is home alone. If so, offer to call someone to come and give support. If the offer is declined, obtain verbal assurance from the person that he or she will call shortly to share the news with other family members or friends.

There are two important reasons for waiting until after the notification to ask if the person is alone. First, if asked this question prior to the notification, he/she may fear a "crank call," and may not accurately reveal the situation. Second, the request may cause extreme anxiety and precipitate a hurried notification. Research indicates that, even when alone, most people still want the notification to be delivered immediately. (See Chapter 13, page 218.)

4. If someone threatens suicide at such a time, stay on the phone and talk it through. For the professional expected to handle such difficult situations, suggestions are offered in the Suicidal Ideation section, in Chapter 8. Otherwise, try to have someone locate a trained professional to go to the home while you continue on the phone. If the person hangs up, call local police immediately.

5. If there is no adult in a home, ask the oldest child how to get in touch with an adult relative. Explain that it is an emergency, but avoid giving any details. You might say, "Your dad was in a car accident (is sick, etc.), and he wants me to talk with your mother (or another adult, if she is not available)." Assure the child that someone will call right back. Then, in contacting the adult, make sure to relate the child's knowledge of the phone call being made to ensure appropriate follow-up.

Case Vignette 4.1

One case example of telephone notification involved a truck driver from New Jersey, who died in California. A home phone number was found in his wallet, so out-of-state contact with his wife was possible:

> "Hello. This is Mr. Leash from the University Medical Center in Sacramento, California. Is this Mrs. Jones?"
> "Yes, it is."

"I'm sorry to call you so early in the morning (6 A.M. her time), but it is important that I talk with you. Are you awake enough to speak with me?"

"Yes. Just a minute. Let me turn on a light. Now who did you say this was?"

"This is Mr. Leash at the Medical Center in Sacramento, California. I'm calling you from the Emergency Room here in the hospital. Mrs. Jones, were you aware that your husband was in an accident?"

"No! Is he all right?"

"Well, we are very concerned, Mrs. Jones. Let me tell you what I know. Okay?"

"Yes. Please! He drives a truck for a living, you know. I always worry about him when he goes on these long trips."

"It appears that John was driving on the freeway to Woodland and fell asleep. His truck left the road, and he sustained some severe injuries to his chest and abdomen in the accident. The injuries were severe enough to require CPR at the scene. Do you know what CPR is?"

"Oh, my! Yes, I do."

"Well, he was flown by helicopter to this hospital and arrived still under CPR. Now, Mrs. Jones, his injuries are very severe. Do you understand what I am telling you so far?"

"Yes. Is he going to live?"

"Mrs. Jones, things just aren't going well. Do you feel able to talk about this on the phone?"

(Again, this question gave her the chance to defer notification, or perhaps to have me speak to another family member in the home. If she were home alone, it would have been appropriate to offer to call another relative of her choice, and have the relative call her back directly. I also would have asked, "Will you be all right until they call you back?" It is important not to hang up the phone until you are sure of the person's emotional stability. If necessary, continue talking until the person seems composed. In this specific case, further delay was not indicated.)

"Yes. I want to know how he is."

"Well, Mrs. Jones, he has the kind of injuries you can't survive." (Pause.)

"Is he dead?"

"Yes. He passed away about 2:30 A.M., our time."

In this type of notification, after sufficient time and support have been given, ask if the person is home alone. If so, offer to call someone else, or get an assurance that others will be called soon. Reassure the survivor that you will be available by telephone to offer any support needed and then, if appropriate, proceed with the practical death-related matters at hand.

Case Vignette 4.2

Another example of telephone notification involved a well-known individual who died on a plane flying to Sacramento. He suffered a heart attack and, before the plane could land, had already stopped breathing. CPR was begun at the scene, and he was flown by Life Flight helicopter to our hospital. Shortly after arrival, he was pronounced dead. I retrieved his sister's telephone number from his wallet, and discovered that she lived in Fresno, more than 200 miles away.

Because of the distance, I decided to make a telephone notification, if the conversation allowed. After reviewing the facts surrounding the death, I telephoned, and the conversation proceeded as follows:

> "Hello, is this Mrs. C.?"
> "Yes."
> "This is Mr. Leash, and I'm calling you from the University Medical Center in Sacramento. I'm here with your brother, Todd. It appears that he boarded a plane to Sacramento and became ill en route. He was brought to our hospital after the plane landed. Has anyone notified you of this, or is this your first call?"
> "You are the first. How is he doing?"
> "Well, things haven't gone too well, Mrs. C. I would like to call his immediate family and talk with them. Is Todd married?"
> "No."
> "Does he have any children?"
> "No, he doesn't."
> "It sounds as if you are his closest family, then, aren't you?"
> "Yes. He doesn't really have anyone else, I don't think."
> "Well, perhaps we might take a few minutes and discuss his condition. Are you where we can talk?"
> "I suppose (tentatively)."
> "If this isn't a good time, I could call you back in a few minutes, when we know more. Would that be better?"
> "Oh yes, why don't you do that."

I was somewhat surprised by her acceptance of my deferral, particularly when my request for immediate family was an obvious clue that something serious had occurred. I arranged to call her back in about half an hour. In that interim, three state officials arrived and requested information on the victim's status. I notified them of the death, and one offered to call a mutual friend of the deceased and his sister. The friend lived near the sister and would be able to go to her home and provide a personalized notification there. After the sister's unusual response to my call, I was relieved to defer to a family friend. The staff person placed this call, and at the appointed time I called the sister back.

> "How is he doing? (Tentatively, again.)"
> "Well, as I mentioned, things haven't gone well. I was just talking to one of Mr. C.'s staff, and he suggested that we call Mr.

L. to go to your home and talk with you there. He has all the information you need. Would that be all right?"

"That would be just fine. So he'll be here soon?"

"Yes, Mrs C., it should be only a few minutes. If you have any questions, please feel free to call me later. Okay?"

She responded that this would be fine, and we closed the conversation.

In reviewing this scenario, it is clear that this woman was not ready to discuss her brother's condition at that time, or at least not by means of the telephone. Had I firmly determined to tell her and abruptly delivered the news, it would have robbed her of the privilege of deciding when and from whom she was to receive the news.

For this reason, it is important always to choose your words in a way that allows family members a chance to defer. A good preparatory phrase is, "Things haven't gone well here. Is this a good time to talk for a few minutes?" If you detect hesitation, you might say something like, "Would you like me to call back later when I have more details?" or "Is there someone you would like me call instead, right now?" You may be surprised how many people will choose to have the notification deferred.

In talking with one family by telephone, the response was:

"Please, don't give me bad news."

"Okay. I understand. Would you like to have me call back, or is there someone else I should call?"

The person then gave me the telephone number of another family member, and I promised that I would ask that person to call directly after our conversation. This arrangement was much preferred, and, again, I carried out the wishes accordingly. If you are sensitive to the tone of voice, inflection, and the words used by family members, you will be more likely to proceed according to their needs and wishes.

Anticipatory Notifications

At times, you will encounter situations in which the actual death has not yet occurred but is expected imminently. In these situations, it is helpful to use a process called *anticipatory notification*, in which you foreshadow the loss and allow the family to begin the grief process more gradually. When a death is expected, or even highly probable, you should not hide this fact from the family. Instead, give those present the opportunity to make preparations, both personal and practical, and, when feasible, to spend additional time with the critically ill family member. This allows relatives to say goodbye (even if the patient is unconscious) and makes it more likely that they will be able to come to terms with the loss.

Case Vignette 4.3

A 19-year-old boy died as a result of a car accident. When he arrived at the hospital with severe head injuries, he was still alive, but the prognosis was extremely guarded. I spoke with his father outside the operating room at length. The victim's mother was out of town but had been notified of the accident and was now en route to the hospital. We discussed both his son's condition and their family.

He told me that this boy was their only child. He and his wife had tried for ten years to have children, and finally, when they had given up hope, this son was conceived and born. As older parents, they had turned their complete attention upon him and enjoyed a full family life. Just recently their son had been admitted to a university some distance from their home, so they had purchased a car for him to use at college—the same car in which he was injured.

The young man apparently had failed to negotiate a freeway off-ramp, and the car had rolled down a steep embankment. He had sustained a broken neck, with spinal cord damage and severe head trauma.

The father asked, "If he were to survive, would he walk again?"

"No," I responded. "It doesn't look as though he would."

"Do you think he can survive?" the father asked intently, with a clear and steady gaze.

"We never know until sufficient time has passed," I responded. "But, no, it doesn't look as if he will survive. I think you should both prepare yourselves for this."

"Oh, if only he could live," the father said. "I don't care if he can't walk." Placing his head in his hands, he said, "I would carry him on my back all the days of my life, if only he could live." His fervent prayers and heartfelt pleas touched my heart, and tears filled our eyes.

Although this was a difficult experience for both of us, it was also a meaningful one. This preliminary notification allowed the pain and sorrow to be felt and managed early on and began the process of preparatory grief, a well-documented and important transition. While this was not the usual "notification after-the-fact," it was a notification just the same.

Just two or three hours later, their son died. The period in which we talked, and the ensuing time prior to the death, allowed both parents to prepare themselves for their loss. Had we not discussed the possibility at all, or had I held out false hope, the time would have been spent in vain, and a valuable and supportive opportunity would have been wasted. In the interim following the statement of expected death, the parents were able to say their "good-byes" and come to initial grips with the impending loss.

Telling Children

When telling children of a death, it is important to be direct and truthful. Amy Hillyard Jensen, a twice-bereft mother, in the pamphlet *Healing Grief*, notes the following:

> Handled carefully, the truth should be good enough. Your own beliefs will, of course, determine what you say about the meaning of death and about life after death. And you can admit there is much more that you do not know. But distortions of reality can do lasting harm. For example, "gone to sleep" may lead to a fear of going to sleep, and "God took her'" may lead to a hatred of God for being cruel. Incidentally, death in a hospital may lead to a fear of hospitals unless the child is reassured.
>
> Do not say, or let others say, to the child who has lost a father, "You are the man of the house now." And no child (or adult) should be told to "be brave." Having to put up a false front makes grieving more difficult.

An appropriate notification should be geared to the child's developmental level. It is important that the physical surroundings and environment not be too distracting. When making the statement, bring the children near to you and look at them directly so that they feel you care and so they will give you their undivided attention. The words chosen might be something like those used with a five-year-old girl whose mother died in a car accident.

Case Vignette 4.4

"Jenny, do you understand what we've been talking about?" She nodded. I continued, "Mommy was hurt real bad in this accident, and they took her to surgery where the doctors tried to fix the things that were wrong. But they couldn't fix them in time, so Mommy died. Do you understand what it means to die?"

"I think so."

"Have you ever had a pet or someone else die?"

"Well, our cat died once," she responded. "Mommy and daddy said he went to Heaven."

"Did your cat ever come back home?"

"Nope, he never did." She looked to her father, as if to be supported in her conclusion. He shook his head, "No." Tears started to well up in her eyes.

"Well, Mommy died, too, honey," I continued. "And although she can't come home again, either, I'm sure she loves you just the same as always. Now, I want you to know there isn't anything any one of us could do to save Mommy. Her death was just a bad accident. No one did anything wrong, not you or anyone. Okay?"

She nodded her understanding and went to her daddy where he hugged and comforted her. Later, the father and I talked about children's grieving patterns, and I prepared him to support her further.

On-scene Notifications

Those who are "first responders" face a most difficult task. Occasionally, a family member who was not seriously injured in the accident, or who arrives at the scene during extrication or resuscitation, will require notification on the spot. If at all possible, defer this to a more appropriate time. If the victim is being transported to a hospital, tell the family member to get more information there, after the accident victim has been examined by a physician.

If death has occurred on-scene, however, and the deceased is going directly to a coroner's office or funeral home (as in small counties without a county morgue), you may need to break the news right away. Here are some suggestions.

Assessment of the Bereft

If the bereft individual is behaving erratically, appears to be under the influence of alcohol or other substances, or has any injuries, use particular caution in exposing the survivor to further stress. Carefully read the section on notification contraindicators later in this chapter to ensure that you do not unduly compromise or distress someone already in difficult circumstances.

Selection of Surroundings

Prepare the surroundings as much as possible. For example, get the family members out of traffic, perhaps into your vehicle (*not* theirs, as you don't want them driving away crazily), or into a secluded area slightly away from the scene. Speak to as small a group as you can (immediate family only), preferably no more than two or three—have others wait nearby or in their vehicles. Don't notify someone by yourself if you can help it. You can control a difficult grief response much better if there are two of you present.

Notification Delivery

Follow the guidelines in Chapters 2 and 3 for delivering a notification statement. Give family members plenty of time to absorb the news and collect their feelings. Keep them in a controlled atmosphere (with you, in relative privacy) until they are able to maintain their composure.

Viewing a Body On-scene

Try to discourage families from viewing a body on-scene *if* a viewing under such circumstances might be overwhelming. However, if the relatives seem under control and cooperative, it is within their right to view their loved one at once. You should prepare the body appropriately first, following the guidelines noted in Chapter 5 as closely as possible. An ideal on-scene viewing location would be in the home, if that's where the death occurred, or inside an ambulance, where the survivors can grieve in partial privacy.

Support and Follow-up

After a notification of death, never leave a family member entirely alone. Offer to call other family members to come; offer to take the person home, to a friend's or relative's family residence, or to a nearby hospital or similar setting, for counseling and support.

If there is more than one family member present, and one of them seems collected enough to drive home safely, make note of this openly. You could say something like, "Why don't you drive the car, Julie. I think your brother is having pretty rough time. Okay?" Your assistance with suggestions and observations may prevent another tragic accident.

A notification of death is a lengthy commitment, and it is important to make time to ensure the safety and emotional well-being of all involved. In a setting in which notifications are likely to occur, it would be advisable to develop a protocol, and to obtain referral resources for just such occasions.

Notification Contraindicators

Certain contraindicators exist in selecting which members of the family to tell and when. These generally involve situations in which the newly bereft individual is mentally or emotionally incapacitated, or where legal situations, such as homicide, prohibit a prompt notification.

Accident Co-victims

Those who have been involved in an accident with the deceased need to be carefully evaluated regarding death notification. They may already suspect the death, in which case they should be told the facts, if they ask for them, when circumstances are appropriate. The general rule to follow in such circumstances is to wait 12-24 hours, or until the patient is intently requesting information. Look for a time when the patient is well-rested and settled in the hospital. Avoid notifying someone who is in great pain or under heavy sedation. As always, if notification is appropriate, follow the guidelines of the Sequential Notification Technique in Chapter 3, page 52.

Surgery or Sedation

Individuals in pain, under sedation, or who are about to undergo surgery will not be prepared to receive such news. Traumatic injury, with the associated shock, or the influence of psychoactive drugs, creates an altered mental state. Although individuals may appear to process and

respond to information normally, the emotional impact may be dramatically increased. Their coping mechanisms may be markedly compromised,
preventing a constructive response.

Traumatic Brain Injuries

Patients with mild to moderate brain injury present a special subset of
accident victims. In such circumstances, delay notification until the
normal functions of the brain have resumed. Of particular mention are
individuals with marked temporary short-term memory impairment.
Notifying such persons should be delayed, when possible, to prevent the
experience of multiple re-notification stress. Again, follow the general
rule of waiting until the person begins asking about the deceased. At
that time, his or her ability to integrate this difficult information is
usually evident, and the notification can be appropriately carried out.

Survivors on Respiratory Support

Patients who have been intubated, and are thus unable to respond
verbally to the news, should not be told too hastily of a death. Postpone-
ment of the news until respiratory support is removed would be ideal.
However, if a patient is alert, writing requests for information or
otherwise clearly pressing for the news, he or she should be told. Select
a time for the notification when several family members can be present
for support. It is critical that both the notifier and the family spend
additional time verbalizing important feelings for the injured person. In
this way he or she can obtain the emotional release that is so important
after a loss.

After the initial notification, encourage relatives to discuss all
appropriate details of the death in the presence of this person. Have
them anticipate and respond to the patient's potential feelings and
concerns. The family should be prepared to review the death many times
over, as the patient may indicate a desire to hear these details again and
again. This is a normal response and stems from the limited ability to
express feelings. If the injured person is unable to attend a funeral,
encourage the family to photograph or videotape the major events and
people there. This will assist in obtaining those important feelings of
closure that a funeral provides.

Alcohol and Drug Abuse

As with persons in intense pain or under sedation, those under the
influence of alcohol and drugs are in an altered mental state. In this
state, information is evaluated and stored differently, inhibiting its later
retrieval and processing. After sobering up, a person may have difficulty
remembering much of what was reported while he or she was in an
altered state. In situations where news of great emotional gravity—such
as the death of a loved one—has been delivered too early, the notifica-

tion may need to be reiterated, with the grief experienced again. This can easily be avoided by waiting until the person has become clear of drugs or alcohol.

An exception to this general practice occurs when a drunk driver has killed someone in a motor vehicle accident. In these circumstances, law enforcement officers are required to tell the patient of the death immediately, regardless of the driver's mental or emotional state, in order to effect an informed arrest. It will then be necessary to provide emotional support to both the driver and the family members when they arrive.

Homicide

Law enforcement officials must always be consulted before attempting any contact with families of homicide victims. On occasion, attempts to notify the family can potentially circumvent officials' efforts to apprehend the perpetrator(s) of the crime. Law enforcement staff members will usually choose to make the notification themselves.

Chapter 5

Notification Follow-up

Once the news of death has been delivered, it is imperative that the notifier provide both psychological and emotional support to survivors. This should include referral for continuing support, when needed. Also, any practical information that you can provide to assist the family with tasks such as funeral arrangements and reports will be appreciated.

Members of one family noted that, at the time of their loss, they felt they received the least support from those in authority. Their daughter, Valerie, was killed in a car accident following a high school graduation party. The driver of the car was drinking, and the car careened off a high embankment and rolled, throwing Valerie from the vehicle and crushing her beneath it. Her grief-stricken parents drove all night to another town to view her body, only to be turned away because of their late-night arrival. They also had difficulty in obtaining autopsy results and police reports.

Timely assistance and accurate information can prevent confusion in accomplishing the many tasks that accompany the sudden loss of a family member. This chapter covers a few important support and informational issues.

Debriefing

When a sudden traumatic event has occurred, people invariably express feelings of unreality. They may say, "This seems like a dream," "This can't really be happening to me," or "This can't be real. I'll wake up and it will be over." These feelings are a natural consequence of events over which they have no control and limited information. Such expressions indicate the lack of a *loss context*, which is needed to organize and give meaning to their thoughts and emotions.

Loss Context

A loss context is created through a process known as "debriefing." Debriefing consists of the orderly staging and presentation of details and information to meet the conceptual and emotional needs of those involved.

Survivors need to be able to visualize the death scene and events to accept them as reality. While in emotional upheaval, people often ask questions that aggravate their confusion and stress. They simply don't know where to begin. It is better to resist responding to ill-timed or extraneous questions ("What will we do with her cat?") and pursue—or repeat—those facts most pertinent to the circumstances of death.

Uncomfortable details should be withheld until such time as the listeners can tolerate them emotionally, building upon what has already been said. An abrupt death notification can prolong these feelings of unreality. The resultant turmoil clouds the thinking processes and further inhibits mental depth-of-view. It is imperative that the notifier present all information in a systematic way, with gradually increasing detail, to avoid confusion. If your presentation seems haphazard and filled with unconnected events, those involved will find it difficult to perceive the death as "reality," and their distress will be significantly prolonged. In such a condition, they are not prepared to view the body, assume the tasks of further family contacts, make funeral preparations, or support each other in their grief.

Religious Support

Many people have active religious affiliations and would greatly appreciate the offer to contact a minister, rabbi, priest, or pastor. In such circumstances, the family may wish last rites for their loved one or baptism, especially in the case of an infant. The family members may not be able to prioritize their concerns, and your assistance in identifying appropriate support systems will help them through a difficult transition.

Where there is no specific religious affiliation, or in the absence of a familiar religious support person, you can offer to contact a hospital chaplain. Chaplains are trained to provide support to persons of all faiths and can be of tremendous assistance to many families.

Additional Family Contacts

Often, those present at the hospital will feel a great need to call other family members promptly. They will appreciate having a telephone available for their use. It may be helpful if you offer to place the calls and to speak first, preparing the person on the other end with a brief, gentle statement of the death, instead of leaving the newly bereft family member to struggle with breaking the news. Under duress, people tend to make blunt notification statements and may thereby compromise the ability of others to provide the desired support.

Helpful Family and Friends

In this follow-up process, try to assist the family in identifying those who can be of the most immediate assistance. In some cases, it may be a friend or neighbor, rather than a family member. Help to screen the selections, considering such variables as the health of the individuals being called and those who live at far distances. Help the family to slow down throughout this process. It is common for people under stress to feel the need to do something, anything, to try to alleviate the pain they are experiencing. Yet many contacts and certain decisions are better left to another time. Once all initial calls have been made and local family members have arrived, with time allowed for emotional composure, the family is usually ready to view the body.

Viewing the Body

You're First

Most family members will want to see their loved one shortly after notification. (See Chapter 13, page 223.) To prepare the family to see the deceased, it is imperative that you have viewed the body first. It is your responsibility to be sure that the body is properly arranged for viewing. Also, survivors will often ask specific questions about the condition or appearance of the body, and they will need to feel that the information given is first-hand and accurate. This is an integral part of establishing the requisite loss context.

Family Reluctance

It has been noted (Shultz, 1980) that the family may need "permission" to see the body, feeling reluctant to request this themselves. In my experience, this happens often.

After the notification of death has taken place, and the family has had sufficient time to recover from the initial shock of the news, the subject may be approached by saying, "If you would like, we can arrange for you to see (your husband) here."

If members are hesitant to view the body, try to find out their reasons. Encourage them, if appropriate, with statements such as, "I think you will be glad you did," and "I'll be right there with you."

Such encouragement is particularly important in situations where the family may feel the body has been mutilated. Even if the body has been badly disfigured, it still may be important for the family to see it. Shultz suggests draping or bandaging the affected areas to shield them from the family, and notes that, even if all that can be viewed are the hands, the family can recognize and find meaning in the part of the body that has been shown. Again, it is important for you to have already viewed the body, so that you can prepare it for viewing, confirm its condition, and guide the family properly.

Viewing and Denial

Sometimes, families will indicate that they have no interest in viewing the deceased. If relatives were at the scene and saw the patient being treated and placed in an ambulance, perhaps an additional viewing is not necessary. But if someone is exhibiting substantial denial of the death and remains hesitant to view, it is usually wise to pursue the issue. As Collins notes, "A 'no' response usually means the survivors need more time."[10] In such situations, simply talking with them longer about the death can provide the additional emotional support and time they need to prepare themselves.

One way to do this is to gently take the person aside and discuss the issue frankly and clearly. It may be helpful to say something such as:

> "I know this is difficult for you, but I am concerned that you may miss this opportunity. [Your son] will never look and feel so nearly alive again. If you want to give him a good-bye kiss on the cheek, now is the time. Are you sure? This may be important for you to come to terms with your loss."

Such comments may seem extreme, placing undue pressure on the family. However, it is often important for families to touch and embrace the deceased and offer a tender farewell. Never again will the body be as receptive to such efforts, and thus as therapeutically effective, as immediately following the death.

It may help to allow those who are prepared for it to see the body first. After viewing, they may easily persuade other family members to do so. Collins notes that she tells family members that they will not be left alone unless they request it. While it is regrettable that our society has engendered such a fear of death, for many the support of knowing that someone will be with them may help them to overcome this fear.

Death Phobias

Although it is important to encourage viewing, it is equally important to avoid pressuring any family member into viewing. There are those whose fear of death borders on the phobic, a situation which cannot be resolved instantly.

If, after encouragement, certain family members still do not desire to see the body, they should be supported in their decision. Openly support them if they appear to feel undue or inappropriate pressure from others. Otherwise, they may participate in an experience that may significantly traumatize them.

A gesture that is often appreciated is offering to clip a lock of hair for the family. Place it in an envelope for them to take home. This can be particularly helpful for family members who were not able to view the body.

---

[10] Collins, S. "Sudden Death Counseling Protocol." *Dimensions of Critical Care Nursing,* Nov.-Dec. 1989. Copyright Hall Johnson Communications, Inc. All quotes reproduced with permission.

Preparation of the Body

In preparation for viewing, the body should be made as presentable and approachable as possible. The rules for this are simple: just ask yourself how you would want your family to see you in such circumstances. Blood, dirt and debris should be washed away from all exposed areas. Using a little hydrogen peroxide will help. In our setting, we keep a comb available for use in such situations.

Bandages and linen are usually changed, as they may have become soiled during the treatment efforts. Collins suggests replacing bandages, "unless there is less than a quarter-sized area of saturation. Leaving some sign of the trauma is realistic." Consistent with that, all gross signs of injury are usually covered or bandaged, but lesser sites (if not bleeding), are left for the family's acknowledgement.

With these techniques and preparations, in the hundreds of viewings I have facilitated, I have never had family members react inappropriately to visible injuries. Occasionally, I have had family members want to lift the sheet covering the body to look for other signs of trauma. In most such cases, I had not given them details of injury sites that they would not normally see. While it is appropriate for them to make their own visual examination, you may need to interrupt them to describe the other injuries they will encounter. At times, they may then forgo the attempt.

Collins also suggests leaving medical equipment at the bedside, as a way of showing survivors that all that was possible was done. While advocating the removal of blood-stained instruments and tubes attached to the body, she notes that the presence of other medical equipment will contribute to the family's acknowledgement of the death as reality. She makes the comment, "Survivors are not shocked at the equipment—they are shocked at the death." This is true with all elements of the viewing.

A caution is added here. In cases of homicide, the endotracheal tube and I.V. lines may have to be left in place until the coroner removes the body. In my experience, during the brief call to the coroner's office to report the death, permission can often be obtained to remove some or all medical paraphernalia if appropriate documentation is made. Permission is especially likely to be granted in cases where the cause of death is quite obvious. Appropriate documentation includes marking I.V. tube sites and other wound sites resulting from medical treatment.

These sites can be marked by drawing circles around them with a pen, and noting the markings on the chart. Notations should also be made of the phone call, the permission obtained, and the items removed. In situations where the survivors' grief is acute and optimum therapeutic value from the viewing is important, the extra effort can be worthwhile.

Positioning the Body

It is also important to position the body carefully for an ideal presentation. Failure to attend to this can sometimes inhibit family responses. If the body is in a hospital bed, elevate the head. This limits fluid accumulation in the mouth and nose, decreases the flow of blood from upper-body wounds, and helps with a more aesthetic appearance. Place a small pillow or folded sheet under the head. This will tuck the chin closer to the chest, helping to keep the mouth closed and more normal in appearance.

In a larger room, do not put the body toward the back, as it may seem ominous and far away. Neither is it ideal to put the body in profile, or where the family will see it from the feet upwards (perhaps looking into the nose and gaping mouth), or with the head of the bed closest to their entry, where upon they may feel they are approaching the body from behind. The best presentation is near the door, with the foot of the bed nearest the entry. This allows them to view the body from a slightly diagonal direction (about 30 degrees). Dimming the room's lights may be helpful, if not made too dark or foreboding.

Escorting Family to the Viewing

Regardless of the nature of the death, it will always be necessary for the family to be escorted to the viewing room. In a hospital setting, this is usually a private treatment room, where you can make all of the preparations just described. It is best if two people can assist the family at the door of the room. This is not always possible, but it is ideal because it is not wise to direct the family into the room in front of you, nor is it wise to leave them unprotected behind you. It is not uncommon for a family member to faint upon seeing the loved one, and someone should be behind to assist.

Give the family permission to touch the body by approaching it first and touching an arm, hand or brow for them. Nearly always at this point, family members will spontaneously come to the bedside and make contact themselves. After making sure that all are managing this initial presentation well, step away from the body and allow the family some semblance of privacy with the loved one. If the viewing is long, leaving the room for a time, if all are comfortable with this, can provide for further family intimacy.

It has been suggested that families be provided with multiple viewing opportunities to facilitate their grief and acceptance of the loss. I do not always find this necessary, but in cases of highly emotive grieving or denial, it is crucial. Sometimes it may require that the body be moved to an area that can be left free for this activity for an extended time. While moving the body may be acceptable for subsequent viewings, always have the initial viewing in the most ideal setting available before moving to another location.

Where excessive guilt or other unresolved emotions are attached to the loss, family members should be given "alone time" with their loved one. This is an opportunity for them to perhaps share feelings and thoughts that had been neglected before. Encourage survivors to talk to their loved ones, out loud if privacy allows, to facilitate the resolution of these feelings.

While this may be early in the grief process to expect extensive catharsis, such communications are always of great value in the grief-resolution process and can take place at the hospital setting or later in the funeral home. Where unresolved feelings are evident, seek opportunities to encourage the survivors to make such communications. Your suggestions may well facilitate this process.

Viewing Children/Infants

More flexible arrangements can often be made for survivors viewing their own children. This is always to be encouraged where possible. As Collins (1989) further notes, "For the parent, a child's death can mean the loss of a future and a dream. A part of the parent can die with the child." With the anguish and intense emotions this loss brings, every effort should be made to assure that the viewing experience is intimate and meaningful. This is especially important immediately following the death, as the body is yet supple and receptive.

Parents should be encouraged, when acceptable to them, to hold their small children and infants. Often, they will want to do so spontaneously, especially in cases where the death occurred shortly after birth. At such times, parents usually have had few opportunities to hold the infant and will often have a great need for a physical expression of love. This will allow them a final chance to "own" their child in their arms.

Sometimes, it may be appropriate for a small child or infant to be removed from a treatment area for viewing in a family room or other similar area in the hospital. Such a setting may seem less clinical to the family and can give them greater intimacy in this last interaction.

Finally, Collins (1989) offers the thoughtful suggestion that a deceased child not be left alone. She narrates an experience in which she had a medical student at the child's side, holding his hand, when the parents entered the room. When she saw this, the mother exclaimed, "How wonderful, you did not leave him alone." In my experience, this has been particularly important with infants. To reassure a parent, when they relinquish their dead infant from their arms to yours, that "we'll take good care of him until you see him again" can be a meaningful gesture. Keeping the baby swaddled in blankets, even into the morgue, is a way of keeping this promise.

As an aside, the careful observations of the caregiver can greatly assist the family. For example, with any death, but especially with the death of a child, the family may be eager for baptism and/or last rites to take place. Your inquiry about the need can assist them in the decision-making process. Further, Jezierski (1989) suggests that, with the death of an infant, you may want to ask if the mother is nursing. If so, provide information regarding delactation or offer contact information for the local LaLeche League or other source of assistance in stopping the flow of milk. It can be extremely difficult for a mother whose child has died to deal with continuing lactation. Again, your observant eye will suggest many things that you can do to make things easier for a family.

Photographs
While not a common request, at times families may desire to take pictures of the deceased. This may seem morbid to some, but in actuality it can prove enormously useful to a family in resolving grief and should not be discouraged. Photographs represent the ultimate reality in grief actualization and can facilitate acknowledgement, emotive responses, and serve as a vehicle for verbal expression. In some situations, such as the death of a newborn, families should be encouraged to consider taking photographs. Indeed, in our hospital setting, cameras and film are provided. These photographs may be the only pictures the new parents will ever have of their child and can become important parts of their family history.

Consent for Autopsy

In situations where the medical cause of death was not clear, or to conduct research (when coroners' laws do not intervene), the attending physician may wish to perform an autopsy. As with organ and tissue donation, this can be a sensitive subject and one that must be approached carefully to improve the likelihood of the family's participation. It is important to raise this issue only after an initial viewing of the body and following an adequate grieving period. This is a situation in which the physician should make the request personally and not defer to any other professionals present. It may be advantageous, however, to have someone accompany the physician to provide family support. While I have successfully obtained many autopsy authorizations, it seems most appropriate when this request comes from a physician.

If there is a large gathering, the physician should select one or two adults, including a legal next-of-kin (a social worker or nurse may be able to assist here), to speak to in private. If too many people are present, it can lend to confusion, and conflicting opinions can interfere with the process. A request can then be made as follows:

"As you know, Mrs. Smith, your husband seems to have died from a heart attack. But we can't be sure without an autopsy. I feel it would be beneficial to you and your family if we could confirm the cause of death. Occasionally, it also can be important to the health of your children for them to know their family medical history.

"In addition, we may be able to obtain medical information from this exam which can help us to better understand how to treat patients in similar situations in the future. May we have your consent to perform this exam?"

Coroners' Laws

At times, an autopsy may be necessitated by the circumstances surrounding a death. In such situations, formal determination of the cause of death will fall to a coroner. Nearly every state has enacted coroners' laws. The purpose behind these laws is to ensure an impartial medical-legal investigation, so that no suspicion of homicide is present, or remains, where suspected. Similar to the regulations in other states, the California Health and Safety Code defines deaths that must be reported to the coroner as:

A. Death without professional medical attendance.
B. Death during the continued absence of the attending physician.
C. Cases in which the attending physician is unable to state the cause of death.
D. Deaths where suicide is suspected.
E. Death following an injury or an accident, either recent or in the past.
F. Death under such circumstances that afford reasonable grounds for suspecting a criminal act.[11]

Virtually all accident victims, and most unexpected-death victims, fall into these categories. Most states follow similar guidelines. Should a death become a coroner's case, the decision to autopsy cannot be avoided. It must be done in accordance with state law. Families should be told of these examinations and helped to understand the purpose of the law if questions arise. They should be informed that they can obtain a copy of the autopsy results. Timely funeral arrangements can be made by notifying the mortician of the location of the body.

Funeral Arrangements

Basic funeral arrangements are not difficult to make. Funeral directors usually make every effort to reduce stress on the family at such a time. Family members will probably want to select a funeral home near the area where they wish the remains to be deposited. They need to let the funeral director know where the body is currently located (hospital,

---

[11] From C.R. Simmons, Sacramento County, California, Coroner/Public Administrator's Office.

coroner's office, etc.), and sign the necessary papers releasing the body to the funeral home for transportation and preparation.

Families often express concern that they may omit important preparations. A checklist, found in Appendix K, can be included in a "bereavement packet" to assist them with the basic requirements of this process.

Funeral Expenses

The family should be made aware that funeral home services and costs may vary. Unless a family is certain of which funeral home to select, you should encourage calls to several places—to determine who offers the services desired at the most affordable cost. Under federal law, funeral homes must offer detailed price information over the telephone.

When finances are a serious consideration, encourage the family to contact a local Memorial Society, which may have a low-cost arrangement with area funeral directors. Inform the family that cremation is usually the least expensive choice. In addition, most local governmental bodies have a department, such as the Public Administrator's Office in California, that will assist with a modest funeral when the family is completely without funds.

Therapeutic Involvement

A family also may be told that, in most states, next-of-kin may handle all funeral arrangements without the use of a funeral director. Lisa Carlson, in her book *Caring for Your Own Dead—A Final Act of Love*, points out that, apart from the financial savings, there is tremendous therapeutic value in being intimately involved with the physical activities of funeral arrangements. Having something to do may make a family feel less helpless. Especially in the case of an unanticipated death, there will be more opportunity to face the reality of a death when the family is intimately involved. Some church groups offer support in this sensitive endeavor.

Carlson's book provides practical details and state-by-state requirements for families and support groups who wish to perform some or all of the tasks that would be otherwise delegated, at high cost, to a funeral director.

Case Vignette 5.1

Some time ago, a close family friend died of colon cancer. She was in her mid-forties and left behind a family of six. The youngest child was only four years old.

When she died, we felt her loss deeply. She had requested that I speak at her funeral, which I did, along with others who had been selected. The morning after the funeral, family members invited me to join them in attending to the burial. Prior to the service, they had carefully excavated a grave in the cemetery where many of her family members were buried. This morning, they were to fill it in.

At first, I was somewhat taken aback, for I had never heard of family members doing such a thing by themselves. It seemed that this task was supposed to be left to others, to ensure the job was done "professionally."

When we arrived, each adult took a shovel, and then all gathered together. We stood quietly while her husband offered a gentle, poignant prayer. Following this, we began.

As we worked, we reminisced. Many fond, loving, and beautiful memories were shared there. Tears were shed, and hearts were touched. Humor seemed appropriate, as well. Stories were exchanged, and we smiled and chuckled as we remembered many enjoyable family experiences. She was a fun-loving and happy person, and I truly believe she would have approved. Most particularly, as we labored together, there was an overriding, encompassing feeling that we were personally and tenderly taking care of those final arrangements made for someone we all loved.

If such involvement seems appropriate for a family, especially if they suggest it themselves, all encouragement and support should be given them. It can greatly aid the grief process and can be an outstanding experience that will be cherished throughout a lifetime.

Assessment and Referral

During the entire process, the caregiver should be alert to any signs of complicated grief that appear. If possible, these issues should be addressed and dealt with before the family leaves the hospital. Always alert family members to special problems that may appear later and educate them about the grieving process. Help them to understand the different ways we all grieve and encourage them to be tolerant of individual patterns. (See Appendices for bereavement resources.)

When the family members are prepared to leave the hospital, help them to make a plan for the evening. Determine who will be driving. Many times, a husband or father will assume the task of driving everyone home, even when the weight of grief may compromise his ability. He may need "permission" to turn that task over to someone else.

In the case of a spouse's death, suggest that the widow or widower spend the night with another family member to lessen the impact of returning to an "empty" home. If this is suggested in the company of other family members, it may spare the bereaved from making an awkward request or the experience of spending a difficult night alone.

If the deceased person committed suicide in the home, it may be critical for all family members to spend a night away. In cases of violent suicide, murder, or traumatic death in the home, it maybe helpful to take aside a family member or close friend who appears capable and consider how the scene of death should be cleaned and put in order. Some cleaning companies provide this service, and, in many situations, the immediate family will appreciate being spared this task. On the other hand, it may be extremely important not to make decisions without involving survivors to some degree. The death has already diminished the sense of control most people need to function with purpose, and being involved with necessary tasks can be therapeutic.

First responders are in a unique position to assist the family. Draining the tub in which a baby drowned, for example, may be a little thing to do, but it can reduce substantial stress for the family later on (if investigating law enforcement will allow it). If a less-than-highly-stable family seems intent on returning to a death scene without site preparation, you might call a neighbor or clergy person to accompany them, if you are not free to follow yourself.

Finally, refer the family members to local support groups where long-term follow-up can be obtained. Give references in writing to help them locate an appropriate source of counseling.

Bereavement Literature

It may be helpful for your organization to develop a "bereavement packet" to assist the family in dealing with various aspects of the death. This packet should include coroner's information, hospital "decedent affairs" resources, guidelines for making funeral arrangements, sources for counseling and local bereavement support groups, as well as literature on the grieving process.

Few families are prepared for dealing with death. Well-selected literature can be a valuable resource in helping them come to terms with their loss. Several good booklets are available through the Centering Corporation, P.O. Box 3367 Omaha, NE, 68103-0367, and through Medic Publishing Co, P.O. Box 89, Redmond WA 98073. Other literature is available from groups that specialize in support for a specific kind of loss—the death of a spouse, a child, a sibling, or by the mode of death—suicide, homicide, AIDS. By learning what to expect during bereavement, family members will be better able to understand and support each other. Many families later express how grateful they were for this material. They often note that reading booklets such as "Healing Grief," over and over again, helped them to gain the strength to move forward with their lives.

Counseling and Support Group Referrals

In addition to bereavement literature, referrals should be provided for counseling, if necessary, and for appropriate self-help groups. These groups consist of peer-counselor staff (unlicensed volunteers), or family members who have undergone similar losses and who have organized themselves into a formal support group. These groups can be very effective and usually provide their services free of charge. The only criterion for referral is loss of a relative, in a context that is relevant to the group's purpose. Examples include Parents of Murdered Children (POMC) and Sudden Infant Death Syndrome (SIDS). Appendix J. contains a list of numerous bereavement groups. Many of these groups are chapters of larger organizations. Check your local telephone book for further information.

In cases of complicated grief, one-on-one counseling or therapy may be indicated. One professional notes, "Grief counseling generally assists in helping the bereaved to resolve normal, relatively uncomplicated grieving. Grief therapy, on the other hand, addresses underlying personality dynamics, and, in particular, areas of conflict which inhibit normal grief resolution."[12] You should seek out appropriate counseling and therapy resources in your area to ensure adequate referrals and follow-up for the families with whom you work.

Follow-up Letters

Lydia Bixby, a Boston widow who lost five sons in the Civil War, read and reread many times the gracious letter sent to her by President Abraham Lincoln. It reads, in part:

> I feel how weak and fruitless must be any word of mine which could attempt to beguile you from the grief of a loss so over-whelming. But I cannot refrain from tendering to you the consolation that may be found in the thanks of the Republic they died to save. I pray that our Heavenly Father may assuage the anguish of your bereavement, and leave you only the cherished memory of the loved and lost, and the solemn pride that must be yours to have laid so costly a sacrifice upon the alter of freedom.[13]

While you may be unable to write so eloquently or with such purpose, any genuine, caring comment that you send to a family will doubtlessly be appreciated and treasured. Such words of condolence can be referred to many times when grief is most acute, and can provide a great support during the recovery process. Jane Pauley, co-host of NBC's *Today* show, referring to the miscarriage which occurred during her first pregnancy, said:

> It was one of the most painful periods of my life. . . . The up side was that I got hundreds of thousands of letters from people. To my surprise, I found that condolence letters from perfect strangers really made a difference.[14]

---

[12] Alexy, W., *Bereavement*, vol. 3, no. 5, p. 11.

[13] Bullard, F. Lauriston (1946). *Abraham Lincoln & The Widow Bixby,* pp. 26-27. Rutgers University Press. Reprinted by permission of Rutgers University Press.

[14] Pauley, J. *Bereavement*, vol. 2, no. 9, p. 9.

In situations where numerous deaths are handled on a regular basis, your department or office could also develop a letter of condolence for routine use. While less personal than a hand-written note, it can still serve as a reminder of your caring thoughts and of your willingness to assist in the future.

Public Information Release

When an individual of some note dies, or where an accident or injury is of public interest, members of the media may arrive at your facility asking for information for immediate release.

Family members should always be notified before public release of information occurs. The media/information release protocol of one major trauma center is included in Appendix G. This is for reference only. For absolute legal clarity, a risk management staff member, legal advisor, or appropriate administrative officer should be consulted prior to the release of any information.

In cases of multi-media source contacts or circumstances in which there is interest from the general public, a written release should be prepared to ensure uniformity and accuracy of information, to document the information, and to minimize potential legal entanglements.

Chapter 6

Organic and Tissue Donation

There are numerous paperwork tasks that must be done immediately following a death. Many are simply informational, to be sure that the family receives needed referrals and that there is an appropriate and timely disposition of the remains. Your familiarity with these tasks can provide comfort and clarity in a time of stress. One important follow-up requirement, however, may offer a great measure of support to the family, if approached sensitively, and thus deserves special mention here.

The Need and the Benefits

Today, more than 22,000 people[15] are waiting, and, unless organ donors can be found, dying. It is estimated that another name is added to a waiting list every 30 minutes[16]. Those needing tissue donations represent even greater numbers.

The average organ recipient lives more than eight years after the transplant, and it is not unusual to live 15 years or more[17]. Continuing research and medical advances are extending these limits further each year. Donated tissues generally remain viable throughout the recipient's lifetime, or, in some cases, until new, regenerated tissues replace or bond with those of the donors. In spite of the enormous need, only about 30 percent of all eligible donors actually donate[18]. It appears that this is due in significant measure to families having not been adequately approached by medical staff.

Overlooking, or even avoiding, the topic with a family can cause considerable dismay at a later date. One father wrote, after later discovering that donation could have been an option for his child:

---

[15] United Network for Organ Sharing UNOS, telephone interview, February 26, 1991.

[16] UNOS, Third Annual National Transplantation Education Symposium, October 11-12, 1989.

[17] *Facts About Transplantation in the United States*, United Network for Organ Sharing, December 12, 1988.

[18] United Network for Organ Sharing, Update, June 1990, vol. 6, issue 5, p. 13.

Dear Doctors and Nurses,

The task of informing someone who has placed his hopes and dreams in your abilities as a physician that a loved one has died must be the most difficult task a human being must face. The feelings of loss, of finality, and of grief which you bring with the news of death are sometimes thrown back at you in emotional outbursts which will hurt you if you let them. Remember, it is our hurt, not our heart, speaking at that moment.

But please remember this also: at that moment, there is a tremendous comfort that will help this hurt. That will lessen the sense of finality. That will reduce the loss. It is the chance to grant permission for organ donation. Please inquire, and give those who grieve that option.

Unless you act, and ask, you cannot help this person. I know it is difficult, but you must be courageous. Without your help, the wait for a needed organ will be longer for thousands, and death will remain a final act.

Please help!

(Signed)

"A father who was never asked."[19]

For those who were approached and did choose to donate, feelings are also deep and poignant. One tissue donor's family wrote the following note to the unknown recipient of their daughter's corneas. Their touching note reads as follows:

Recently, my wife and I lost a beautiful and vibrant twelve-year-old daughter to heart failure; hers was a longstanding illness which we knew to be terminal, and yet we had hoped and prayed that one day her life would be sustained through heart transplantation.

Our quest has been denied and we deeply grieve that fact; however, in some small measure we benefit and take solace in knowing that her gift in death has assisted you with the legacy of sight. . . . We find comfort in the knowledge that a part of this special child lives on.

Thank you for perpetuating her memory and giving meaning to her passing.[20]

Recipients are, of course, deeply grateful to those who participate in donation. A heart-transplant recipient wrote the following to newspaper columnist Ann Landers:

---

[19] From the Medical Eye Bank of Maryland. Reprinted with permission.

[20] Note from the Sierra Eye and Tissue Bank. Used with permission.

> I am a heart transplant recipient, the 38th done at UCLA Medical Center. Eighteen months after the surgery, I am 41 years old, healthy, happy and leading a completely normal life. It is like a miracle. I feel so blessed.
>
> I owe this life to someone I have never met, some healthy young person who died unexpectedly. And I will be eternally grateful to the family who allowed their loved one's heart to be donated.
>
> My message is to that unknown donor and family: There is no way I can adequately thank you. I think of you every day and pray for you every night and I shall do so for the rest of my life.[21]

Clearly, the need is real and the benefits are tremendous. To realize these benefits, however, all health care professionals must actively participate in identifying and approaching the families of potential donors, for both organ and tissue donation.

Nearly 50 percent of all people questioned for the research in this writing were in favor of organ and tissue donation. (See Chapter 13, page 224.) Forty-three states *require* that medical staff at least present the option of organ/tissue donation and thus give the family an opportunity to participate. Donation, of course, must be done in a timely manner to ensure the viability of the organs and tissues.

Organ donation may involve donation of the liver, kidneys, heart, lungs, pancreas, thyroid, and parathyroid. Tissue donation may involve donations of corneas, or full ocular globes, dura mater, middle inner ear bones, intercostal cartilage, facia lata, heart valves, saphenous veins, skin, tendons and ligaments, and other bones and joints. After initial screening for eligibility (see Appendices B and C), and if the patient meets the criteria for one or both forms of donation, family members should be approached about this possibility as soon as they are appropriately prepared.

There are many reasons why a family may be reluctant to donate. Some people express reluctance to have their loved one "go through anything more." They also may feel that letting some part of the body be given away means losing their loved one even more completely. To mitigate these and other concerns, follow the protocol suggested below.

Family Preparation

In arranging the donation request, it is important to not broach the subject too early. In cases of brain death, always wait until the family has spoken with the physician and has again viewed the loved one. Make sure all questions regarding brain death and its irreversibility have been thoroughly answered. Again, it is critical that the family has viewed the

---

[21] *The Sacramento Bee,* Ann Landers, August 2, 1988. Reprinted with permission of Ann Landers and Creators Syndicate.

body, perhaps several times, before a donation request is made. Viewing allows the family to regain feelings of "ownership" of the loved one. These feelings are critical for the "letting go" that is necessary for a successful donation authorization.

Always limit any discussion of donation to immediate family members only. Friends and relatives may cause confusion, or may discourage donation when, in fact, they have no authority to consent or refuse and need never know that donation took place. To facilitate this, escort the necessary family members away from any other group present, taking them to a quiet room for uninterrupted discussion. Direct yourself to the legal next-of-kin so that he or she may recognize and assume the primary decision-making role. (See Appendix D for definition of next-of-kin.)

Note that, although the person designated as legal next-of-kin has the final say, it is important that all family members present be in agreement, or at least not in active disagreement about donation. Explain clearly the benefits of organ and tissue donation. Dispel any misconceptions and concerns family members may have. Allow them ample time for a meaningful decision.

Here is a possible approach if the issue is tissue donation:

> "There is something very important that I need to talk with you about. It concerns tissue donation. There are many people whose lives could be greatly improved by the donation of certain small tissues we all have. These people include those who are blind or deaf, crippled, in chronic pain, or suffering from correctable birth defects. 'John' [the deceased] is in a position to help many of these people. Since he isn't able to speak for himself, it falls to you to voice his wishes for him. What do you think John would want? Has he ever discussed this with you?"

Reassure the relatives that tissue donation will in no way affect a viewing at the funeral service. The tissues are generally small and subtle, and no one except immediate family members needs to know of the donation. If they begin to voice personal opinions, remind them that this is a decision they are making for John, and that they should consider what they feel he would want. If the situation becomes complex, with many diverse opinions, reassure them that it is important that they also feel good about the donation and that they are in no way obligated to consent. Most families will respond positively to such an approach.

Organ donation involves a much more complex medical process. Organ donors must be brain dead, but with a heartbeat still intact. Such conditions do not arise very often. Typically, at least two clinical examinations, by separate physicians, must be performed to declare a patient legally brain dead. It is the physician's or nurse's task to ensure that the family fully understands brain death and its irreversibility.

Failure to make this completely clear will likely obviate any organ donation request.

One way to do this is by using a dialogue such as the following (tailored to an accident situation):

"Mrs. Doe, Dr. Henderson and I have just finished examining your son and want to talk with you about what we found. As you know, David received a profound blow to his head in this accident. It has caused tremendous swelling of his brain. If a great deal of swelling of the brain occurs, it can squeeze closed the blood vessels to the brain itself. Just like any tissue in our body, without the oxygen our blood brings to it, it dies. If enough of our brain tissue dies, then we die too.

"This is what has happened to David. In our examination of him we have found signs that the life-saving functions of his brain have all stopped. One of these is his reflex to breathe on his own. Without the respirator we have breathing for him, David's body would have already stopped all of its remaining functions.

"Other signs include the absence of any pupil function, the absence of his gag reflex, and the absence of his reflex to blink his eye if touched. These functions are what we call 'autonomic.' That means they are an automatic function of the body that always works if we are healthy.

"These functions originate in the most guarded area of the brain, the area that is last to be affected by injury. When functions in this area are lost, it is because the brain itself has died. In your son's situation, we find that all of these functions have ceased. David's only remaining reflex, if you will, is his heartbeat, and it, too, will shortly stop.

"What this means is that David is brain dead. The person you know as your son has already died, even though his heart beat may continue for some time longer."

Following such a discussion, answer the family members' questions fully and give them time to absorb this information. *Do not* approach them about donation until they have had time to fully consider this news and to ask any follow-up medical questions they may have. This is the first stage of their emotional preparation for the loss. Be sensitive to this need.

At this point it may be appropriate to escort the family back to see the loved one (the above dialogue should *never* take place in a patient's room). After sufficient time has passed to be sure that the most acute grief reactions have abated, family members may then be approached about their willingness to participate in donation. Again, the donation request should not be delivered at the patient's bedside. It is much better for immediate family members to be escorted to a quiet room for an undisturbed opportunity to consider the request carefully and fully.

Later, if necessary, reiterate that complete death is inevitable, that in a short time the remaining vital signs will begin to deteriorate and death will then quickly follow. At this time, a medical professional should approach the family for an authorization. This person need not be the physician; indeed in some cases it is better if it is not. Some families may need to feel that the physician is continuing to attend to the sustaining needs of their loved one's life right up until the end. If they think that the physician is eager to remove the organs, trust can be damaged, and undue anxiety may result.

A dialogue similar to that for tissue donation may be used for organ donation. For example:

> "There is something very important that I need to talk with you about. It concerns organ donation. While I know your son's body appears very much alive to you right now, something has occurred that we call "brain death." We've talked about this before.
>
> "Although we are able keep your son breathing, and his heart beat is still present, the injury to his head is so significant that his brain has stopped functioning. His brain has died, and at some point this will cause his heart to stop beating, too.
>
> "In situations such as this, your son has the opportunity to give a remarkable gift to others. There are many people whose lives could be saved, or greatly improved, if they were to receive an organ donated to them by your son. I am sure this is difficult to think of right now, but we have to act quickly, before his heart stops beating completely.
>
> "Since your son isn't able to speak for himself, it falls to you to voice his wishes for him. What do you think he would want us to do?"

The major emotional obstacle to overcome here lies in the family's feelings about the body. When the loved one is still warm, still breathing on a respirator, and a heartbeat yet remains, it is easy to feel that the person is still alive. This makes it difficult to relinquish the body to surgery, knowing that, upon removal of the usable organs, all life supports must be discontinued, and the remainder of the death process will then be completed. It is important for the caregiver to validate these feelings and allow the relatives to discuss their reactions fully. Always make sure that all involved have a complete understanding of the concept of brain death. If all steps are carefully pursued, many families will gratefully authorize a donation.

Most, if not all, organ and tissue procurement centers send thoughtful letters of appreciation to those families who participate. These letters can serve as a special reminder to the family of the benefits their loved one was able to give. The following is a letter sent out by the Sierra Regional Eye and Tissue Bank:

Dear Mr. Smith,

I would like to take this opportunity to thank you for your thoughtfulness of others at the time of the loss of your wife. I know this must be a difficult time for you and all who knew and loved her. I hope you may be consoled with the knowledge that due to your generosity, two people have had their sight restored. In addition, the cartilage will provide necessary tissue for facial reconstructive surgery for many patients, the middle-ear bones will be used in hearing-restoration surgeries, the donated bone will be used for many patients needing orthopaedic transplants and spinal fusion surgeries, and the dura mater tissue will replace dural defects for patients needing cranial surgery.

The decision to give consent for donation takes a great deal of courage. I can think of no greater memorial to your wife than (her) gift of a better quality of life for others.

On behalf of the Sierra Regional Eye and Tissue Bank staff, the physicians, and, most of all, those who now enjoy a better life, thank you.

With sincere condolences,
Mary Beth Danneffel, R.N., B.S.N.
Executive Director

Religious Perspectives on Donation

Some families may express reservations about organ and tissue donation due to religious beliefs. In Appendix F, many religious views on this subject are summarized by authorized spokespersons representing the various beliefs. While some religions do prohibit organ or tissue donation, most do not. It may be helpful to refer to the official view on the subject to assist the family in coming to a decision.

Cautionary Notes

In seeking consent from a donor's family, take great care in choosing a proper approach. While the need for organs is great, so is the need for genuine, wholesome, and informed consent for procurement. Anything less, and family members may experience complicated post-traumatic symptoms related to the donation itself.

Note that, in the suggested dialogues above, the entire focus for consent is on the deceased's wishes or intent, whether expressed or implied. Further, no real attempt is made to assuage the family's feelings of grief via donation, although secondary benefits are pointed out (the knowledge that someone in need was helped, and assurances that a letter for family remembrance will follow).

Consider the following experience related by a donor's family member:

Case Vignette 6.1

The neurologist's words were so shocking, I simply couldn't comprehend them. "Your sister is brain dead." Before the news could sink in, he tossed out something else, nearly as stunning. "I feel obligated to point out that she would be an excellent candidate for organ donation."

And so began the most devastating and confusing day of my life. Within 12 hours, I would call the family members back home to Vicksburg, Miss., to mourn the loss of our brightest star, Jennie Katherine Johnson, killed in a car accident. I would inform my mother, critically injured in the same accident, that her only daughter was dead.

And I would give permission for an organ procurement team to take the heart, liver, kidneys and corneas out of my 18-year-old sister's body before unplugging her ventilator.

It was April 13, 1986. I was 25.[22]

He continued by describing recent media events surrounding the court battle of a family to donate the organs of their baby—a baby born without a brain, and doomed to die soon. That battle, with its intense media coverage, had brought his experience with organ procurement forcibly back to his mind. The recollections caused him to acknowledge troubling thoughts that continued to haunt him some six years later. As he wrote:

Finally, a six-year standoff with my feelings has ended. For the first time, I can admit to a lot of bitterness, not just at Jennie's death, but also at the process that converted her so swiftly and almost casually from a lovable college freshman and aspiring artist into a human organ farm.

I'm talking about the darker side of organ donation. It's much more complicated than any news story can convey.

I still don't remember who put the idea in my head that organ donation was one of the few ways to make some sense out of a senseless horror. I just know that somewhere in the middle of the craziness, I latched onto that concept. I had another recurring thought: Maybe Jennie wouldn't be as dead if part of her lived on in someone else's body. I saw that same one-two thought process echoed in words printed throughout the media during (the recent events coverage). The child's family and doctors said it. Lawyers pleaded it. A court case and legislation were built on it.

But I can tell you, it's faulty thinking.

The fact that a loved one's heart keeps beating in another person's chest doesn't lessen the blow you feel from the loss. And nothing can ever explain untimely death, whether it comes to

---

[22] Johnson, Hayes, "Learning to bury the anger after donating his sister's organs," *The Sacramento Bee,* Wednesday, April 15, 1992.

an 18-year-old or an infant. Yet the experts in the field of organ donation and transplantation will let you fixate on those two concepts—making sense of tragedy and creating a sort of living memorial to lost loved ones—in order to win your support for organ donation.

For a long time after my sister's death, I had nightmares about allowing the mutilation of her body. I even began to have doubts about the doctors' claims that she had been brain dead, and that she could feel no pain while they took away her vital organs. These reactions hit me like aftershocks for years.

Beyond such irrational fears, there also is a cold reality most donor families must face: Once this act of human kindness is completed, so is your usefulness in the transplant world. Except for the collection of reusable body parts, the whole of transplant science is geared toward organ recipients.

Their right to privacy overrules a donor family's right to know who received the organs. Any communication between recipient and donor family has to be initiated by the recipient. In our case, there apparently have been no attempts by any of the six people who got my sister's organs to contact our family.

Six months after the accident, my mother made a quixotic journey from Mississippi to Richmond, Va.—where a young man received my sister's heart—in hopes of locating the recipient. She found the right hospital, but never made it past staff members, who refused to give any information for fear that it might upset the recipient's family. They made it clear they thought her mission was more than a little morbid.

After recovering from her injuries, my mother went back to college to become a social worker, determined in another way to make good out of bad. One of her pet projects now is to establish a support network in Mississippi for organ donors' families.

She has made me swear, however, that when her time comes to join my sister, I will not allow anyone to take her organs. I won't.

For my part, I carry a driver's license that lists me as an organ donor. They can have my whole body if they want it. But when I'm gone, I don't want anyone standing around trying to explain how death got cheated a little on the day they took a piece of my flesh and planted it in someone else.

I want experts to take the time to explain all the negative sides of organ donation to other people I love. Then I want those loved ones to say goodbye and get on with their lives.

Its time I did the same.[23]

What went so tragically wrong in this experience? How could it have been improved? Are all families inevitably going to feel such emotions and have such thoughts? Shouldn't donation be an experience of some

---

[23] Ibid.

meaning and support to a family? Why is it that some families report great comfort from donation, when this family experienced such emotional upheaval?

It is imperative that we learn from this experience. We must better protect and aid those in such circumstances in the future. To do so, let us look at each point of concern just mentioned.

First is the delivery itself. The doctor announced, "Your sister is brain dead," and immediately encouraged the stunned survivor to agree to organ donation. No time was given the family for the reality of death to sink in. This is an error of monumental importance. No human being, in the shock of fresh grief, could ever conceivably give informed consent to relinquish any part of a loved one. Time is an absolute necessity, to set order in one's heart and to clear away thoughts, pain, and tears. Only then can such a sensitive issue be broached.

Next, let's consider the meaning of the donation. The writer cites feelings he "latched onto" for comfort, but that later troubled him: that donation was a way "to make some sense out of a senseless horror," and that, "Maybe Jennie wouldn't be as dead if part of her lived on in someone else's body . . . creating a sort of living memorial to lost loved ones."

Let me caution you about the use of these or any other concepts. Never tell others how to grieve. Never tell them what an act of kindness should or would mean to them. Never tell them why they should accept donation. The process of grief, the meaning of their kindness, their reasons for donation—these are intensely personal things. Such feelings of the heart are theirs alone to define. Should you infringe upon this sacred, emotional ground, they may feel violated and coerced.

At the very most, you may share that others who have actually participated in the donation process have expressed taking comfort. But your primary focus should be the intent of the deceased and the very real need identified. Given sufficient time, next-of-kin will fill in the rest for themselves and will feel much stronger for having found their own reasons for having accepted, or rejected, donation.

Another issue of concern is the fear of "mutilation" of a loved one, and the fear that pain may be felt by a victim who has already endured too much pain. These questions caused the writer years of "nightmares" and "aftershocks."

While we do not have the luxury of hearing the full discussion provided this family, it is likely that they were not sufficiently informed of the meaning, irreversibility, and finality of brain death. It is not enough to tell the family that a loved one is brain dead. It is not enough simply to state the fact that the person cannot feel pain. Survivors must actually be *educated* on the subject, and able to understand the extensive roster of changes in the body that lead to such a conclusion. The presentation should be tailored to the situation and to the family's ability to comprehend, but the important concepts are:

1. The loss of autonomic neurological control. This includes no reflexive responses, no pupil function, no response to noxious or painful stimuli, instability of blood pressure, no natural inspiratory effort.

2. That such autonomic functions originate in the most guarded part of our brain, that all other cognitive activities already will have ceased before compromise of the brain stem occurs (except in cases of brain stem infarct, or other direct stem compromise, where death yet remains inevitable).

3. That the swelling associated with a bluntly traumatized or anoxic brain gradually cuts off all blood flow to the cerebrum, leaving the tissue to die.

4. That while a heartbeat may remain, and other organs may continue to function, neurological tissue is very sensitive and fragile and would not withstand the insults other tissues in our bodies may weather more easily.

When these and other issues are addressed in full, families may then vest faith and trust in the medical personnel serving them and the judgments they render. Armed with such knowledge, they may then more successfully gauge the reality of the situation when their emotions overwhelm them.

After all else is said and done, organ donation is ultimately, purely and simply, the giving of a gift—a gift of absolutely priceless value given at a time of tragedy. One ought to feel uplifted and supported by any act of generosity and the more so for a gift that was accompanied by such pain.

However, a gift, no matter how well given, ceases to be such when it is not appreciated. Consider the writer's comments that, "Except for the collection of reusable body parts, the whole of transplant science is geared toward organ recipients. . . . Their right to privacy overrules a donor family's right to know who received the organs. Any communication between recipient and donor family has to be initiated by the recipient."

In my experience, organ donor program personnel have been most willing to convey communications initiated by either the donor's or recipient's family. When this is not the case, a gross error exists. One need not relinquish confidentiality to convey messages from one family to another. Should both families be willing to communicate with each other, so much the greater support they may both receive.

Of greatest importance in this, however, is the need for real and expressed appreciation. This completes the giving circle—a gift is given, and then gratefully received. For those who need such reassurance, support in their communication efforts can be critical. And, where mutual sharing is not welcomed, the personnel from the organ procurement agency can fill the need in some measure by expressing on behalf of the recipient families the heartfelt appreciation they surely feel.

On that issue, most procurement agencies follow through well. But at every convenient opportunity, those of us who work with generous families in times of intense grief should emphasize the extreme importance of a simple, heartfelt, thank-you note.

Part II

Grief Management

Chapter 7

Typical Grief Responses

Case Vignette 7.1

I remember feeling cold as the night nurse steadily hopped her stethoscope over my distended abdomen in search of sound, movement—anything to verify that life still existed below. Icy cold is how I felt inside when she quietly put her instrument away and left my hospital room. She didn't say a word. She didn't have to. My silent womb bespoke the unfathomable and tragic end to my fairy-tale pregnancy. My dream baby was dead inside me.

No sound could possibly be as loud as the silence heard at the end of a stillbirth. No lusty birth-cry like the books promised; no . . . pictures, no "oohs" and "aahs" from ecstatic onlookers. Just sickening silence. His tiny body was quickly hidden from our eyes, and placed in a metal basin, lest we be horrified by the sight of our new son. I asked to see him, but the nurse shook her head. I asked if I had given birth to a boy or a girl. No one responded. I didn't find out that my baby was a boy until I heard my OB say, "stillborn male" into a hospital tape recorder. "His name is Jesse," I said to myself.

The stillbirth of my son was devastating, the pain so real I thought it would kill me. Nothing in life could have prepared me for the death of my precious baby. He was an unrepeatable gift, and dying before he had a chance to even draw one tiny breath simply went against the laws of nature.

I remember being angry over the way the situation was handled at the hospital where I delivered. I felt as if the instant Jesse's heart stopped beating, I was somehow tainted. I went from being a doted-upon pregnant woman to being a baby-less mother. I felt out of sync on the maternity ward, and definitely a threat to the staff's comfort zones. I was a marked woman. At the time, I felt as if I had failed to do the only natural thing a woman was created to do: produce live offspring.

In the days following the birth, I was ignored, denied the routine medical care given to other postpartum patients, and left virtually alone in my room to try to assimilate what had happened to me. Because I never saw Jesse, nor held him, I never got the chance to say hello or good-bye to my fourth-born child. He simply disappeared without a trace. No one seemed to want any reminders of a dead baby around, and certainly no one told me I could bury or even memorialize a one-pound baby. It took me years to realize the devastating effect this additional loss would have on me.[24]

Making Room for Grief

Medical facilities are dedicated to the physical improvement of health, and are generally staffed with caring and considerate professionals. However, in the haste to care for the physical well-being of our patients, we may overlook their mental and emotional needs. Considerably more could have been done for this mother to assist her in accepting and overcoming her loss. In contrast, consider this next experience.

Case Vignette 7.2

On August 1, 1989, a 29-year old expectant mother of two was involved in a car accident. Upon her entry into the Emergency Room, the fetal heart tones indicated that her eight-month pregnancy was in distress. She was rushed into surgery, and the baby taken by Cesarean section. However, we were unable to save the child.

She was a beautiful baby, even in death. One of the nurses found a pink jumper that fit and dressed her. A matching pink ribbon was put around her head, and her hair, a beautiful auburn, was smoothed and combed. Then pictures were taken, both instant and better-quality 35-millimeter, in a variety of resting positions. She was then wrapped in a soft blanket and readied for the family.

Upon waking from the surgery, the mother asked immediately about her child. Prior to her awakening, we had placed her in a quiet, private area of the recovery room. There we could talk freely. At that time she was told that her child had not survived. Many tears flowed, and we talked long and openly about her plans and dreams for her child. She had two other children, both boys. This would have been her first girl. More tears. The sharing continued. When asked if she would like to see her child, she requested that we wait until her husband could be with her.

When he and the grandparents arrived, all were notified of the death in a quiet conference room. After preparing them with caps and gowns, they were then ushered into the mother's room where they could talk. When the mother requested it, her child, Amanda, was brought in. She had her father's features and hair color. Her skin was soft and supple, gentle to touch. Each of the family, beginning with mother, took turns holding her, cradling her in their

---

[24] Erling, S., "Tattered Dreams," *Bereavement*, vol. 3, no. 5, March/April issue, p. 34. Reprinted by permission of Bereavement Publishing, Inc., 8133 Telegraph Drive, Colorado Springs, Colorado 80920.

arms. Father held her for more than an hour. We all talked more. The instant pictures were shared. They were beautiful. More tears. A warmth of parenting, of family, was in the room. The loss was painful, very much so, but strength was found in sharing.

Upon leaving the recovery room, the mother was moved to an area of the hospital away from other postpartum mothers. Here I met with her daily to talk and help her resolve her loss.

These circumstances greatly facilitated the family's grief process. Staff treated the parents and other family members sensitively and with compassion. Death, even prenatal death, was accepted as a normal, although painful, part of life. As a result, efforts were made to recognize their parenthood and their family's feelings and to create memories for all involved.

Opportunities for sharing continued throughout the hospital stay. When appropriate, funeral information was presented so that the family could make informed choices on how to formally recognize the brief presence of this new member. Such a process empowers families to acknowledge and accommodate grief. While these efforts can never be forced on others, when they so desire, each step will contribute immeasurably to their acceptance and healthy closure after the death.

Understanding Grief

Intense grief and sorrow are unavoidable consequences from the loss of a loved one. Indeed, these difficult feelings play a critical role in the healing process, preparing us to ultimately relinquish our dead, to risk further and care again. Because of this vital role of grief, full grieving is to be encouraged, and neither the family, the medical staff, nor the counselor should attempt to abbreviate or obscure the painful feelings that occur in each phase of the resolution process.

There are, however, ways to assist the surviving family members in coping with a loss and in maximizing their potential to heal their pain, appropriately moving forward with their lives. These include viewing the body, open recognition of the loss, verbal sharing, and an accepting atmosphere. To assist in this process, the care-giver must possess a clear understanding of grief, the stages involved, and both normal and pathological grief responses. Beyond this understanding, the care-giver will then need to develop various approaches and methods to facilitate optimum grieving and to ensure a healthy resolution.

Following the death of her husband, British journalist Mary Stott wrote, "To have grief spelt out, its pattern charted, is something we all obscurely need."[25] The purpose of this section, Part II, is to provide a

---

[25] Stott, M. (1973). *Forgetting's No Excuse.* London: Faber and Faber.

brief introduction to grief patterns and normal responses, and to suggest management techniques that may assist in guiding families through the resolution process.

The Physiology of Grief
First, it is important to understand the physiological responses that accompany acute grief. By so doing, the care-giver can better appreciate the level of compromise the loss creates and the specific grief management requirements that result. Since acute grief is best described as a state of emotional stress, let us look at the physiological reactions stressful states induce.

Monat and Lazarus (1977) define stress as a perceived imbalance between demand and resources. Harris (1984) defines it as "any threat to physical or emotional homeostasis." Since no two people perceive a given threat or imbalance in exactly the same way, some people will react to a situation with an ergotropic (stress) response, others will not.

One factor, however, that affects the potential for and severity of a stress response is the degree of control the person can exercise over the threat. The greater the perceived lack of control, the greater the stress. The loss of a loved one—especially a sudden, unexpected loss—is a threat of extreme proportions, fully outside one's control. As such, it elicits a stress response in virtually any person involved.

Dr. Jeffrey S. Harris (1984) describes the physiological changes in the body that rapidly follow extreme stress as the body's "Flight, Fight (FF) response." The basis of the FF response is the instinctual need for self-preservation. When a person is injured or in combat, the FF response can improve the chances of survival. However, in situations of purely emotional stress, these same changes can inhibit the person's capacity for healthy adaptation. In Dr. Harris' writings, he describes the changes brought about by the sympathetic nervous system. The physical symptoms, with their associated psychological responses, are as follows:

Direct Sympathetic Nervous System[26] Response to a Stressor

Increased muscle tone: chest pain, reduced tidal volume, abdominal guarding, headache, back pain, joint pain, muscle pain, bruxism, tics, globus hystericus, and dysphagia.

---

[26] Reprinted with permission.

Increased neural tone: cough, dry mouth and eyes, tachycardia, myocardial sensitization, urinary urgency, hyperreflexia, intestinal cramping, dysmotility, increased glucagon, and glucose release.

Perceptual inaccuracies: changes in time sense, accident proneness, communication difficulty, and memory alterations.

•

Sympathetic Adrenal Response to a Stressor

Effects of epinephrine: dilation of bronchi, increased cardiac output, increased blood volume, increased dilation of coronary vessels, increased myocardial contractility, increased heart rate, myocardial sensitization, increased blood pressure, increased blood supply to the brain, heart and skeletal muscles, increased perspiration, dry eyes and throat, increased mobilization of glycogen, decreased peristalsis, increased metabolic rate, sensation of bladder fullness, enhanced blood clotting, resistance to fatigue, increased concentration, and dilation of pupils.

Effects of norepinephrine: peripheral vasoconstriction; increased blood pressure; cool, pale skin; renin/angiotensin activation, including (a) vasoconstriction and (b) aldosterone secretion leading to sodium and potassium secretion.

With your heart pounding, your skin sweating but feeling cold and clammy, your breathing growing rapid, a slight feeling of nausea coming on, and a great increase in muscle tension, you're likely to feel overwhelmed! Compound this with the tragedy of the loss of a family member, and perhaps you can begin to empathize with the tremendous strain being experienced by survivors. Because of these changes, heightened intensity of reaction is very evident in death notification.

Obviously, if a person has a preexisting illness, such as vascular or cardiac instability, extreme fluctuations in these changes can lead to worsened illness or even death. As a result, minimizing the intensity of the response with a carefully prepared and delivered notification can be very important.

Keep in mind that the person may be experiencing "perceptual inaccuracies" just described, with reduced ability to process information and make appropriate decisions. You can compensate for this compromise with clear, thematic, easily understood information.

By speaking slowly and not assuming a full grasp of events and outcomes, you can maximize the effectiveness of your contact with the person who is experiencing grief.

The Behaviors of Grief

In his work *Grief Counseling and Grief Therapy*, J. William Worden, assistant professor of psychology at Harvard Medical School, discusses the psychological influence of attachment (relationship bonds) on the grief process. He and others cite the need we all have for attachment security and emphasize the stress caused if an intimate loss is threatened or realized. For example, Bowlby (1975) notes:

> The greater the potential for loss, the more intense these reactions and the more varied. In such circumstances, the most powerful forms of attachment behavior become activated—clinging, crying, and . . . angry coercion. . . . When these actions are successful, the bond is restored, and the activities cease, and the states of stress and distress are alleviated.

Indeed, the need to maintain intimate attachments appears to be the primary source of most grief reactions. In this light, one can better understand the "clinging, crying, and . . . angry coercion" so common with the bereft. Providing opportunity and permission to release these intense and deeply rooted behaviors can greatly enhance progress toward recovery.

Theories of Grief Resolution Patterns

Erich Lindemann (1979), in his classic study of the survivors of the 1940 Boston Coconut Grove Fire, was the first researcher to demonstrate that acute grief presents a definite syndrome with fairly predictable stages. He noted that, with a significant loss, there usually ensues a pattern of psychological disturbances, physiological disturbances, and some disruption of social relations. While everyone grieves in his or her own unique way, by recognizing these predictable steps in the grief process and encouraging a healthy outcome, the counselor can assist in moving the process forward appropriately.

There are numerous theories of grief that have gained acceptance in recent years. One researcher, Nancy Weinberg (1985), notes that successful grief work has three significant components: (1) the acceptance of the painful emotions involved, (2) the active review of a variety of experiences and events shared with the lost person, and (3) the gradual development of new relationships that can replace some of the functions the deceased fulfilled.

Dr. Elisabeth Kübler-Ross has given us a model that helps to describe the emotional integration of these three components. She indicates that families generally undergo five stages in the grief process: denial, anger, bargaining, depression, and acceptance. This theory was designed to elucidate the grief processes undergone by families of the terminally ill, in which the death is typically slow and protracted.

Families undergoing _sudden_ catastrophic loss appear to go through a slightly altered grief process from that presented by Dr. Kübler-Ross. This has been well described by another researcher, Margaret Epperson (1977). With the absolute loss of the loved one already evident, "bargaining" appears to be generally absent, and "depression" is replaced with a response more akin to remorse, due in some measure to guilt feelings associated with the loss. Epperson's resolution process includes six phases:

1. High Anxiety is described as a time of great stress, with many physical manifestations of emotional upheaval. These include agitation, rapid respiration and increased heart rate, irritability, muscular tension and fainting, along with digestive/bowel changes which may result in nausea and diarrhea.

2. Denial appears to be an emotionally protective reaction, seeking to postpone the realization of the loss until sufficient psychological preparation has been made. As such, it is a phase that generally should not be hurried. Often, efforts are made to hasten this phase, out of concern for the family member's stability. In practice, a short period of acute denial is normal and to be expected so long as it does not persist beyond the viewing of the body and after the family has departed the hospital.

3. Anger is a common emotional response and can be directed inwardly, toward another family member, or toward the psychotraumatologist and others. Usually, it is a diffuse kind of anger that lashes out at society or life in general, feeling that the loss was somehow "allowed" to occur. Many times, it seems to be an attempt to affix blame on someone. This reaction is usually brief. If it persists, it will have a more complex underlying cause, such as a cover for hurt or fear, and will need to be addressed further.

4. Remorse includes feelings of both guilt and sorrow. Families regret not only that the accident or illness occurred, but that they did not, or could not, do more to prevent it. It is the "if only . . ." stage. In such a phase, families may need repeated reassurance that their actions were reasonable, that more could not have been expected of them. In situations of true culpability, family members will need intensive support to be able to come to terms with their role in the loss and to recognize that we all make mistakes, sometimes with tragic results.

5. Grief is an intense period of overwhelming sadness that can eclipse everything else. The greatest assistance that can be rendered in this phase is verbal sharing and encouragement. The duration and intensity of this stage will depend on factors such as the medical condition of the patient, the strength of existing support systems, and factors such as family culpability in the disease or injury scenario.

6. Reconciliation, as described, is generally the last phase to be experienced, and it seems to be an end-point to the acute family crisis. This is the time when the family begins to adapt to the existing circumstances and is finally able to move on with life as a renewed unit.

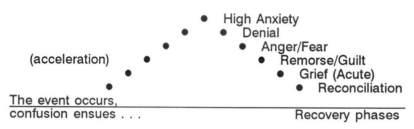

**Responses to
Traumatic Bereavement**

Epperson (1977) has further noted, as has Dr. Kübler-Ross, that people may skip over certain stages, or change sequences, or eliminate other stages altogether in the adaptive process. Also, all family members do not go through the phases at the same time or in the same way. The description given above, however, offers an excellent model of appropriate grief responses to the catastrophic losses so common in emergency trauma care.

Identifying Coping Patterns

Reactions of individuals and families to a traumatic loss vary greatly. Every reaction stems from a preexisting, dynamic, highly differentiated coping pattern or defense mechanism. The presenting behaviors can be significantly influenced by circumstance and environment, but, in general, what you observe immediately following a notification represents an exaggeration of the predominate stress-coping pattern of that person.

This is important to understand for two significant reasons. First, in times of stress we revert to the familiar. If there is too much damage to basic, familiar structures, we become unable to cope. Because of this, it is critical that you find some way to support, directly or indirectly, the exhibited coping patterns. If these patterns are destructive, or inhibit the resolution of the loss, you may seek to modify them, but don't try to totally alter them. Doing so could strip people of important protective buffers and leave them exposed to more pain than they may be prepared to bear.

All families learn to accommodate the previously experienced coping patterns of each of their members. To abruptly alter the behavioral paths that have been already recognized and adapted to by the family—particularly if there is a significant level of dysfunction to which all other family members have previously adapted—is to risk compromising not only the dysfunctional individual, but the entire family structure as well.

Occasionally, this can prove enormously disconcerting. For example, a family member may react with overt anger that subverts or circumvents a healthy grief response on the part of the other family members. While this may concern you, as well it should, you must use great caution in engaging the response. Before doing so, consider _all_ variables that are necessary for a successful outcome, including intervention time available, willingness of the family to participate, the degree of current emotional compromise, etc. By so doing, you can assume an appropriate stance for an optimum resolution.

Typical Notification Responses

A few common notification responses are described here to assist you in assessing the behaviors you may observe in practice. Each of the responses described here is generally within normal limits. Even so, there will be aspects of each that may not foster a full and healthy grief response. In all situations, your task will be to optimize outcome and nurture stability.

Holistic Grief

This is the idealized model, usually exhibited only in degrees. It is highly dependent on circumstance, hence rarely fully manifested. It is evident to the extent that individuals are open to the ensuing events and honestly meet their fear. They gather others around them and pour out their grief, allowing others who are present to do the same. There is great pain evident; they have lost a loved one and have not escaped the burden. Yet somehow, windows are opened to the heart, from which flow tender feelings. The key elements necessary for holistic grief are a lack of ambivalence in the relationship with the deceased, the willingness of all present to share without prejudice or reluctance, and a genuine love and concern preexisting among those present.

In such situations you may find yourself drawn in and allowed to grieve and care, with and for all present. You may feel entitled to take some credit for this scenario, but, in reality, you were simply present at a choice interaction of life in which people, without emotional impediment, faced a great challenge in a meaningful way.

Action-oriented Grief

This response is characterized by rapid movement toward organization and activity. It can initially be functional and useful, so there is some tendency to encourage it. The goal of this response is to emotionally buffer oneself, and often others, from any experience perceived as painful or tumultuous by remaining preoccupied with the other tasks at hand.

A person exhibiting this coping style will often be the one making plans for family contacts, assessing the status of others present, and coordinating other ensuing events. At best, the person may provide assistance, organization, and support that will be valuable to other family members. At worst, the person may try to control, manipulate, and coerce others. An excessive need to control may be demonstrated by hurrying others along, arguing, pressing for an immediate viewing of the deceased, asking brusquely to complete any needed paperwork "so we can leave," and, in general, exerting pressure on you and all present.

In managing this response, it is usually best to avoid confronting such people in a power struggle. Instead, work with them. Find a way to allow their active participation in some aspect of the tasks at hand—getting warm drinks for those present, moving a car for some family member who left it in an ambulance driveway, or any other constructive task. Coordinate viewing of the deceased in groups, accommodating both those willing to begin the emotional work of the grief process and those exhibiting avoidance behaviors.

Gradually, you can introduce circumstances and conversation that will more appropriately engage action-oriented responders in the full grief process. By so doing, you may succeed in initiating an appropriate grief response for all involved. The prognosis for most action-oriented responders is good, because they are usually less reluctant than others to give vent to their feelings later, in a more private setting.

Inordinately Calm Response
This grief response usually represents a mild degree of denial. It is not pathological, as there is no active refutation of the death reality, but it does indicate a deliberate attempt to set aside the emotional reality for another time. This is a generally workable initial response, but it does hamper the goal of appropriate grief expression. While virtually everyone should be allowed to grieve at his or her own pace, if you can at least initiate an early grief response while family members are still in your presence, you can more fully assess the situation and encourage healthy grieving. To this end, you should use all tools available to you, such as viewing the body and conducting dialogues, to encourage initial grieving to the extent that family members will allow.

Emotional Withdrawal
Certain individuals will place barriers to communication and interaction and turn inward, circumventing some or all of the elements of discussion. Most commonly, this response is identified by a down- or outward-turned gaze, an effort to avoid spontaneous discussion or comments, or even a refusal to respond to direct questioning.

This indicates an overt withdrawal from the dynamics of the experience. In the extreme, it represents a pathological response, but for most it is simply another kind of emotional buffer that will mitigate shortly. Because of the severity of the withdrawal, however, it can easily become more intense after the person leaves your facility. Thus, gentle attempts should be made to gradually engage such a person while he or she is still there.

To do so, use your usual methods of grief interaction, but focus more closely on this individual. Never actually pressure the person into involvement. Instead, offer subtle verbal and physical contacts that foster participation. Be near the person at critical moments, such as the viewing of the body (and viewing should be strongly encouraged), and maintain an open, comforting dialogue with other family members to allow the person an easily accessible window for verbal, and hence emotional, entry.

Extreme Guilt

Feelings of guilt are common at the loss of a loved one. Survivors routinely make statements such as, "I shouldn't have let him leave," or "I should have been there." Usually, these feelings are mitigated easily with reality testing. Occasionally, true culpability exists. In such situations, great care must be taken to achieve a balance between acceptance of reality and supporting the person. Using techniques such as that of the "perfect parent," found below, will help.

Situational Blaming

This is a common response and is quite sensitive to environmental influences and circumstance. It is most evident when there is an element of culpability present, whether perceived or real. In such situations, it must be dealt with promptly to return the bereft person to appropriate progress in resolving grief. Let's look at a case example.

Case Vignette 7.3

In the winter of 1989, a young mother hurried from her home to purchase groceries for the family. She left a babysitter—the 14-year-old daughter of a neighbor—with the children. In her haste, she didn't see her four-year-old open the front door, nor did she see her two-year-old son dart out of the house. The mother started the vehicle, slipped it into gear, and rapidly backed into the street. In her haste, she had no idea her son was now beside the car. He was struck as the car rolled over the roadside gutter so the "thump" and associated movement of the vehicle were insufficient for her to even realize that the accident had occurred. She continued to the store without knowing what had happened.

The baby sitter, responding to cries from the four-year-old, came running and, upon seeing the injured two-year-old, called for an ambulance. The brain tissue exposed in the little boy's head had a dramatic impact on all present. When the mother returned from the nearby store, she found the house in turmoil. An ambulance and the police were out front, and the injured child was just leaving the scene under CPR. She was stunned to learn what had happened. Following the ambulance to the hospital, she arrived just behind her son.

At the hospital, I made the usual guarded overtures, preparing her for the inevitable loss. Although the child still had a heartbeat, the prognosis was certain death. While providing her with updates on the resuscitative efforts and preparing her for the possibility of a loss, I assisted her with a call to her husband. Their relationship had been "rocky," I was to learn, and when he arrived he began lashing out at her, citing her "neglect" of the child as the primary cause of the injury.

When the death news was given, some 20 hours later, the father's anger and pain increased. His pain now turned outward toward his wife. We talked at great length, gradually reducing, though never resolving, his blaming response.

In such situations, resolution efforts often involve two specific steps on your part. First, acknowledge the pain of the blamer, appropriately focussing it on the loss (e.g., "I know you must be feeling great pain at the death of your child."). Second, in the presence of both, openly acknowledge the spouse's very real pain, as well. Discuss the loss openly, moving, if they allow it, into ventilation of emotions. This can sometimes bring them into greater harmony with each other. Later, when some emotional stability has returned after the viewing, if significant blaming persists or escalates, utilize a reality-testing tool such as the following "Perfect Parent" dialogue:

"You seem extremely angry with your wife. Can you tell me why?" (Even though I already knew why, I wanted him to say it himself).

He then made comments to the effect that if she had not been so careless, this would have not happened. I then agreed with him that her lack of forethought and attention appeared to have contributed to the accident.

However, I then said, "I want you to know that in spite of her involvement, she cannot be entirely blamed for this loss. Some of the events were purely coincidental. No one could have immediately known that the baby was in harm's way when he had just been left in the house.

"There is something more important to us, however, in our situation. In life, we *all* make mistakes; it is a constant part of the process of living."

I paused and evaluated his reaction. Then I personalized the concept by asking, "Could you ever promise me that you could be a *perfect* parent and *never* make a mistake, ever, even once, with your children?" I persisted until the response was appropriate and honest.

"Then this, or something like it, could have happened to you, or to me, just as it happened to your wife, couldn't it."

After reflection and much discussion of the real capacities of all persons, including ourselves, he began to agree. Conversation was then gradually moved toward more direct grief work, and the process was more fully engaged.

When you pursue this vein of thought for a brief period, the initial blaming reaction will usually end, or at least abate. This will allow time for both parties to return to the primary grief issues and to begin again to work toward resolution. Know, however, that in families with a high level of conflict, this blaming response will most likely reoccur and may well escalate. If the marriage is to survive, both spouses must receive support from other sources. Referrals to bereavement support groups and counseling centers are critical in this scenario. Be sure to provide them.

Grief and Anger

Closely associated with a blaming response is that of anger. The anger may be directed toward life, toward circumstances, or toward oneself and others. It may even be directed toward you. This is a common response to an irretrievable loss. I mention this to reassure those of you who are new to the delivery of notifications that hostile coping responses do not necessarily indicate that your delivery of the death news was poorly structured.

The most difficult anger-related situations you are likely to encounter, within a normal grief context, are those in which people direct their anger pointedly at you and those in which people exhibit assaultive behavior, such as breaking objects and throwing things.

While most people will respond to you with deference, occasionally you will meet people whose mechanism to cope with stress is to vent their feelings on the most emotionally removed but available person— you, the care-giver. Generally, you need not worry. Just give them time and they will nearly always apologize after the tension subsides. However, if their reaction is unduly prolonged, or if they appear to be becoming assaultive, you will need to respond appropriately.

Often, just removing yourself from their presence for a brief period, allowing for private family time, will help. If anger does not then subside fairly rapidly, you may reasonably conclude that there is either an underlying pathology or some other unaddressed circumstance causing the poor grief response to continue. Such issues should be sought out and attended to when possible.

Another form of anger that should be noted is that of the survivors toward the deceased. This the quite natural feeling of having been abandoned, of being left in a compromised state, and being helpless to rectify it. Worden addressed this when he wrote:

> A woman whose husband died of cancer said to me, "How can I be angry? He didn't *want* to die." The truth is that she was angry with him for dying and leaving her. If the anger is not adequately acknowledged, it can lead to a complicated bereavement.[27]

The bereft are often reluctant to acknowledge such feelings at or around the time of the death notification, but they occasionally do become evident. Your acknowledgment of the validity of such feelings can greatly hasten their resolution.

Demonstrative Notification Responses

While the most common responses are those described above, every person is unique, and you may encounter a wide variety of acceptable grief responses. Sometimes a response can be extremely demonstrative and may appear unusual, but this should not prevent you from helping to move it to a wholesome outcome. To assist you with your evaluations, here are a few less common, but normal, grief responses. You might note that several of these responses may be combined, as they are not mutually exclusive. Each response is illustrated by a mini-vignette.

Highly Vocalized Grieving

> The news was broken. She stiffened for a moment, then her eyes widened and she began to scream loudly. I stepped toward her, pulled her into my arms, and held her, allowing her to cry. The screaming stopped. She made no attempt to turn away but buried her face in my shoulder and sobbed.

Upon notification of a death, one of the more disconcerting family responses is that of overwhelming, soul-wrenching anguish. The depth of this pain can bring about impassioned reactions, including screaming and yelling to vent emotional pain. On occasion, this has brought other staff to my office to see if I was having difficulty with a potentially dangerous person. An initial reaction such as this can be of such magnitude as to cause you undue concern and to wonder whether you somehow "blew it" in your presentation of the notification. This is not usually the case. At times, you may find it necessary to intervene with someone who seems near hysteria, but generally the vocal catharsis will run its own course.

---

[27] Worden, 1982, p. 20. Quoted with permission.

Striking Out Reactions

> He put his head in his hands for a moment, then, seizing the waste basket beside him, stood and threw it across the small office. Turning to his left, he smashed the glass covering of a picture with his fist, cutting himself badly. I quickly obtained gauze coverings and called a staff nurse to care for him. In a moment, he was calm and tearfully began to apologize for his outburst.

Some people may also throw themselves upon the floor, pound on the furniture, and otherwise dramatically act out their grief. In these situations, your own anxiety can be heightened when other family members fix their gazes upon you, either accusingly, for having brought about the traumatic response, or with fearful "do-something" looks, hoping that you can quickly resolve the pain. Careful management of an extremely demonstrative individual may be in order if the behavior escalates, but generally you will need only to reassure the family that the demonstrative individual is responding normally, while you keep yourself calm.

Self-striking Reactions

> Upon hearing the news, several family members stood, openly wept, and started to wail and groan—not typical weeping sounds, but a wailing and moaning in rhythmic expression of emotional pain. In concert with this, many began striking their chests and slapping their heads and bodies. No one struck anyone else, only themselves as they brought forth their grief. One young woman knelt before her chair and began rocking back and forth before it, occasionally slapping the seat with her outstretched hands.
>
> After a time, the grieving subsided, and we continued with other matters at hand. Upon viewing the body, the pattern of grief renewed again with some vigor and again it subsided normally, without significant intervention on my part. I simply stayed near and offered the comfort of a gentle touch of an arm or shoulder from time to time.

More common with Asian and Middle-Eastern peoples, this grief pattern consists of striking oneself or objects with substantial force. However, the pattern *never* involves striking anyone else. While an observer may be concerned, it is rare for this behavior to cause injury. Care should be taken, however, to carefully steer those exhibiting this behavior away from any objects that could injure them. In practice, this is usually quite simple, and you may find yourself surprised at the degree of direction the bereft will allow you to provide in physically guiding this expression of their grief. Usually, this behavior will be expected by involved family members. Therefore, they will not be alarmed by it and will not expect you to try to curtail it.

Emotive Chanting

> After the delivery of the news, the mother stood and turned to the wall. She cried out loudly once or twice and then turned to face the room. Her eyes were closed and she extended her arms out in front of her. Gradually becoming louder, she began to chant rhythmically, using the name "Jesus" over and over. She suddenly appeared ready to fall. Two of her sons and I rushed to support her, and, as she was a large woman, when her knees buckled, we lowered her to the floor. She rolled over and began to cry. The family members looked toward me. I calmly reassured them that she was fine, and they then calmed somewhat.

Exhibited by many cultures, and also typical with some individuals of Pentecostal religious beliefs, chanting is an acceptable form of grief expression. It usually involves the rapid repetition of single words or short phrases, often with religious connotations. Sometimes you may not be able to distinguish the actual words used, but you can always recognize the behavior by the rhythmic nature of the sounds uttered. The purpose of chanting appears to be the establishment of a briefly altered consciousness to escape the emotional pain. It can be very effective and therefore should not be interrupted too quickly.

Management Strategies

While much could be said regarding the appropriate management of these responses, an effective strategy incorporates three basic steps.

1. **Remain calm.** Family members will often look to you in seeking appropriate responses to a difficult situation. Their reactions can be strongly influenced by your calm presentation.

2. **Verbally reassure** others present that many forms of grief expression are appropriate. Even staff who are present during such episodes may need to be reassured. When those present see that you are relaxed and comfortable with the reactions, they will feel secure that you will be able to manage the events without incident.

3. Allow those reacting demonstratively to express a full and complete initial grief response. **Don't hurry their natural reactions—** just allow them to expend themselves. Most will find a reasonable and healthy end-point.

During the reactive process, stay close by the most demonstrative griever. Your presence and gentle touch (a hand on the shoulder or back) may serve to comfort and calm the bereft, and will foster more appropriate outcomes. When encountering angry or self-abusive behaviors, *never* respond to a physical reaction with physical restraint (e.g, trying to hold the arms of a thrashing griever). These demonstrations of grief are an important avenue of release and should not usually be curtailed. Instead, after a reasonable time has passed and you sense that the person is beginning to regain control, gradually indicate the need for an end-point. This can be done verbally using comments such as, "I know this is difficult for you, but we need to take a minute and talk now, okay?" or, "We need to talk now. I know this is hard, but it's important that we take a few minutes together." Usually, this is all that is needed for grievers to collect themselves and return their focus to you.

Obtaining well-timed closure to demonstrative grief reactions can be important, especially with those exhibiting particularly vocal or angry responses. After sufficient time has elapsed, to prevent further escalation of these reactions, begin intervening at a lull in events. When you sense that these individuals are starting to work themselves up to higher levels of expression, carefully indicate a need for limitation, using such comments as those noted above. By carefully modeling and shaping appropriate responses, you can optimize a family's grief experience.

Family Crises
Notifications can also bring up preexisting family problems. In times of crisis, normal personal and social barriers are weakened, and individuals may move into "root" behaviors. While crisis intervention and initial grief counseling are *not* substitutes for marriage or family therapy, these issues can be thrust upon you.

Always try to bring your therapeutic interventions back to the issue at hand—the loss—in order to accomplish your primary task. Substantial progress in other areas of family functioning may also result from your efforts.

Case Vignette 7.4

A young couple entered the office, escorted by a hospital registration staff person. Their three-year-old child had been hit by a passing automobile in front of their home and was in the trauma room under CPR. The mother was in tears. The father was stoic, standing somewhat away from her. I invited them to be seated. She sat on the couch and held her head in her hands, continuing to cry. He sat down with her, but offered little if any support, staring at the wall in front of him. Occasionally, she would turn toward him, but he subtly deferred any contact.

We discussed the accident scenario. Mother was the sole provider of information. Both parents had been at home, and the wife was preparing dinner. It appeared that an older child had exited the house, leaving the front door open. No one noticed when the younger child left, also. Within seconds, the motor vehicle accident occurred.

After a lengthy resuscitation effort, the child died. A notification was effected, followed by a viewing, and discussion of coroner and funeral information. Somewhat prematurely, the father terminated the conversation by standing and saying to his wife,

"Come on, let's go," then leaving the room. She stayed behind and after the door closed behind him said, "He's going to blame me for this, you know!" Having seen his stoic manner and his limited efforts at engaging her in mutual support, I could accept her concern and elected to pursue it further. I left to get the father and found him in the parking lot. I told him there were a few more things we needed to discuss, and he accompanied me back to the office.

When we reentered the room, he sat conspicuously across the office and avoided eye contact with his wife. I began speaking with them again.

"There are several things we need to discuss, but first I think we need to talk about what's going on between the two of you."

"What do you mean?" he asked almost angrily.

"You are avoiding one another," I responded. "Just look at where you're both sitting now. Your wife tells me she feels you are going to blame her for this accident, and it's clear that neither of you is able to offer the other any support."

Just then, the wife spoke up, "Well, I think we need to talk about it. We are having some problems, and it needs to be said."

With those opening comments, we began what was to become a very productive dialogue. Numerous personal and marital issues were shared. Tears were shed, and grief was begun. Finally, we were able to address the many important issues awaiting them at home, including the needs of their other children. The child who had left the door open would very likely be feeling great guilt, and would need to be attended to. The other children would have questions. We discussed ways to manage the questions and indicators to be aware of in monitoring their grief resolution. While there were still many problems we couldn't address in the brief time available, they left better able to support one another, with better tools to manage their own grief and to respond to their children.

Generally, acute grief lasts much longer than society recognizes. The most substantial portion of grief work is usually completed in the first year. But holidays, anniversaries, birthdays and the like can "bring it all back," fresh, real, and very painful. This can be very discouraging to the survivors, who become weary of the efforts required to manage their feelings. It can also cause supporters to become concerned that the grief is too protracted. However, it is only when the responses are overtly destructive (to self or others), when social or occupational functions are greatly compromised for an extended period, or when constant grief work is needed beyond a year, that there is genuine concern about a pathological response.

Physiological Problems

Frequently encountered physiological responses following the death of a loved one include loss of appetite or overeating. There is often a feeling of being "tied in knots" inside. Muscular problems, or physical symptoms involving the heart or stomach, are common. Disturbances of sleep are also experienced—either having difficulty falling asleep or awakening often in the night. Even with sleep, feelings of exhaustion often persist.

For couples, sexual difficulties may also arise. The loss may be severe enough to preclude many previously pleasurable activities for a time, although this should gradually resolve as grief diminishes.

The bereaved may also find great difficulty in concentrating. Their minds may wander easily, causing difficulty in reading, writing, and decision-making. For this reason, important decisions should be postponed until the emotional intensity subsides.

In Appendix H, a more exhaustive list of signs and symptoms of grief is provided, ranging from uncomplicated reactions to problems requiring immediate medical attention. In addition, Appendix I lists a variety of responses to grief and offers coping strategies. It will be helpful for caregivers to become familiar with these reactions to bereavement and the suggested coping skills, and to be able to inform families about the grieving process.

A healthy diet, rest, and appropriate exercise are important at this time for all involved. Opportunities to talk and share feelings safely are especially important in resolving grief. Tell all families of these issues in advance, so that they can prepare themselves to understand and deal with symptoms as they arise.

Chapter 8

Pathological Grief

Grief, being an intense and painful experience, can bring about pathological responses where any predisposition exists or in cases of preexisting crises. When confronted with the loss of a loved one, even genuinely stable individuals can find themselves feeling entirely unable to cope and respond appropriately.

The counselor can best assist those involved when he or she has learned to anticipate and deal with unusual responses, so as to not feel surprised or threatened by the newly surfaced emotions.

Following are descriptions of grief responses that demonstrate varying degrees of pathology.

Family Dysfunction

Case Vignette 8.1

After his death, I made the call, and his wife soon arrived. Gently, I broke the news. She was able to respond to questions and concerns in her behalf and cooperated fully. Then I helped her call local family members to obtain full support for her at the hospital. Little did I suspect the scene that was to follow.

After the arrival of the family, very intense, vocal, and aggressive grieving began. The coffee maker, along with its stand and extra water, were thrown to the floor. Paper work was torn, and one adult child began repetitively striking her head forcefully against the wall. No help from any family quarter was forthcoming, with the exception of the husband of the woman banging her head—he tried to hold her head in his arms.

Anger, as well as fear, was all around—I could see it in their eyes and faces, but no direct reference was made to any event, neither to past issues or even to the death itself. With so many people present (about 15 eventually arrived), mutual sharing and support were strikingly absent. On the surface, family members seemed absorbed in grief demonstrations of their own and spoke little if at all with each other.

Adult sons and nephews stalked in and out of the room, almost in an attention-getting fashion. Indeed, this seemed to characterize the family's grief. Whenever one person escalated in wailing, even when the group as a whole had begun to settle down, intense renewed group expression followed, almost competitive in nature rather than as a natural emotional need.

Any attempts on my part to offer tissues or seating were rebuffed. When I tried to start a dialogue, to speak of essential facts and arrangements, I was met with anger or refusal. The spouse, who earlier had been composed and generally appropriate, now became dazed and helpless. She seemed fully dependent on those about her, which was surprising when so little help seemed forthcoming.

All my efforts seemed to no avail. Nothing was "right" or helpful, gauged by their responses. Viewing the body was a chore, as the demonstrative, hostile behaviors intensified, and I got no sense of "closure" for them at all. In the end, staff had to demand their departure from the treatment room, with an injured patient at the door, before the family members responded with haphazard compliance (long lingering and loud grieving).

What went wrong with this family? Could the presentation of the news have been changed? Was there some dramatic "personality clash?" What could have been done differently to mitigate the total chaos, the anger, and the acting out? The answers, I have come to believe, may be surprising.

In this case, the notification of death was well-delivered, gentle and appropriate. The initial reaction of the spouse was well within normal limits. The change in behavior occurred later and only after additional family members arrived.

This was a family system significantly marred by dysfunction. Instead of mutual support, theirs was a family in which attention was doled out by the competition of drama. Help openly supplied could not be accepted—this would reduce the individual's "need-position" in the hierarchy. The only way to be assured of support was to remain overtly in "pain." Thus, this family was unwilling to let me or any other staff member help. Furthermore, the interactive mechanism was so strong that it was likely to draw anyone else into the same emotional "dance."

In similar situations, what could any counselor's effective role be? When this degree of dysfunction is displayed, the only solution would be to minimize interactions and remove oneself from the drama, retaining some capacity on the sidelines to assist anyone desiring to escape from the family competition. As difficult as this is to do, it is the greatest service left for you to offer.

Note that never before or since have I seen this degree of dysfunction by a group. Such an occurrence should be rare, indeed. However, if you encounter this, even in substantive degrees, it is important to reduce your interactions and avoid what will become an escalating power struggle in which you have no place.

Suicidal Ideation

Following is an excerpt from a suicide note, written by a 25-year-old man, found on July 26, 1989:

The reason I'm writing this letter is to let everybody know why I am taking my own life. I QUIT! I can no longer handle the fact that I am alone and unwanted. I cannot bear the thought of not being loved. So I decided that I don't want to live anymore. . . .

Tell my mom that I love her, and that I'm sorry.

Goodbye,
Kevin[28]

I quote that note only because it is a typical example of the feelings expressed by victims of suicide or attempted suicide.

Similar feelings—of being hopeless, helpless, and unloved—often occur when a person is notified of the death of a loved one. It is very important that you recognize, and prepare for, this possibility. If threats of suicide occur, they *must* be examined and dealt with immediately. These issues should be addressed by a mental health professional. Call for assistance, if at all possible. If not, or if you are that professional, use the following outline to examine and deal with the potential. The outline includes some of the variations that are inevitable, depending, for example, on whether the suicide threat occurs in person or over the telephone.

1. Ask the question.

Even if the threat has not been verbalized, but you suspect the potential, *always* ask something like, "Are you thinking of hurting yourself?" If the question is unconvincingly denied, leave it for now but come back to it later when it feels more comfortable. Be tactful and gentle at such a time, but never ignore a potential tragedy.

2. Find out if the person has already made a suicide attempt.

If the contact scenario would have allowed time to have acted on a suicidal thought, ask the person if he or she has already done or taken something. If the answer is "yes," find out the following as fully as possible:

• The person's name and exact location (if unknown, as may be the case early in a telephone notification).

• *Exactly* what the person did and what physical condition he or she is in at that time.

• If drugs (including alcohol) were taken, find out what, how much, and when taken. Find out if the person is currently on

---

[28] Name has been changed.

any medication, has an allergy history or active medical problems. Get the person's age and weight, if you have time.

• Help the person get medical attention. Ask permission to call, or have someone else call, for medical assistance. If there is hesitation on that issue, maintain a rapport but continue to pursue the need for help. Call 911, if available in your area. If this is a telephone contact and the person resists and begins losing consciousness, stay on the line, as tracing can be initiated.

3. Explore the depth of the threat.

Learn if the thought had been present prior to the loved one's death. See if the person is considering a mechanism for ending his or her life (e.g., a gun, pills, or auto accident). Ask if a time and place had been considered. Such questions will enable you to more effectively judge the likelihood of the threat being put into action. The more thorough the plan is, the more likely the person is to act on it.

4. Have the person remove the threat.

If you are on location and someone has a method in hand (e.g., a gun, pill bottle, knife, or razor blade), ask the person to put it down. Never try to take something away. Never say, "Give it to me," as you can be injured when approaching the person. Once it has been put down, *then* you can more safely retrieve it and remove it from sight.

If this is a telephone contact, ask the person to put the item away—in a drawer, box, or cupboard, perhaps. By so doing, the person can establish distance from the threat and bring more attention to the problem that precipitated it.

5. Explore the reasoning.

Help the person to test his or her fears. Never belittle or negate the concerns; instead, help the person obtain a realistic perspective of the problems and to understand how the problems can be resolved.

One powerful approach that often helps is to ask the grieving survivor how the *deceased* would want him or her to respond to the loss. Care should be used that this suggestion not become a barrier to the honest expression of fears and feelings, but rather to help the person recognize that many times the strength to continue comes from those whom we love, even after their death.

Nearly always, when asked this question in a tactful fashion, the bereft person will readily acknowledge that the deceased would want a positive response, with growth and increased understanding, not withdrawal or self-destruction.

6. Counsel the person.

Listen. Empathize and reflect on any ambivalence you hear. Offer support. Through extended conversation, gradually help the person to understand that, frequently, our greatest strengths come through adversity—that through such experiences, we add depth to ourselves and meaning to our lives, increase our ability to love and care, and become a greater source of strength to others. To experience and come to accept a great loss is to learn what it means to love.

7. Respond appropriately.

If, after all your efforts, the threat is not relinquished, select an appropriate professional response. Emergency psychiatric services should be sought. If no licensed mental health professional is immediately available, contact a local law enforcement agency to report the situation. The person will be taken into custody and transported to an evaluation facility or local mental health agency for further evaluation and protection.

8. "Contract" with the person, if reasonable.

If the threat is not firm, then the professional may safely attempt to establish a verbal contract with the person. This contract should, in substance, commit the person to contact a designated individual before attempting to inflict self-harm. That person should be a counselor, another family member, or a good friend. Both parties must be aware of the contract and must agree to participate. If they are willing to accept the conditions of the contract, only then can the counselor relinquish further immediate intervention, releasing the person with follow-up referrals for additional counseling and support.

9. Follow up.

See to it that other family members are aware of the follow-up appointments to ensure the person's participation in further counseling. In addition, don't leave the person alone for the next few days. Obtain a commitment from appropriate family members to stay with him or her, to provide support, and to call for help should the status deteriorate.

Note: All these suggestions are intended for use by professional personnel. If you do not have designated responsibility to resolve such situations, or, if for any reason you do not feel competent to make such a disposition, *always seek further professional assistance.* The goal is to ensure the safety of all involved. The outline is no substitute for detailed training in this subject. It recognizes, however, that a person making death notifications may encounter an emergency of this nature and should be prepared to be as constructive as possible until outside assistance can be obtained.

Case Vignette 8.2

One evening at the hospital, someone hurried into my office, saying, "A man has a razor blade in the men's room, and he's trying to cut his wrists." I immediately responded and entered the rest room.

He stood in front of the sink, looking into the mirror. Blood ran down his right arm from a cut in the wrist. In his left hand he held a razor blade. The blood was bright red and created brilliant round blotches on the light composite floor. He appeared to be under the influence of a depressant substance. His hair was tousled and unkempt, his face was unshaven, and his clothing was soiled and stained.

I immediately noted that the room was humid and close, giving a "trapped" feeling.

As I entered the room, the man looked up and paused briefly from his efforts, and then continued sawing at his wrist. The blade seemed dull. I approached him and began talking in a slow, reassuring manner. I was able to divert his attention from his arm to myself, causing him to interrupt his efforts for brief periods, but he would not engage me in conversation and would return to cutting himself.

After each successful interruption, I drew closer to him and eventually extended my hand, asking for the blade. He immediately changed his posture and began to lash at me with the instrument. Slowly, I backed out of the room, caught the attention of a passing nurse, and hurriedly requested that law enforcement be summoned. At our facility we have 24-hour peace officers on staff, so I knew they would arrive soon.

Re-entering the room, I continued to divert his attention as regularly as possible while maintaining a distance until the officers arrived. Upon their arrival, the man essentially gave up and was handcuffed and placed in protective custody. Later, he was taken to a locked psychiatric facility for further treatment.

While following most of the standard crisis intervention techniques, I deviated in three significant areas that should be noted:

1. I pressed his "space," drawing fairly close when he was armed.
2. I asked him to "give me the blade," instead of simply requesting that he put it down.
3. I had not arranged law enforcement backup before pursuing a lengthy discussion.

I strongly suggest that you do not repeat these errors! Each put me inappropriately at risk.

To more fully understand suicide and the skills required for long-term intervention, I recommend the following books: *Concerning Death: a practical guide for the living* edited by Earl A. Grollman (see the section entitled "What You Should Know About Suicide"), and *Grief Counseling and Grief Therapy* by J. William Worden. Also check the Bibliography for other valuable readings.

Violent Behavior

When grief causes a person's behavior to escalate beyond the realm of verbal interchange, pathology is in evidence. Violent overtures are not uncommon when a family member is told of the death of a loved one. One researcher (Turner, 1984) notes that the bereft person's age, sex, and family situation relate to the potential for violence. Young males, particularly those between the ages of 15 and 30, tend to be the most violent. All individuals, regardless of race, without intact nuclear families, such as spouses or children, tend to be more violent than those who have ready sources of support. Turner also notes that, while family members can provide great solace, they also can become specific targets for violence. You should be alert to any signs indicating that potential.

Understanding the cause of the violent behavior is a prerequisite to its effective management. Many people, when they perceive a significant loss of control, become violent or aggressive in an attempt to regain that control. The sudden loss of a loved one is a blatant emotional assault and an assertion of vulnerability, hence the heightened potential for violence. By recognizing this, you can anticipate a violent response and better manage its outcome.

Once a chance of violence has been recognized, staff should take definite steps to avoid confrontation (Turner, 1984). It is important not to show anxiety or fear. If a family member appears imminently violent, try to put that person at ease physically. For example, find a quiet, private area with comfortable seating, away from disturbing noise and intrusion. Offer a hot cup of decaffeinated coffee or other beverage and wait until the person has relaxed to some degree. Later, you can formally assess the potential for violence by posing straightforward questions such as, "Are you concerned about losing control and hurting someone?" This will allow the person to vent any violent impulses in a more socially acceptable manner through verbalization.

Do not, under any circumstances, attempt to counter threats with other threats. Instead, attempt to understand the angry person's viewpoint and to help resolve his or her frustration. One way to do this is to help the person become *actively* involved in the situation at hand. It may be possible to direct the person's energies toward the obvious and pressing practical issues—contacting family members, release of belongings, and funeral arrangements. Often, as people proceed with the resolution of these concrete issues, they gradually begin to verbalize their feelings, and their behavior becomes a model of a successful coping response.

Suggestions offered to foster appropriate responses include the following:

• Assume the role of the person's advocate. This has a calming influence. Make clear your willingness to help. An offer of food or drink also serves to calm angry people. Such an offer underscores an interest in their welfare and is thus encouraging to those in crisis.

• Provide family members with privacy, helping them to feel less vulnerable. Choose an area that is as private as possible, away from the confusion of the emergency room and provocative or disturbed patients. However, use care not to place yourself in a situation of potential harm.

• Don't leave a bereft person alone in a room. If you must leave, arrange for another staff member to remain nearby, so that the person feels another's presence.

• Never approach potentially violent persons too rapidly or move too close to them. While comforting touches may be appropriate in other circumstances, many violent or aggressive people consider touching to be an intrusion, and this could escalate their violence. Proceed very cautiously.

Homicidal Ideation

As with suicide, homicidal threats are *never* to be ignored. Such threats occur commonly when the loss of a loved one is due to negligence (whether real or perceived), drunken driving, or intentional violence. Usually, after a "cool-down" period, most people will begin to calm, and the potential for violence will diminish. This does *not* mean that they are no longer angry or bitter, but rather that they have begun to exercise sufficient self-control to stabilize themselves.

In some cases, however, agitation increases. Individuals have been known to rush from a notification situation, breathing out threats, to search for those whom they feel are responsible for the death. In such circumstances, *always* contact local law enforcement immediately. The police will take whatever action they deem appropriate and will obtain the necessary information required to make an appropriate disposition of the case.

Tarasoff Regulations

Further, by law, you *must* make every effort to also contact the threatened individual as quickly as possible and to the extent you are able. The purpose is to warn him or her to take whatever action may be needed to escape harm. The legally applicable reference is to a case known as *Tarasoff v. Regents of University of California*, 551 P.2d 334 (Cal.) (1976). It reads in part:

On October 27, 1969, Prosenjit Poddar killed Tatiana Tarasoff. Plaintiffs, Tatiana's parents, allege that two months earlier Poddar confided his intention to kill Tatiana to Dr. Lawrence Moore, a psychologist employed by the Cowell Memorial Hospital at the University of California at Berkeley. They allege that, on Moore's request, the campus police briefly detained Poddar but released him when he appeared rational. They further claim that Dr. Harvey Powelson, Moore's superior, then directed that no further action be taken to detain Poddar. No one warned plaintiffs of Tatiana's peril.

Plaintiffs' complaints predicate liability on two grounds: defendants' failure to warn plaintiffs of the impending danger and their failure to bring about Poddar's confinement. Defendants, in turn, assert that they owed no duty of reasonable care to Tatiana.

We shall explain that defendant therapists cannot escape liability merely because Tatiana herself was not their patient. When a therapist determines, or pursuant to the standards of his profession should determine, that his patient presents a serious danger of violence to another, he incurs an obligation to use reasonable care to protect the intended victim against such danger. The discharge of this duty may require the therapist to take one or more of various steps, depending upon the nature of the case. Thus, it may call for him to warn the intended victim or others likely to apprise the victim of the danger, to notify the police, or to take whatever other steps are reasonably necessary under the circumstances.

In the case at bar, plaintiffs admit that defendant therapists notified the police, but argue on appeal that the therapists failed to exercise reasonable care to protect Tatiana in that they did not confine Poddar and did not warn Tatiana or others likely to apprise her of the danger. Defendant therapists, however, are public employees. Consequently, to the extent that plaintiffs seek to predicate liability upon the therapists' failure to bring about Poddar's confinement, the therapists can claim immunity. No specific statutory provision, however, shields them from liability based upon failure to warn Tatiana or others likely to apprise her of the danger, and Government Code section 820.2 does not protect such failure as an exercise of discretion.

Two significant findings are highlighted in *Tarasoff*:

Once a therapist does in fact determine, or under applicable professional standards reasonably should have determined, that a patient poses a serious danger of violence to others, he bears a duty to exercise reasonable care to protect the foreseeable victim of that danger. While the discharge of this duty of due care will necessarily vary with the facts of each case, in each instance the adequacy of the therapist's conduct must be measured against the traditional negligence standard of reasonable care under the circumstances.

Within the broad range of reasonable practice and treatment in which professional opinion and judgement may differ, the therapist is free to exercise his or her own best judgement without liability; proof, aided by hindsight, that he or she judged wrongly is insufficient to establish negligence.[29]

There are numerous factors to be considered in the determination of danger. One legal counsel has noted:

> A therapist first must determine whether his or her patient poses a serious danger to an identifiable third party or parties. If such a danger is posed, the therapist then must determine what protective action must be taken. Several factors are relevant to these determinations, among them the seriousness of the threatened harm, the likelihood that the patient will harm the third party, the standards in the therapeutic community for assessing the danger and its likelihood, and the impact of protective action on the third party and the patient.
>
> The more serious the threatened harm, the more likely it is that some action is necessary to protect the third party. A wide difference exists between harm threatened with a dangerous weapon—such as a knife, a revolver, or poison—and a threatened punch in the mouth or slap across the face.
>
> The likelihood of the patient carrying out the threatened harm may require consideration of many factors. Were similar threats of serious harm made in the past carried out? Is there any other history of threats or overt acts of harm? Is the likelihood of harm based solely on the prediction of dangerousness without any recent overt threat or harm as a basis? Is the patient suffering from a delusion involving a third party, upon which he or she may act in a violent way? Other factors that may be relevant are the degree of psychotic manifestations, the patient's cultural background, and whether the patient has a history of being physically assaulted as a child. The more likely the harm, the more likely it is that some protective action will be necessary.[30]

Know your facility's protocol for such situations, or obtain specific directions from your supervisor. In practice, when a homicidal threat is expressed, most individuals will remain with the notifier if requested to do so. In situations such as this, it is the professional's responsibility to attempt to resolve the issue. Much like dealing with someone who is suicidal (described earlier in this chapter), the psychotraumatologist needs to follow a protocol. Here are the steps that you may take:

1. Ascertain the depth of the threat.

Do so by discovering the reasons that the individual has for threatening such an act. There may be further rationale not previously known to you, depending upon the circumstances surrounding the death. Get the facts.

---

[29] Brieland, 1985. Reprinted with permission.

[30] Beis, 1984.

2. Empathize.

Validate the feelings when possible. Allow for expressions of anger. At this stage, it is possible to resolve the threat. If not, proceed with the following steps:

3. Reality-test the individual's reasoning.

Pursue the rationale to justify taking another person's life to its ultimate conclusions.

4. Provide counseling.

Elicit family support. Help the person to understand the consequences, personally, to his or her family and to the family of the threatened individual. Highlight the full meaning of the proposed action, helping the person to see the intermediate and end-point results such a course of action would bring. Be thorough.

5. Obtain a commitment.

Solicit either a commitment to make no attempt to do harm, or a commitment similar to the verbal contract described in the suicide section—that if the person later feels impelled to take any action, a designated individual must be contacted first. This person could be a counselor, a family member, or a good friend. Make sure both parties are aware of the contract and agree to participate fully.

6. Evaluate and follow up.

If _any_ concern still exists (and it should if "contracting" is necessary), contact an appropriate licensed mental health professional for further evaluation and action. If you are that professional, follow through with appropriate legal and administrative consultation to ensure a proper disposition. Learn the policy of your facility in advance to ensure appropriate action.

By following such a protocol, the professional counselor can successfully intervene in critical situations and avert what could otherwise become a terrible tragedy for all involved.

Grief Influenced by Drugs and Alcohol

When family members arrive at the hospital under the influence of mood-altering substances, working through grief becomes extremely difficult. Emotive responses tend to become exaggerated and uncontrolled, and the ability of the family members to unite in support of each other is greatly reduced.

There seems to be no specific management strategy that is particularly effective for such situations, except to call in other family resources (other relatives or close friends) to provide extended support. This is particularly important when young children are involved.

Care must be exercised in releasing such family members from the hospital. Note who will be driving and make suggestions to maximize family safety. If you are seriously concerned, quietly contact local law enforcement and convey your concerns *prior* to the family's departure.

Extreme Denial

In normal or uncomplicated reactions, grief usually reaches its peak within three or four months after the bereavement (Weinberg, 1985). However, when the essentials of grief resolution do not take place, the process is delayed, and psychosomatic, psychoneurotic, and psychotic reactions occur with increased frequency (Lindemann, 1979).

An early predictor of an individual's ability to successfully complete the grief process is the degree of protraction and severity of the denial phase. If extended acute denial is noted—such as a family member who *emphatically* verbalizes a factual disbelief of the situation for 30 minutes or more, even after having seen the body—the notifier must utilize aggressive crisis intervention techniques to bring the family member into the *process* of resolution. In other words, even if some components of denial may still be present, the family member needs to begin to *emotionally* recognize reality at some internal level.

Case Vignette 8.3

In December of 1988, a truck driver was brought in under CPR. On receiving the first radio report, we wondered if he had been in an accident, as he was found in the driver's seat of his 18-wheel truck. However, we shortly learned that the vehicle had been parked, and he had been found slumped over the steering wheel.

Upon his arrival, the medical staff quickly worked to revive him. He had been intubated in the field, and the initial course of cardiac medications had been given. Following extensive efforts, he was pronounced DAR (dead after resuscitation) in the emergency room at 10:34 P.M. The cause was a presumed myocardial infarction (heart attack).

I completed his clothing search and in his wallet found a telephone booklet with his home phone number. I also noted that it contained the phone numbers of many women other than his wife. I quickly placed a call, using the usual technique to avoid a telephone notification. His wife took careful directions and headed for the hospital.

Upon her arrival, I met her in the E.R. lobby and escorted her to my office. She was a slight woman, approximately five feet tall, and was dressed in a pullover shirt and light blue slacks. Her hair was short and blond but had begun to grow out, with grey shafts. Her mannerisms and speech were decidedly unsophisticated, but her expression was intent and clear. She had arrived alone and said that there was no one available to come with her; she had no transportation, so had taken a taxi to the hospital.

After a brief narrative of the events surrounding the death, I broke the news. She sat for a few moments in stunned silence. She asked no questions and looked down, as if studying a single spot on the floor. Gradually, she began to cry softly. She then looked at me and asked, "Are you sure he's gone?" "Yes," I responded, "We're sure."

Suddenly she looked up and said emphatically, "He's not dead. He can't be gone. I'm goin' home, and he'll be at the house when I get there. You ain't tellin' me the truth, I know you ain't." She arose from her chair as if to leave, moving toward the door.

I met her there and put my arm around her shoulder, saying, "Mrs. Smith, I know this is hard for you. Losing anyone in your family is always difficult to handle. Why don't you take your seat for a minute and collect yourself. Then we can go in and see him together. How would that be?" She nodded and sat down again, with tears welling up in her eyes.

I asked how long they had been married. "Thirty-six years," she replied. Almost immediately she became quite talkative. Her tears cleared, and their life stories began to tumble from her lips without pause. She became quite animated for a time. They had married young and had no children, she said, and they had always been happy. Then her expression changed, and she described years of separations, alluding to regular episodes of infidelity on his part.

"We were just gettin' back together," she said tearfully. "And we was doin' so good. He just can't be gone, he just can't." Her voice and mannerisms became somewhat childlike. Clearly, she was regressing emotionally, overwhelmed by the magnitude of her loss. I intervened briefly, bringing her back to reality by expressing my sorrow for her loss at such a crucial time. She then seemed to calm and reorient herself.

Shortly after this, the nurse arrived and invited us into his room. We entered it together, and I approached the gurney first, drawing her after me. She moved to my side and leaned over and hugged her husband. Commenting on his new growth of beard, she suddenly spoke to him saying, "You ain't dead. Come on, get up. We're goin' home." She pulled at his arm again and again, becoming increasingly insistent. Then she began to cry and pleaded further with him to come with her.

Again, I intervened, reaffirming the reality of the situation. We left the room and talked more about the death. This continued for several hours into the night. A call was placed to her sister-in-law, who came in promptly. She responded very constructively to the news and became a great support in working with the wife. From time to time, we would re-enter the room and view the body again, reality-testing the death each time. (The coroner's staff had delayed picking up the body until further notice at my request.)

Just when it seemed that we had made progress, she stated, "Please, I've gotta go now. My husband will be home soon. He always brings donuts home in the mornings, and we eat 'em together."

As the night wore on, she eventually began to recognize the death but was unable to bring herself to verbalize the loss. I understood her reluctance and gave her time. Finally, at about 7 A.M., she looked at me and said, "He really _is_ dead, isn't he." I nodded my reply, and at long last she bowed her head and wept.

The gradual-but-persistent efforts had paid off, and grieving had begun. Her sister-in-law, who had remained patient and caring for these many hours, offered to take the wife to stay the day at her home. They left together, offering mutual comfort and support at the loss.

In examining the reasons behind this prolonged denial response, I came to two conclusions. First, the recent reunification represented for her a new beginning and hope that the marriage might bloom again. Apparently, the husband had treated her better during this period than he had in the past. This hope was rudely and prematurely wrested from her by his sudden death. Second, the many times he had left her or been unfaithful in the past, were, for her, very real and unhealed losses. They had left her less able to cope with this final, "ultimate" loss.

By recognizing mitigating circumstances and allowing for them in your interventions, you will be much more successful in resolving those acute barriers to normal grief.

Signs of Pathological Grief

There are many other subtle indicators that grief may be moving toward pathology. The following list has been suggested as warning signs applicable to children:

- Absence of grief—shows *no* emotion
- Persistent blame or guilt—other anxieties
- Aggressive and destructive outbursts
- Depression and suicidal thoughts or actions
- Unwillingness to speak about the deceased
- Expressing only positive or only negative feelings about the deceased
- Prolonged dysfunction in school
- Always assuming a caregiver role
- Accident proneness
- New stealing or other illegal acts
- Signs of addictive behavior: drugs, food, certain activities

"These are only warning signs," the author notes, "and do not necessarily indicate a severe problem. The *intensity* and the *duration* of these behaviors are the deciding factors indicating the need for professional help."[31] While many other indicators could be added (recurrent nightmares, etc.), these certainly give the needed flavor.

For adults, many similarities could be noted as well, especially in regard to mood changes and age-related behaviors such as job difficulties. Typically, either the bereft individual or close adults will recognize

---

[31] Papenbrock, 1990, p. 11. Reprinted with permission.

a problem. Earl Grollman has written, "In general, one is able to distinguish normal from pathological grief not by the latter's being abnormal *per se*, but rather by emotional reactions being so intensive and prolonged that the physical and mental well-being are jeopardized."[32]

Whether it is a dramatic change or a more subtle-yet-persistent one, if a person is experiencing difficulty in bringing grief to a wholesome, successful conclusion, further professional help should be sought.

---

[32] Grollman, 1974, p. 329.

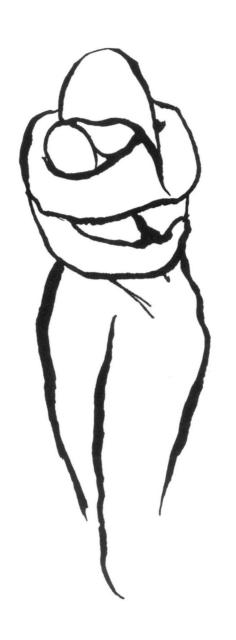

Chapter 9

Bereavement Perspectives

Bereavement Relationships

The nature of the familial relationship with the deceased can significantly affect the process and outcome of the grief response. The resolution challenge for the bereaved is greater or lesser depending on the role the deceased played in the person's life. For example, the loss of a spouse can be a much greater loss to overcome than the loss of an elderly parent. Because of the importance relationships play in the grief counseling process, bereavement perspectives for various family ties are detailed here.

Death of a Spouse/Significant Other

In a life-stress scale developed by Holmes and Rahe (1967), the death of a spouse was ranked as the highest external life stressor possible, followed by losses such as divorce, job transition, and so on.

There are many reasons for the depth of this trauma. By far the greatest is the loss of the intimacy and comfort provided in marriage. Even in a relatively recent marriage, the spouse was selected to be someone with whom the individual would choose to share all of his life. Permanent, concrete plans have been made; deep emotional investment has been granted. Thus the loss is felt with extreme acuity. Further, as married life progresses, both partners develop patterns of accommodation for, and dependence on, each other. With the death of one, these patterns are completely disrupted, leaving the survivor with feelings of loneliness and a perceived inability to cope.

A significant variable in a person's ability to handle grief is the emotional preparation that comes with the knowledge that death is impending. The critical amount of forewarning appears to be about two weeks. Clearly sudden death, with no forewarning at all, presents a tremendous obstacle to overcome (Carey, 1979).

Glick, Weiss, and Parkes (1974) conducted a longitudinal study with the main finding that the forewarning of the death had a "salutary effect" on how adequately and fully the bereft adjusted. Among widows, a lack of forewarning and emotional preparation for the death was associated with a phobic response to future remarriage. And while widowers without forewarning might remarry, they seemed more likely than other widowers to continue to feel tension and anxiety long beyond the usual resolution period (Carey, 1979).

With this in mind, management of the initial grief process after a sudden loss takes on crucial importance. The need for the spouse to view the body, to be encouraged to fully grieve the loss, and to identify and maintain a well-defined support system should be of paramount concern to the helper.

Shortly after the death, numerous problems may develop. In asking widows and widowers to name the main problems faced after the death of their spouses, Carey (1979) noted that *loneliness* was named by 27 percent of widowers and 54 percent of widows as being a great problem. Loneliness was most difficult at specific times of the day, such as near the time of the evening meal and throughout the evening. Many also expressed loneliness when doing things by themselves—for example, while involved in routine household activities or recreational pursuits.

Indecision about the future and the loss of personal goals were also problems expressed. The need to be needed by someone became more acute. The widowed, particularly if childless, found it difficult to find others with whom it seemed appropriate to share grief.

Carey also noted that many widowers had difficulty learning how to run their households and tend to the needs of their minor children without their wives. Widows found that making decisions alone often produced anxiety, especially regarding family issues. Also, some women expressed fear about their personal safety and noted nightmares about people breaking into their homes. Those who were not accustomed to dealing with finances found that the task presented great difficulties.

For any helper, an awareness of these issues can greatly assist in supporting the bereft spouse. The spouse and other family members can be educated about these problems, and preparations can then be made to assist.

Death of a Child

The loss of a child can be acutely difficult for parents to resolve. It can jeopardize their emotional stability and compromise crucial marital and family ties. One couple shared the following note with me after the death of their son.

Case Vignette 9.1

A miracle, created from love, "our prince, our angel" was born on Sunday, February 26, 1989 at 12:36 A.M. He was eight pounds, two ounces. What a joyous day! He was placed immediately on my stomach while John cut his umbilical cord. He gazed into my eyes and I kissed him again and again. He was perfect. The joy and elation were unbelievable! Upon discharge, 24 hours later, my husband picked me up with our precious son.

On 3/4/89 at 6 P.M., Derek was hospitalized for hyperbilirubinemia (jaundice) and congestion. [He] was released 48 hours later. He was healthy and home with his family. I continued to take him to his family physician for follow-up bilirubin levels. On 3/9/89 he was still slightly congested, and I returned to his physician. She alleviated my fears.

Derek slept in a bassinet next to our bed. On 3/11/89 at 5:30 A.M. I placed him between John and me, and finished nursing him. Sometime between 5:30 and 7 A.M., he died in his sleep between us. John, my husband, woke up at 7 A.M.—horror on his face. There was frothy discharge from Derek's nose on his yellow nightgown and on the sheets. I gave him CPR immediately. There was no pulse. I think I knew he was dead, but I could not believe it. When the ambulance arrived, they continued to try to bring him back to life. I was hysterical! He was taken to the hospital. John and I were placed in the social service room, and a doctor came in and said, "Your son is dead." I demanded to see Derek immediately.

We were brought into the trauma room. His precious body was wrapped in a white sheet. I unwrapped the sheet and held him close to me for hours. I told him how much I loved him, the plans we had for him, and all about his extended family that loved him whom he would never know. I wept and wept and knew it would be the last time Derek would be in my arms.

I miss him. I yearn for him. My arms ache for him. Grief is an intense, lonely, and personal experience.[33]

The loss of a child can be among the most traumatic of all deaths. It is a death that is seen as "out of turn." Rando (1985) notes that parents keenly feel responsible to protect and to nurture their children, and there is a natural expectation that the child will outlive the parents. When this does not happen, there is a universal feeling that a primary parenting role was somehow unmet.

These feelings are particularly evident in dramatic, unexpected deaths. For example, the child may have been a passenger in a motor vehicle accident in which the parent was the driver. At such times, the parent experiences a tremendous degree of "survivor's guilt"—with feelings of failure, or "it should have been me instead." Therefore, it is imperative that the notifier obtain as thorough an understanding of the accident scenario as possible. More often than not, the accident can be explained as a tragic but unavoidable event. Occasionally, however, true culpability is present (e.g., drinking and driving, or child neglect), and the grieving process will, of necessity, be prolonged.

---

[33] Lisa Morris, _Letter of Loss_. Printed with permission.

In such situations, castigation or even subtle disapproval of the parents is *never* acceptable. Your job is not to "teach them a lesson," as it is sometimes expressed. The loss speaks for itself in that regard, usually too effectively. One might think that such a warning to health care providers would be unnecessary, but you may find yourself easily drawn into such behavior, especially if you are a parent. Spare the grieving parents. As one writer described it, "A child's death is the minute that lasts an eternity." No reproof will be necessary from you.

As previously noted, Holmes and Rahe's research indicates that the death of a spouse may be the most traumatic loss of all. Johnson's investigation (1983) contradicts this finding. In a study of couples who had suffered the loss of a child within the previous year, all but one stated that the death of a spouse would not have been as traumatic as the death of the child. Johnson puts forth the explanation that a child's death is more profound and difficult to resolve because the child is seen as a literal, physical extension of the parents and a joint, personal creation.

One of the most difficult aspects of parental bereavement is that usually both parents are equally devastated and thus unable to give full support to each other. Rando (1985) notes that the situation is made even more difficult by the closeness of a marital relationship. Parenting can add a sense of purpose and become a source of mutual support and strength. The death of a child may interfere so fully as to compromise that support.

The age of the child at death seems to make little difference. The emotion appears to be the same: "How could parents outlive their child?" Parental grieving is further complicated by the social stigmatization many experience following the death. It is all too common for parents to experience feelings of abandonment. They often complain that they feel like social "lepers." (Rando, 1985.)

A corollary to the negative feelings sometimes experienced by caregivers, mentioned earlier, this isolation may result from other parents' fears that such an experience could happen to them, too. In addition, friends and neighbors may feel awkward in openly enjoying their own children and choose to avoid the bereaved family entirely. In working with a bereaved couple, it is crucial that strong support systems be identified and mobilized. Parental bereavement self-help groups can play a critical role in this process. Note the many bereavement self-help groups listed in Appendix J.

Death of a Parent

Of all deaths within an immediate family, for *adult* children, death of a parent is *usually* the least difficult. Sanders (1980) reports that adult children are quickly caught up in the fast pace of life. Families, jobs, and daily responsibilities allow little time to dwell upon the loss.

Many times, however, there can be a heightened feeling of vulnerability to death expressed by adult children, particularly when the parents died in old age. Sanders (1980) notes that, while a parent is alive, there is a feeling of a generation still ahead. When the parent dies, this places the son or daughter, particularly the eldest, as next in the natural order of things, causing some anxiety. Such feelings need to be noted, validated, and discussed to enable the survivors to effectively manage the primary loss and also to prevent debilitating preoccupation with death.

Death of a Friend

Death of a friend brings its own complications. This is a loss that is often largely unrecognized or underestimated. When a patient dies, in the haste to deal with family grief issues, many times no one acknowledges the grief felt by those without blood or marriage ties.

Often, others will arrive at the hospital with family members of accident victims, only to find that everyone—staff and family—expect that these friends will step in as the primary supporters. In the helping role, they are expected to "be strong" and may, indeed, be very capable in providing such a service. However, in the process, many are given no opportunity to grieve themselves.

In working with all gathered, acknowledge the very real grief that close friends may feel. Provide ventilation opportunities similar to those given the family. Present these opportunities in the presence of the family. By so doing, "permission" is given the friend to grieve without feeling that he or she is a burden to others present. Most family members will then spontaneously include such friends in the grief process, to the benefit of all parties involved. Friends, when allowed to grieve their own loss, provide stronger support than those with unresolved feelings.

Children's Perceptions of Death

Children also undergo a complex grieving process, particularly at the loss of a parent or sibling. However, with their immature understanding of death concepts, resolution of the loss may be more difficult. For example, one study (Sanders, 1980) noted that, among the younger participants, feelings of unreality were prominent. It seemed impossible to them that such an event could actually have taken place.

For this reason, and to bring children's grief to a wholesome resolution, it is important to include children in all aspects of the grief process. Barring an unusually disfigured body, children should be allowed to view their loved ones, *if they desire to do so*. They should also be involved in funeral arrangements and be allowed to grieve with the entire family. One writer suggests:

Rely on your own judgement and on whether your child wants to attend the funeral. Older children (some say age 10 and up) should be *encouraged* to attend, but no child should be forced.[34]

Families should not hide their expressions of grief or try to present a "business-as-usual" facade. Allowing (not forcing) children's full involvement in the grief process will aid them in gradually resolving their own grief.

Even news of impending death may be shared with children, especially when the death process is prolonged. During my research, one participant noted that he felt "cheated" that, as a child, he was not allowed more involvement both prior to and after the death of his father. He was nine years of age at the time, and family members were hesitant to discuss the terminal nature of his father's illness. When the death occurred, he was shocked to learn that it had been expected and that no one had allowed him to prepare for it and to spend additional "special" time with his dad.

The concepts of death that children must master to fully understand a loss are irreversibility, finality, inevitability, and causality. These concepts develop in a natural maturation process. While there is some disagreement regarding the exact ages at which children grasp these concepts, it is generally accepted that a child of two or younger has the concept of "here" and "not here." A child of three to five years sees death as temporary. At six to ten years a child understands the reality of death and is curious about its biological aspects and the details of burial. From 11 on, a child conceives of death in a manner similar to that of an adult.[35]

In describing these conceptual steps, and recognizing the problems that may occur for children at different developmental levels, Schonfeld (1989) has provided the following outline:[36]

Irreversibility: Death is a permanent phenomenon from which there is no recovery or return.
Example of incomplete understanding: The child expects the deceased to return, as if from a trip.
Implication: Failure to comprehend prevents the child from detaching personal ties to the deceased, a necessary first step in successful mourning.

---

[34] Papenbrock, 1990. Reprinted with permission.

[35] Staff, *Compassionate Friends* newsletter, Fall, 1982. Reprinted with permission.

[36] Reprinted with permission.

Finality (Non-functionality): Death is a state in which *all* life functions cease *completely*.

Example of incomplete understanding: The child worries about a buried relative being cold or in pain; the child wishes to bury food with the deceased.

Implication: May lead to preoccupation with physical suffering of the deceased and impair readjustment.

Inevitability (Universality): Death is a natural phenomenon that no living being can escape indefinitely.

Example of incomplete understanding: The child views significant individuals (i.e., self, parents) as immortal.

Implication: If the child does not view death as inevitable, he/she is likely to view death as punishment (either for actions or thoughts of the deceased or the child), leading to excessive guilt and shame.

Causality: The child develops a realistic understanding of the causes of death.

Example of incomplete understanding: The child who relies on magical thinking is apt to assume responsibility for death of a loved one by assuming that bad thoughts or unrelated actions were causative.

Implication: Tends to lead to excessive guilt that is difficult for the child to resolve.

To identify a child's maturity level regarding death, simply discuss the death and determine how completely the child understands each of these concepts. Offer information that may narrow identified gaps in understanding, using language appropriate to the child's age. Answer questions directly and simply. Undue embellishment is not necessary. Give answers to build on later, not ones that will have to be unlearned later. Most professionals agree that, "even a child of two or three can understand 'his body could not work anymore'." (Staff, 1982)

Resolve specific concerns. For example, explain to the child our reasons for tears. As one author suggested, "Death is something that happens to everything that lives, and in time it will happen to everyone who is alive now. But death itself does not hurt, and the person who has died is beyond all physical pain. The pain that is felt is the pain of loss among those who are still alive and able to feel." (Jackson, 1965) Even if the child doesn't directly understand a given death concept, if the specific concerns of the child can be addressed and put to rest, the child can successfully set aside that aspect of the loss until age and maturity allow for complete resolution.

Another situation that may need intervention is "wish fulfillment." Many times children may think or say something to the effect that, "I don't love you," or, "I wish you were dead." Even if the thoughts had not been outwardly expressed, if they occurred in close proximity to the death, many children will need to share these thoughts and have it explained to them that they could in no way contribute to the death. Otherwise, in their minds they may feel that they carry the burden of the loss, which becomes unbearable when they witness the grief of the family.

To address such concerns, parents should allow plenty of time to talk with their children. Encourage open sharing of positive, or even negative, feelings and memories. These can be expressed orally or through art or writing. If the loss is seen as an open topic in the family, children will in natural course seek opportunities and ways to express themselves and will put their fears and concerns to rest.

When developmental gaps are obvious, you can educate support persons about identified problems in the grief resolution process and assist them with appropriate responses. Help them to identify when the grief process requires the help of a professional and when actions are simply "normal" for a child. Help them realize that children often mourn "at a distance." They shouldn't be concerned if younger children at first make jokes or continue normal play as a distraction. Some children may have frightening thoughts they fear to share, and such play provides a needed diversion until their feelings can be more fully defined.

Later, if children feel left out or have not found a way to express their feelings, they may misbehave to obtain the attention and help they need. Parents and others can recognize these behaviors and respond appropriately. In this way, many of the potential problems for children can be resolved, in spite of developmental obstacles.

In educating parents about managing their children's grief, help them to understand that the initial preparation work is primarily personal. Of greater importance than what a child is told is what the child sees. Children model us surprisingly well, and they model our fears with the greatest alacrity of all. If the parents respond to a death with feelings of catastrophe and horror instead of simple and genuine sorrow, a child will respond in like manner, possibly overwhelmed with fear. Thus, parents first need to come to some semblance of composure and acceptance themselves and explain and reassure as needed. Encourage parents to take the time necessary in this preparation, thus allowing their children the greatest support and stability possible.

Finally, a child who may be too young to understand a death, or certain of its aspects, needs a high degree of love and attention to nourish feelings of personal security. Deeper understanding will come with time.

Special Concerns

Some losses will require special assistance at the outset. For example, when a young child loses a parent, there are often feelings of abandonment that are very difficult to deal with. For young children, life is defined and ordered within the context of family. "Family" is most fully defined by one's parents. This loss can be particularly disturbing.

In regard to sibling loss, children may, for a time, seem preoccupied with the deceased's belongings and may even insist on wearing his or her clothes. These are normal responses at the time. Gradually, given input as they request or need it, they, too, will work through a grief process at their own level, allowing the loss to be resolved (Staff, 1982).

In situations where a death leaves a surviving twin, be prepared for the potential for greater problems. The loss may be traumatic enough to require counseling for the entire family. Specific symptoms to watch for in children include nightmares, bed-wetting, difficulty in school, persistent acting-out behaviors, and other disturbances. If symptoms are severe or persist longer than one to three months, seek the advice of a qualified professional.

A particular note of concern was provided by one author, a psychologist, who writes, "Children between the ages of five and seven are a particularly vulnerable group. They have developed cognitively enough to understand some of the permanent ramifications of death but they have very little coping capacity; that is, their ego skills and social skills are insufficiently developed to enable them to defend themselves. This particular group should be singled out for special concern by the counselor." (Worden, 1982) The need for special time and attention should be emphasized to parents and other family members.

Schonfeld (1989) adds another caution. He notes that ". . . numerous studies have illustrated that adolescents are particularly vulnerable to long-term behavioral and emotional complications resulting from a personal experience of death, despite the attainment of an increased developmental level of the concept of death." It may be easier to see the needs of young children than the needs of adolescents. Watch them carefully. Look for long-term effects from a loss. Don't quickly assume that all is going well unless expressions of grief resolution are fully in evidence. They, too, may need extensive support before becoming able to move on with their lives in a healthy manner.

Cultural Issues

While death is a universal experience, cultural responses to it vary greatly. Examples of this diversity—in this case among peoples of Southeast Asia—are provided in this excerpt from a UCD Medical Center Interpreting Services newsletter:

> In many cultures . . . discussion of death is forbidden in the presence of a terminal patient. Death is a reality in the hospital, and something UCDMC interpreters deal with often.
>
> Hmong (a Laotian group) elders believe their "death date" is predestined; if you talk about death out loud, you are tempting fate. As such, any discussion of death, wills, funeral arrangements, or autopsies

is forbidden. Physicians and health care providers treating people from this culture are advised to tell only family members of an impending death, away from the patient's bedside. Because the Hmong prefer to keep their loved ones' bodies whole, they will rarely agree to a biopsy, autopsy, or the removal of any organ such as the brain, lungs, heart or tongue. Otherwise, they believe the next generation would be born with these parts missing.

The Mien (another Laotian group) believe each human has three spirits: one that is reborn, a second that stays with the family, and a third that becomes a ghost or "bad" spirit. Like the Hmong, the Mien believe the dying are going to another life and will need their body whole to survive. It is also commonly believed that "it is better to die at home; the spirit of a family member who dies in the hospital is believed to be lost without a home." These beliefs vary slightly among cultures and age groups.

Decisions about burial sites and disposal of a loved one's property usually are made by the entire family. Location of the grave site is very important; preparations for the funeral are extensive. The older the deceased, the longer and more elaborate the funeral ceremony will be. Expenses in the Hmong and Mien cultures are covered by a collection taken from each family in the clan; hence monetary obligations such as funeral costs, grave sites, and food for the ceremony commonly are paid for in cash.

Some cultures, such as Cambodian and Thai, believe in cremation, with the ashes kept in beautiful urns placed in special places. This also applies to Vietnamese and Chinese who practice Buddhism.

The one belief that is common to all Southeast Asian cultures is the taboo about speaking of death. A loved one's remains are always put to rest in a dignified and honorable way. Below are a few examples of UCDMC patients' families' experiences with death:

1. A 24-year-old Vietnamese man checks himself into the hospital. After several days of testing, he is diagnosed with cancer of the liver. Since he is alone, the physician, through the interpreter, must tell him he has only a few months to live. He has one sister in the Bay Area; the rest of the family in Vietnam. He begins to plan his short future and decides to write his family members telling them he is well and not to worry, rather than worry them with the thoughts of his dying. He is trying to be a very good son by not wanting to worry his mother.

2. A Hmong teenager commits suicide and is taken to the coroner's office. The family comes to the hospital looking for their loved one. Interpreting Services takes the family to the coroner's office, where they discover an autopsy has been performed. The nine members of the family are furious and insist on viewing the body, checking it from head to toe. They blame the hospital, even after the function of the coroner's office, our laws on mysterious deaths and accidents, and the separation between the office and the hospital are explained.

3. An 80-year-old Chinese grandmother dies of natural causes, leaving behind a request that her older son have her body laid out in seven sets of clothes, one for every day of the week in her next world. The request is passed on to the funeral director, who is happy to comply.

4. A Mien baby is born two months premature; the baby is severely deformed and lives only two hours. The mother is upset not only because the baby has died, but also because she was given a Cesarean section operation that has left her "damaged."

5. A 15-year-old Mien boy drowns in the American River. An autopsy is performed by the county coroner, upsetting the family, who wants to know if body parts have been taken out. Interpreters, social workers, and county personnel spend six hours explaining the procedure.

6. One Vietnamese and four Cambodian children die violently in a school yard. The families involved consider that place a "bad omen." Because the children died so violently, it is believed that the "bad spirits will stay there," and the families likely will relocate.[37]

Perhaps one final example will be useful. In 1986, an elderly Laotian man died of cancer, which originated in his tongue. Because I speak Laotian, I became involved in the case, assisting the family with viewing and arrangements.

Case Vignette 9.2

An authorization was successfully obtained for a post mortem medical examination in the hospital pathology department. In process of this, his entire tongue was removed for further clinical tests. Upon release of the body to a funeral home, the family discovered this and became angry with the hospital and staff.

About 18 months later, a great-grand-niece of this individual was admitted with headaches. Upon examination, it was discovered that she had terminal brain cancer. When notified of this, the family became extremely angry, stating that it was due to the removal of her great-grand-uncle's tongue.

After further questioning, it was learned that the elderly man was a patriarchal leader of the clan. After his death, it was expected that he would continue to have contact with the family, telling them, among other things, how to heal themselves in the event of disease. By removing his tongue during the autopsy, we had effectively prevented him from telling the girl how to heal herself.

In their minds, we had not only violated the elderly man, but we were responsible for the girl's death, also.

---

[37] *Cultural News*, January/February, 1989. University of California, Davis, Medical Center. Reprinted with permission.

These examples should suffice to illustrate the point: exercise great care in dealing with any family representing another culture. While we cannot expect to be experts in every culture, we can take additional care to minimize conflicts and to accommodate the family's cultural beliefs.

Mode of Death

Deaths are commonly categorized by the NASH method—natural, accidental, suicidal, or homicidal (Worden, 1982). How well survivors cope with a death is greatly affected by the circumstances that brought it about. Extraordinary, precipitating events will invariably prolong the resolution process. The following are special circumstances to be considered in working with the bereaved.

Stillborn

Large numbers of stillborn births occur every year, many near or at full term. These deaths are often misunderstood. Feelings of parenthood are real, even when the life, struggling into the world, has not survived. One mother recorded her story (Hall, 1991) of such a loss. From her we can learn a great deal.

Case Vignette 9.3

There is a time to be born, a time die—and sometimes, no time at all between.

At 39, I couldn't believe I was really going to be a mother for the first time—even when I saw the baby cavorting around on the scan (ultrasound) and heard the heartbeat. But all the tests had gone fine, I felt strong and healthy, and I began to think about nannies and nursery schools.

November 19, 1987, I was 27 weeks pregnant, nicely rounded, and feeling good after a week's vacation. Bad traffic made it harder than usual to get to my prenatal appointment that day, and my husband, Greg, had to drop me off and search for a parking space. "I'm slightly concerned because I haven't felt any kicking yet," I said to my doctor, "but I suppose that's not unusual."

He immediately looked more attentive and checked me over. All seemed fine until he listened for the heartbeat and couldn't find it. He tried again, this time with the old-fashioned stethoscope.

Gentle and unalarming as he was, I sensed that something was very wrong. Why was he suddenly uninterested in my weight? Why was I to go for another scan at once? Where, oh, where was Greg?

On one level, I continued as though everything was all right and I was just having a test to confirm that; on another level, I knew, but couldn't acknowledge, that something terrible was happening. When Greg arrived, I tore into him and then cut out emotionally altogether when we went in for the scan.

Nothing in either of our lives had prepared us for that silent, motionless screen. The radiologist turned it slightly away from me, and

Greg gripped my hand. My doctor had come in by now. I looked at his face, and I knew. "I'm sorry," he said quite simply. "The baby's dead."

"No . . . no!" In sheer primitive pain Greg collapsed over me. "Are you sure?" I asked.

Yes, they were sure. We clung together like two lost children.

My obstetrician was wonderful. He helped me by explaining how important it was to see the baby after the birth. For that was the next thing. Though I couldn't believe it, he was talking about a normal delivery the next day. Most people probably have no idea that you still have to go through the whole, but greatly increased, trauma of birth even if the baby's dead. Or that your milk will come in (unless prevented by drugs), your breasts ache to nurse, and your hormones continue to behave as if you were a proud, happy mother.

When I came back from the operating room after the delivery, Greg was waiting for me. He'd gone out to buy flowers for our baby. I was still tethered to drips and drains, conscious but feeling heavily drugged. Two nurses appeared with a cot containing our little son—for son he was—wrapped in a pale blue blanket with two yellow roses on his pillow. They told us he was big for his age and would have been tall—words of recognition and kindness which meant so much.

I regret now that they didn't give me my child to hold, but laid him beside me on the edge of the bed, where Greg's arm supported him. I needed to hold him. But at the time it didn't seem possible, what with all the wires, my drugged feeling, and the awesome fragility of his skin.

Instead, we gave him his name, Philip, and I stroked the dark rivulets of downy hair on his tiny head and felt the anguish of my love for him. Birth is momentous enough in itself; to experience birth and death together is really beyond words. I was a mother—this was my son—but all my feelings were too late. Beside me, Greg was wrenched with sobs. My tears wouldn't come till later. After a few more minutes, Greg carefully picked Philip up, put him back on his cot, and kissed him good-bye. The nurses bore him away.

Now we had to face the pain of going on. All our hopes, our expectations for the future, our new sense of life's meaning had died with Philip. (One of the hardest things is how little other people understand all of this. Nor do they realize how long—a year, two, perhaps more—the process of mourning takes.)

Thankfully, I had the operation to recover from, and the funeral to organize. I knew instinctively that we must have one, just as I knew—I don't know how—that the nurses must take photographs, that we must give the baby the name we'd thought of and not "save" it for another child, and that we must create as many memories as possible.

That was one reason why the funeral was so important to us. It marked Philip's life not only for us but for our family; it created memories and forged bonds. There were only four of us at the service, but we clung together, swept up by the music, something primal flowing among us like an electric current. The tiny coffin lay at our feet, Philip's name engraved upon it. We scattered flowers and then left, feeling everything was as right as it could be in such very wrong circumstances.

The postmortem came to no definite conclusion, though an infection was suspected as the cause of death. But even if you have logical answers, they don't address the real whys. Why me? Why now? Why this innocent baby?

I think the search for answers to those questions—the search for the very meaning of life—is a lifetime's work. We hope to have more children and we believe we will—but nothing and nobody can ever replace Philip.[38]

(Note: June Hall and her husband have since become the parents of a healthy boy.)

This short, poignant record underscores the feelings of a stillborn birth and provides several valuable clues to managing the grief process. Creating memories is essential; active, physical involvement of both parents is primary in accomplishing this. The husband's gesture with the flowers at the birth is both touching and concrete, indicative of the tremendous grief he felt as a spouse and a father. Professional care--givers should note the mother's desire to hold the baby, the need for photographs, and how much the mother appreciated the nurse's comments about the baby—how big he was, and the man he might have grown to be. These comments and gestures, while painful, were important for the parents to manage their grief, and, combined with the funeral service, will serve as important events for coming to terms with their grief. The loss of a stillborn is an emotion-filled loss. It must be acknowledged and appreciated as such.

Sudden Infant Death Syndrome

Sudden Infant Death Syndrome (SIDS) is the major cause of infant deaths between the ages of one month and one year. It is annually responsible for nearly 6,000 deaths in the United States alone.[39] SIDS may also be referred to as *crib death,* or *cot death,* and strikes infants who are almost invariably reported to be healthy and whole.

These deaths are particularly traumatic for a variety of reasons. First, there is a great deal of expectancy and preparation for the birth of a child. Parents plan for all aspects of the addition of this new family member to their lives. Rooms are painted, clothing is bought, and plans are made. Following these preparations is the intense experience of labor and delivery. All this makes any pregnancy a major event.

In these early months of childhood, there is an especially intense attachment between the vulnerable child and the parents who care for it. To interrupt this with an infant's death is a loss of overwhelming

---

[38] Quoted with author's permission.

[39] National Center for Health Statistics, Public Health Service, Hyattsville, Maryland. Advance Mortality Statistics for 1989; monthly report, vol. 40, no. 8, supplement 2, January 7, 1992.

proportions. The feelings of grief are extremely acute and are manifest in many ways. Here is a description of typical reactions to a SIDS death:

> Mothers nearly always say that their arms "ache to hold their baby." Many times there is an irresistible urge to escape. Some parents dread being alone; others experience unreasonable fears of danger. If there are other children, parents may fear for their safety and may not want to let them out of their sight. At the same time, they may be afraid of the responsibility of caring for them.
>
> Because (of these conflicting feelings), parents may experience extreme irritation and impatience with (surviving) children's behavior. Further, parents often rely on family and friends (immediately after the loss); yet, at the same time, they may resent their help and feel guilty about this. The situation is made worse if the parents' community does not understand SIDS. Friends or relatives who are trying to help may say the wrong things.[40]

One step in attending to their grief is to educate the parents about the syndrome. While Sudden Infant Death Syndrome is not yet well understood, there are suspected causes. One hypothesis is that death results from a failure of the body's autonomic reflex to breathe. It is postulated to occur in infants because of the immaturity of their nervous systems. Currently, however, SIDS is a diagnosis given when all other causes of death have been medically ruled out. The National Sudden Infant Death Syndrome Resource Center provides some of these basic facts:

• SIDS is a definite medical entity and is the major cause of death in infants after the first month of life.

• SIDS victims appear healthy prior to death; at this time SIDS cannot be predicted or prevented, even by a physician.

• SIDS is *not* caused by external suffocation, vomiting or choking, and is not contagious.

• There appears to be no suffering; death occurs very rapidly, usually during periods of sleep.

Providing parents with this information may ease their feelings of guilt, and help them to explain their situation more easily to others. For additional information, write to the National Sudden Infant Death Syndrome Resource Center. (See Appendix I, page 256)

As with other complicated grief situations, special attention should be given the survivors. Support groups can be of invaluable assistance. In cases of prolonged grief, the death of a twin, or situations where the infant died in the care of relatives or friends, further counseling may well be necessary.

---

[40] The National SIDS Clearinghouse Fact Sheet, "What Is SIDS?"

Abortion

Abortion is a much-underrated loss. As one author put it, "When I worked at a university health service, I counseled many women who had had abortions, and frequently they did not recognize that the unresolved grief from a previous abortion lay behind what was currently troubling them." (Worden, 1982)

This loss history, although perhaps not expressed, can provide a subtle complication to the grieving process later when there is the sudden, unexpected loss of a child. While it is not likely to surface in the early crisis period, should it do so, it indicates a need for professional follow-up.

Suicide

Worden (1982) has estimated that, worldwide, about 750,000 people grieve a suicide loss each year. Thornton (1989) cites statistics showing that in the United States at least 20,000 people take their own lives each year, with suicide being the leading cause of death in the 5-24 year age group.

Few events devastate a family as much as a suicide. All the grief feelings are intensified. The bereaved struggle to understand the loss and may question again and again what they could have done to prevent it.

The need to validate feelings and provide ventilation opportunities takes on crucial importance in working with surviving family members. During this process the caregiver must be alert to even subtle family dynamics, noting particularly if marked blaming or extreme hostility begins to appear early in the bereavement process. This can necessitate aggressive crisis intervention before the family leaves the hospital. The goal of such intervention should be to restore or improve cohesive family responses to the loss, while endeavoring to ensure family integrity until more long-term counseling is begun.

In working with the bereaved, it is important to understand the dynamics that commonly lead someone to suicide. For our purposes, these motivations will be discussed in simplistic terms only, leaving more in-depth dialogue to books devoted solely to the subject.

There are usually four major precipitants: lost goals or dreams, performance fear, isolation perception, and, on occasion, retaliation. These factors may be present in any combination and with varying degrees of intensity. Each situation brings its own unique set of feelings for a family to process. Invariably, the feelings are painful and deep.

Lost Goals/Dreams. By far, the most common precipitants of suicide are lost "dreams" or goals. A divorce, dismissal from high-profile or strategic employment, failing health, or profound injury or illness may lead to the desire to end one's life. In concert with such significant loss is usually a feeling that no one else cares, knows, or is genuinely interested in the person and his/her feelings. Consequently, the individual perceives a loss or absence of external support—perhaps, even, a lack of deserving such support—and thus carries out the death act.

Performance Fear. Another common precursor is a fear of life and its challenges. The individual feels overwhelmed and unable to deal with life's stressors. A variation of this theme occurs when the individual feels he or she has "failed to measure up" to some external or internal performance standard. Examples may include failure to be admitted into a prestigious school, failure in professional studies, or perhaps the disclosure of some moral or character flaw. Such events may trigger a profound sense of performance failure that leads the individual to inflict self-harm. Usually, of course, other life issues exacerbate the situation, catalyzing the need for escape.

In such situations, families will need the opportunity to share their feelings about this aspect of the death and will need to feel that someone has heard and understood their efforts, or inability, to alleviate the deceased's problems or fears. Invariably, family members will feel severe guilt about not having done more to support the deceased or to resolve the precipitating stressors. Do not negate their feelings. Validate those that are real and work through those that are not. Support them in their grief and allow them to express their very real sorrow at the loss.

Isolation Perception. Features of isolation perception are usually evident in, but not necessarily a primary motivator of, every suicide. They are characterized by a preoccupation with oneself and with one's own fears, needs, and desires. Such feelings of isolation may be transient, but if powerful enough they may cause an individual to view his or her world so narrowly as to be unaware of other valued opportunities or other valued roles in the family and society. The person may then ignore or underestimate the loss and pain his or her death would cause others.

Such scenarios are not uncommon with impulsive and highly emotional adolescents. Often, they are unable to fully comprehend the implications of their actions. Helping the family understand this shortsightedness, for example, can give them great comfort if it is sensitively discussed.

Retaliation. On rare occasions, a suicide act may have been precipitated as a form of retaliation for some perceived wrong that may or may not have existed. Again, this is most common in highly impulsive adolescents. An example I recall is a 14-year-old girl who shot herself in the head while talking to her father on the telephone. He was at work when she called and had refused to let her go out that evening with her boyfriend. While other troubles had existed in the home, the primary motive appeared to be that of an angry child who did not understand the irreversibility of her actions. Of course, such an act always arouses suspicions of deeper problems, but they are not always present.

When this factor is involved, it is not uncommon for family members to speculate that the suicide act was motivated by the deceased's desire to "get back at someone." Great care needs to be used by the helper to not validate or refute these expressions too hastily. Do, however, allow the family members their full expression, if that does not cause open hostility or pain to those present. Discuss with them the possibility of retaliation and be open to the expressions shared. Gradually turn the discussion to more productive avenues of grief work.

Because the motivation for the suicide act may be veiled, it is important for the care-giver to carefully observe all family dynamics that may lead to an understanding of *the family's* perception of the meaning of the death. The helper must obtain a reasonably clear understanding of the relationships involved before any real intervention can take place.

Also, care-givers must recognize and mitigate the social pressures on families following such a loss. In his research, Thornton (1989) noted that social perceptions and reactions to families experiencing a loss by suicide can be very negative. There is a tendency to see the family as flawed in some way and bearing blame for the event. While this is less intense at the death of a young child, it increases with the deceased's age and is more particularly directed toward female family members.

Thornton further suggests that it is important for the care-giver to understand both the increased burden the family bears and the reduced support system that then remains. To mitigate this, assist the family to identify friends, relatives, and immediate family members who continue to be supportive. Introduce them to new avenues of support such as self-help programs, community support groups, and counseling services.

Substance Abuse

This loss usually involves a history of legal/illegal drug abuse patterns. Many times, families are unaware of the abuse, or at least the extent of it, so the manner of death may come as a great shock. As a result, notification of the cause of the death should be carefully staged to minimize further complications or distractions in dealing with acceptance of the death.

A suggested pattern of notification of the death (see the description of the Sequential Notification Technique in Chapter 3) would be to first identify to the family the clinical physiological cause of the death (e.g., cardiopulmonary failure), and later provide the extenuating details as family coping patterns indicate readiness.

Great care should be exercised in the release of *any* information relating to substance or alcohol abuse. Conditions of confidentiality may entirely preclude this. When some of the information has been publicly released (e.g., the deceased had been arrested, and a law officer stated that he or she was "found in possession of . . ."), it may be possible for the situation to be more frankly discussed. Consult your facility's protocol.

Murder

This loss brings with it a unique need for retribution or retaliation. It is nearly always viewed as a terrible and premature loss, complicated by the fact that most murders involve relatively young people. The counselor must exercise extreme caution to ensure that the family's grief is channeled in constructive expression. Be sure to convey that it is possible—and important—to acknowledge angry feelings without resorting to additional violent behavior.

Drunken Driving

This is seen by family members as a useless death, indeed another form of murder. This feeling needs to be validated and yet guided so as to not provoke the family to aggressive behavior. It is not uncommon for the drunk driver to be brought to the same facility for treatment; therefore care must be exercised to keep the perpetrator and the family separated during visits, preferably unaware of each other's presence.

It should be noted that the driver's family also is often devastated by the death of another. Again, exercise care that the driver's family remains distant from the victim's, as the victim's family is usually unwilling to accept an apology, however sincerely extended, at such a difficult time. In unusual situations, the transfer of messages of condolence through the social worker may be appropriate but must be conveyed with extreme discretion.

Conclusion

Age, relationship to the deceased, cultural factors, and the way a death occurred all contribute to the ways in which families cope with a death and will influence the time they need to resolve their loss. By being aware of this, you can give timely, well-tailored direction that will anticipate potential problems that might arise long after your contact with the family is over.

Chapter 10

Family Assessment and Crisis Intervention

In working with family members, the counselor needs to constantly evaluate them to ensure appropriate grieving patterns. A few areas of concern should receive special emphasis.

Physical Assessment

Use care in assessing the physical status of grieving family members. Those who are in precarious health may find themselves in acute distress when given tragic news. If such problems surface, always ensure that any presenting symptoms are noted and examined by a medical professional. Common problems include high blood pressure and cardiac conditions. If *any* symptoms become manifest, or any family member notes such conditions and asks that an examination be performed, *always* be prepared to take action on behalf of the person in question.

To further ensure the physical health of those present at the hospital, help them make appropriate plans for departure. Do not overlook details such as where family members will spend the night. No one should be required to be alone. You may want to suggest a place other than the primary residence of the deceased. This may give them needed "permission" to choose a location where they will not have to deal with too many intense memories right away.

Note who will be driving and assess the person's condition to navigate the highways safely. Suggest another driver, if necessary. If you do not do so, no one else may be willing to mention the problem, and an individual may default to a responsibility he or she should not assume.

It may be helpful to discuss with family members how best to notify others of the death. Help them to understand how to prepare others properly for the notification. Too often, family members simply blurt the news out, catching others unprepared and causing them undue distress. You might even offer to make certain difficult calls for them, if phone notification is necessary or appropriate.

Emotional Assessment

Although it may seem incongruent, generally speaking, those who grieve the most demonstratively at the outset usually exhibit the most fundamentally sound initial outcome. After their emotive outburst, my experience has been that they are usually in much greater control of themselves and better able to support others in need.

A person who is initially reserved or withdrawn is likely to have difficulty integrating the reality of the loss and therefore will need greater emotional support. This restrained response is more common with men than with women. Culturally, men are expected to be more emotionally resilient and thus able to deal with losses with less difficulty. The "strong, silent male" façade may mask an inability to cope.

Also, as mentioned previously, anger is a common defensive response. When confronted with an irretrievable loss, many feel the need to lash out at others to compensate for the emotional pain they feel. It appears that the more fragmented the family lifestyle, the greater the likelihood of this behavior. Anger, or other marginal coping responses, can often provide your first clue that significant personal and family matters remain unattended and unresolved. Always note such irregular behavior in your assessment and carefully seek its root cause. By so doing, you may successfully improve or resolve issues that might otherwise inhibit normal grieving and closure.

Support Systems Assessment

It is important to ensure that there are appropriate support systems in place before the family leaves the hospital. This means that other relatives have been notified or have been identified for notification upon return home, that no individual who arrives at the hospital alone leaves alone, and that resources and lodging are available.

In situations of violent death in the home, such as suicide or homicide with a firearm, it can be extremely helpful to identify someone less intimately involved who will accept responsibility to clean and reorder the home before the immediate family returns. This can be a difficult task, but one for which the family is likely to be grateful. Be sure to verify, however, that such a gesture is not perceived as an intrusion.

In short, the social worker should endeavor to ensure that all areas of support are identified and are intact, or will be shortly.

Mental Status Examinations

If a person begins to present behaviors that lead to *grave* concern regarding his or her mental balance, a *Mental Status Examination* should be performed. Such behaviors include marked regressive child-like actions or expressions, excessive threats of violence, and suicidal ideation.

Be aware that in circumstances of crisis some degree of apparent pathology may be evident. The bereft are _not_ undergoing a normal experience and cannot be expected to experience fully rational thought patterns. However, statements or behaviors that indicate a serious loss of contact with reality, or that indicate dangerous behavior, must be addressed.

Use caution not to antagonize or challenge the person directly, but rather continue to be supportive and caring while recording details of the following (Yau, 1987):

Appearance/Behavior/Body Kinetics: Note the general appearance of the client, including hygiene (clean, neat, disheveled, dirty, odoriferous); body appearance (well-nourished, under/over weight, appearing of stated age, bruised or scarred), and whether the client is agitated, aggressive, anxious, or fearful.

Orientation Status: Note clients' orientation to _persons_ (who they are), _place_ (where they are), and _time_ (day of week, morning/evening, month, etc.). If answers seem in any way vague, ask for state, city, county, current season of the year, or other information to clarify their orientation. If all spheres are clear, a person is usually described as "oriented X 3;" or "X 4," if orientation to "situation" is included.

Thought Processes: Look for evidence of thought disorders or psychotic symptoms such as delusions, hallucinations, or marked ambivalence. Note if thoughts are tangential, referential, illogical, scattered, concrete, abstract, blocked, "flight of ideas," paranoid, grandiose, phobic, obsessional, or depersonalized; also look for signs of thought insertion, thought broadcasting, ideas of reference (thought projection), belief in personal "special powers" such as mind control of others.

Mood: Note if the mood is depressed, manic, hostile, angry, fearful, or cooperative. Especially note if the mood is appropriate to the thought content expressed.

Affect: Note if the client's affect is tearful, worried, blunted, flattened, elated, hysterical, labile. Also note if the affect is controlled, consistent, and appropriate to the content of the discussion. Certain deviations from the norm may be present in crisis.

Memory: Note if the individual's memory is intact. Some loss of short-term memory is common in deep grief; differentiate between long- and short-term memory. Note such things as attention, concentration, and the fund of general information available.

Hallucinations: Note whether hallucinations are absent or present. If present, are they auditory, visual, tactile, olfactory, or gustatory?

Vegetative Signs: Note if the person acknowledges any preexisting vegetative signs such as increased or decreased appetite, poor sleep patterns, decreased sexual activity (use discretion), and/or markedly reduced pleasure from previously pleasurable activities.

Speech Patterns: Note speech patterns that are unclear, slurred, mumbled, or even mute. Lack of cogent articulation or illogical sequences should be noted. Also note if the tone is normal, soft, loud, subject to wide swings, pressured, or halting. Note any lisp or other impediment, and expressions in another language.

Insight/Judgment: Note the client's own statements describing the problems and his or her ideas about how to overcome them. Note the degree of impulsiveness or rationality.

Ideation (Homicidal/Suicidal): Ask, "Are you thinking of hurting yourself? Someone else?"

Previous Psychiatric History: Include any counseling received, past psychiatric hospitalizations and/or medications, past attempts at suicide, name and telephone number of any current clinician.

Family Psychiatric History: As above, for other immediate family members.

Medications: Include any medications currently being taken, dosages, and the prescribing physician. Especially note any psychiatric medications, with name and dosage.

Brief Health History: Focus on health problems that could impair mental functioning, e.g., history of head trauma, brain tumors, stroke, or seizures.

Drug/Alcohol Abuse: Note drugs of choice, frequency, any history of rehabilitation treatment, and any family history of substance abuse.

Other: Note any history of physical or sexual abuse, and your assessment of any potential for violence (present, suspected, absent).

Psychosocial History: Include birth order, number of siblings, highest level of education, employment history, marital status and children, parents (including their current marital status), family death history (especially recent losses).

Cognition: Finally, test the client's cognitive capacity, if necessary. Include concepts such as similarities, proverbs, and hypothetical problems, e.g., "What would you do if you smelled smoke in a building?"; the person's capacity for numerical calculations (addition and subtraction by serial threes, fives and sevens); the ability to spell "world" forward and backward; administer a formal written and scored Mini-Mental Status Exam (i.e., Folstein or equivalent), if serious questions remain.

The information described above is required for a complete mental status exam. In practice, however, not all areas may be required to rule out pathology. It is important to describe all areas of examination with the actual _behavioral and verbal_ responses noted. By so doing, the problems can be more easily recognized should a follow-up examination be required. If a person appears to exhibit a markedly maladaptive response or frank psychosis, or if there is genuine concern about the safety of the client or others, it may be necessary to consider psychiatric hospitalization.

Although this should be a carefully weighed decision, under no circumstances should follow-up be neglected, especially when suicidal or homicidal ideation is present. I might note, however, that in the years that I have been involved with grief counseling, I have never had to hospitalize a family member psychiatrically at the time of initial notification.

Counseling Techniques for Crisis Intervention

To understand the need for crisis intervention, it may be helpful to consider the atmosphere in which you work and the reactions it might engender in those unfamiliar with it. For example, I work in a hospital setting.

Not many years ago, most deaths occurred at home. Accidents and illnesses were commonplace, and the family was readily involved in dealing with death. If medical help was available, the physician called was often a local practitioner, a family friend, someone with whom the family had long been familiar.

In our modern social system, medical care has become institutionalized and specialized. Often, patients are treated in a building they have rarely entered before, by physicians they have never met. The historical roots of hospitals provide little comfort—the earliest hospitals were usually places where people went to die; they were places to quarantine those unfortunates who had contracted diseases for which there were as yet no cures. Even as late as the 1950s, hospitals loomed large and foreboding, with enormous tuberculosis wards.

The advent of antibiotics, improved anesthetics, and advanced surgical techniques has given formalized medicine the opportunity to shed its past images. Ironically, because of these same rapid advances, many of the fearful images persist. Unknown physicians and technicians perform complex and unfamiliar tasks, rendering ambiguous results couched in technical jargon that permits little understanding by the patient. As a result, while modern medicine is able to work miracles by past standards, as a by-product it has effectively removed medical care, and most particularly death itself, from the home. Today, when trauma or death occurs, families are taken from familiar surroundings and thrust into a previously unknown world to witness confusing events.

As a result, the grieving process has also become more complex and difficult. With little experiential foundation, families face the huge challenge of coping with death in what may be perceived as an impersonal environment.

In recent years, much research has been done to explore the relationships between the stress of major life changes and subsequent morbidity and mortality. Indeed, a new and intriguing field of study—psychoneuroimmunology—is devoted to the relationships between psychological states and the status of the central nervous and immunological systems. The results of such research demonstrate that psychological stress does affect the physical body, placing it in a compromised position, thus less able to carry out its functions.

The death of a loved one qualifies as a significant loss leading to great mental and emotional stress. Compared to the general population, bereaved persons have more visits to physicians, greater rates of hospitalization, and more frequent surgeries. They are more susceptible to depressive illnesses, anxiety states, personality disorders, rheumatic and arthritic conditions, disturbances of various autonomic functions, and ulcerative colitis. Further research indicates that bereaved persons also suffer a higher mortality rate from coronary thrombosis and arteriosclerotic heart disease.[41]

In the light of such research, it becomes obvious that skilled and effective crisis intervention and grief therapy at the time of a loss can yield great benefits. Many individuals experience difficulty in resolving the emotional pain and adjusting to the changes associated with the loss of a loved one. Family functioning can be jeopardized, and those who might otherwise be able to resume productive lives may find themselves hospitalized in a health system that is already struggling to deal with the increasing demands being placed upon it.

A substantial proportion—estimates run as high as 80 to 85 percent—of all hospital beds are filled, directly or indirectly, by psychosocially induced disorders. These are, in effect, preventable hospitalizations. The root causes cannot always be identified, but they include such factors as alcoholism, drug abuse, unwanted pregnancies, preventable sexually transmitted diseases, domestic and urban violence, stress-inducing life patterns, and the like.

Certainly, we must make every effort to avoid adding to this load the medical complications associated with a protracted grief process. The

---

[41] Weinberg, 1985.

direction and assistance that many people need to reconcile themselves to a significant loss can often be met through _crisis intervention_.

The Crisis Intervention Model

The standard crisis intervention model fits well with the limited time a care-giver will have at the hospital with the family of a deceased person. There is normally very little time for history-taking, assessment, and discussion. The care-giver must quickly assess the presenting variables and take appropriate and _timely_ action.

Quentmeyer (1983), notes that the crisis intervention model differs from the psychotherapeutic model in the following ways:

1. Crisis intervention is time-limited, often with only one to six sessions, while psychotherapy is usually long term and may continue for years.
2. Crisis intervention focuses on resolution of a specific problem. Psychotherapy focuses on the cure of an illness or personality dysfunction.
3. Crisis intervention, in general, focuses on the _inter_personal. Psychotherapy focuses on the _intra_personal.
4. Crisis theory is derived from a model of life, while traditional Freudian psychology is derived from a model of illness.[42]

To understand and utilize this treatment model, one must understand that a true crisis is a situation in which the person's usual coping mechanisms fail to function properly.

Zastrow (1985) notes that the crisis intervention model is based on a belief that, in a crisis, current levels of functioning are disrupted so that, in addition to the crisis situation at hand, internal psychological difficulties that are usually manageable or suppressed become evident, needing attention. Even so, people are viewed as being basically normal in their life adjustment, with the crisis being the major cause of a person's emotional difficulties.

Golan (1979) suggests that a minimal effort at such times can produce a tremendous positive effect, as the individual is in a situation to effect changes in his or her life. Consequently, a small amount of help, appropriately focused, can prove more effective than extensive efforts during a period of less emotional accessibility.

Whittaker (1974) provides a summary of crisis counseling services and describes how crisis intervention generally progresses in the following manner:

1. An attempt is made to alleviate the disabling tension through emotional ventilation and the creation of a climate of trust and hope.

---

[42] Reprinted with author's permission.

2. Next the worker attempts to understand the dynamics of the event that precipitated the crisis.
3. The worker gives his or her impressions and understanding of the crisis and checks out these perceptions with the client.
4. The client and worker attempt to determine specific remedial measures that can be taken to restore equilibrium.
5. New methods of coping may be introduced.
6. Finally, termination occurs—often after a predetermined number of interviews—when the agreed-upon goals have been realized.

In the medical setting, such a model serves both the family and the practitioner well. For example, crisis intervention assumes normalcy of the individual and family. Many of the families encountered do, indeed, cope well and simply need a facilitator and liaison with medical staff. Even in cases of complicated grief, often all that is needed is for someone to facilitate the grieving process, assisting people in catching their emotional balance.

To illustrate the practical application of these concepts, it may be helpful to present a case with details of the crisis intervention process. The following case occurred in the emergency room in 1987.

Case Vignette 10.1

A call came to provide crisis management for a young mother whose child had just died. Upon arrival at the hospital, I noted that the staff was feeling some frustration due to their inability to resolve the situation.

The mother was a 20-year-old, unmarried, Caucasian female with twins approximately four weeks old. Both were boys, identical in appearance. The father was a Caucasian male. He was not present at the hospital and had not been in contact with the mother since shortly after she became pregnant. At this time, the children and their mother lived with the grandmother, who had accompanied them to the hospital.

I was told that the mother awakened that morning to feed the children and discovered that one twin was still warm but not breathing. The grandmother called 911, and an ambulance was dispatched to their home. Medics began cardiopulmonary resuscitation at the scene and continued until the child was pronounced dead in the trauma center emergency room. The mother and grandmother had accompanied the ambulance to the hospital and waited in the clinical social work office for news of the resuscitative efforts. It was there that a physician notified them of the death. The mother was invited into the trauma room to see her child. Upon her arrival in the treatment room, the mother gave the living twin to the grandmother and took up the dead child, clutching it tightly in her arms.

The mother then began a complicated grieving process. She began to insist that the baby was yet alive and asked for a bottle to feed it. She also complained to nursing staff that the child was being poorly cared for, as it was much too cold. The staff and grandmother gently tried again and again to explain that the child was dead, but the mother seemed impervious to all efforts. She sat staring blankly ahead, firmly holding the baby, insisting that it was alive. Staff decided that perhaps time would help and elected to allow the mother to remain with the child until the coroner arrived. Some two hours passed.

When the coroner arrived, the mother flatly refused to release the child, maintaining that it was still living and again requested a bottle so that she could feed the child.

The hospital chaplain was called and was successful in persuading the mother to release the dead infant, but together with the medical staff concluded that, given mother's complete denial of the death, it would be unwise to remove the body from the hospital until she had come to some point of resolution. At this time, staff contacted Social Services, and I was summoned.

After obtaining the above information from the nursing staff, I gathered a presenting impression. I viewed the dead twin's body in the trauma room; he was cool to the touch and somewhat stiff. No signs of abuse were noted, and the child appeared to have been well-nourished.

I found the mother in the emergency clinical social work office with the grandmother and the remaining twin. The mother was dressed neatly and cleanly in casual clothing. Her face wore a rather detached expression, with reddened puffy eyes. She would occasionally talk softly with the surviving child, assuring him that they would "all" be going home soon, and that, "Your brother is just fine."

The grandmother was also neatly dressed and was very alert to the situation. She appeared extremely concerned and uncertain how to proceed. The nursing staff joined us and again recounted to the mother the medical events surrounding the death of the infant. At this point, the grandmother addressed the mother and asked, "Wouldn't you like to go home now, dear?" While the mother had appeared oblivious to all other comments made, she firmly responded to the grandmother that she would not leave without the other child.

Staging the Intervention

At this point, I requested that all but the mother (who held the surviving twin) leave the room. In privacy, I was able to gently interview this young woman on a more intimate level. I found that if I maintained direct eye contact, the mother could follow and respond to a limited discussion. To facilitate this process, it was necessary that close physical proximity be established. This is a common need when acute emotional withdrawal is evident, as an individual's range of perceptive accommodation becomes greatly reduced.

Next, I summoned the grandmother. She arrived together with one of the nurses who had been integrally involved in the entire episode. I asked the nurse to bring the dead child to the office. I then asked the grandmother to sit next to the mother, and the expired child was placed in the grandmother's arms.

Then I requested that the mother and grandmother exchange children. The mother readily complied. Taking the dead child in her arms, she again complained that we had not kept the child warm and further requested a bottle, saying that the baby would surely be hungry. To the surprise of the staff but to fully engage this mother, I elected to comply with this request.

A bottle was obtained, and again everyone was excused from the room. Seated directly in front of the mother, I discussed what a beautiful baby she had. The mother was given the bottle and encouraged to feed the baby. Placing the nipple in the child's mouth she commented, with some surprise, that the child did not appear to be hungry.

The Intervention Process

It was at this point that the actual intervention began. Using regular reminders to maintain eye contact, I gently discussed the process of death. In response to careful questioning, the mother was able to identify all of the major life signs that must be present in a living being such as movement, breathing, warmth, suppleness, heartbeat, and hunger. Then I asked the mother, if death had occurred, which if any of these signs of life would be missing. Hesitatingly at first, the mother reviewed each of the points that had been discussed and agreed that each would be absent. Finally, I reviewed each point again and asked the mother to identify its presence or absence in her child.

After completing the review of each point, the mother began to cry. She never verbally acknowledged the death but she consistently responded emotionally to the realization of the facts. After each realization, I asked the mother to identify whether the baby was alive or dead. Again and again, there was no verbal response, only tears. These consistent tearful responses characterized the mother's gradual acceptance of her child's death.

After sufficient time had elapsed, I called the grandmother and the nurse back to the room. The mother eagerly took the living child in exchange for the dead child and nodded her approval to the grandmother's request that they leave the hospital.

In this situation, the initial crisis intervention was highly successful. However, follow-up counseling with more extensive grief therapy was also recommended, and referral information was given. Until the mother could discuss the death and share her feelings about it, complete grief work could not take place.

Crisis intervention may not always constitute the end-point of a difficult situation, but it *does* play a vital role in the process.

Follow-up Needs Assessment

Those who work with newly bereft families—physicians, nurses, social workers, trauma counselors, and chaplains—stand at a unique vantage point to evaluate the current and anticipated coping skills of survivors. For those who are coping poorly, or are expected to cope poorly in the future, early referral and intervention can be crucial.

Numerous studies indicate that bereavement is closely linked with a surprisingly large number of morbidity factors and has led to increased mortality as well. Hardt (1979) cites a number of studies indicating that depression (a common disorder following a loss) is ". . . suspect to being the cause of a great many ills, including obesity, rheumatoid arthritis, heart failure, even cancer." Further, he cites "an extensive study" completed in 1972 that demonstrated an increased susceptibility to illness in situations with frequent life changes. "Of 43 life-situation changes that led to illness or disease, the most serious were death of a spouse, death of a close family member, and death of a close friend, respectively." [43]

Worden notes, "There are a number of studies in the literature which point to the impact of grief on morbidity and mortality. Grief exacerbates not only physical morbidity but psychiatric morbidity as well; this is especially true of conjugal bereavement, the loss of a spouse." [44]

Eustress Vs. Distress

The rationale for this predisposition for morbidity lies in the intensity of stress precipitated by an irreconcilable loss. Mild-to-moderate levels of stress are common in all lifestyles. Such stress has been demonstrated to improve performance and even personal satisfaction. However, when stress levels become extreme (as occurs with profound grief), overload of the emotional and physical systems can occur. Consider the following graph.

The Stress Response[45]

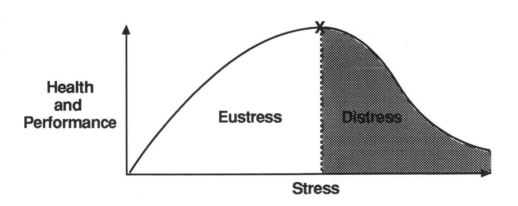

---

[43] Hardt, 1979.

[44] Worden, 1982.

[45] Girdano, D.A. & Everly, G.S., _Controlling Stress and Tension: a holistic approach_, 1986. Englewood Cliffs, NJ: Prentice-Hall.

As can be seen, when stress is increased beyond individual tolerance, both performance and health begin to deteriorate. Persons experiencing extreme stress, therefore, will need additional support and assistance to mitigate the extreme nature of the change (loss) that has taken place.

Preventive Intervention

With this in mind, those involved in grief management should consider the value of adopting a preventive model of intervention. To do so requires identifying variables that put the bereft at high risk and referring those individuals for professional assistance. "If we can predict in advance who is likely to have difficulty a year or two following the loss, then we can do something by way of early intervention to preclude an unresolved grief reaction." [46]

Numerous studies and models of predictive quality were also put forth by Worden.[47] Synthesized and adapted, here is a composite of these studies:

High-risk Bereavement
Follow-up Indicators Checklist

Mode of the death:
- Suicide*
- Homicide*
- Traumatic accident
- Sudden illness (less than 14 days anticipation)
- With survivor culpability (e.g., driver)*

Relationship to the deceased:
- Loss of spouse
- Loss of child
- Loss of nuclear family member or very close friend

Historical Factors:
- History of recent family deaths
- Ambivalent feelings toward the deceased
- Current history of drug/alcohol abuse

Social Support System:
- Poor social support system (as perceived by the survivors)
- Cultural/familial background that inhibits expression of feelings
- Perceived non-support by social network

---

[46] Worden, 1982.

[47] Studies included the following: Parkes, C.M. *Bereavement: Studies of grief in adult life.* New York: International Universities Press. 1972; Raphael, B., "Preventive intervention with the recently bereaved," *Archives of General Psychiatry*, 1977, vol. 34, pp. 1450-1454; Sheldon, A.R., et al. "A psychosocial analysis of risk impairment following bereavement," *Journal of Nervous and Mental Disease*, 1981, vol. 169, pp. 253-255; Parkes, C.M. "Determinants of outcome following bereavement," *Omega*, 1975, vol. 6, pp. 303-323.

Socio-demographic Factors:
- Younger in age   _____
- Loss of spouse, with minor children still at home   _____
- Other losses, when children are under age of majority (18)   _____
- Lower socioeconomic status   _____

Personality Factors:
- Timidity   _____
- Overly dependent (on others, or the deceased)   _____
- Presence of a personality disorder (DSM III-R)   _____

Emotional Factors:
- History of depression   _____
- The presence of a concurrent life crisis   _____
- Prior psychiatric illness/hospitalization   _____

Response to the Loss:
- Anger—high   _____
- Suicidal/Homicidal ideation*   _____
- Self-reproach—high   _____

* Indicates persons for whom follow-up should be mandatory.

Should numerous loss factors on the check-list be involved (perhaps five to ten factors, excluding those where follow-up is considered to be mandatory), further contact should be considered. A follow-up letter to applicable persons could indicate your interest and desire to remain available and supportive, inviting a return call.

Opportune times for contact seem to be at one, three, six, and twelve months after the loss. You could include a small pamphlet indicating common challenges to grief and other writings on bereavement each time. In this way, you may provide the encouragement, information, and further referrals that high-risk families may need.

Chapter 11

Grief Management Strategies

Primary Goals

The primary task of any professional interaction with the bereft is to facilitate mourning and its resolution. To understand the thrust of the work to be performed, it is helpful to possess a concept of the grief resolution process, and the stages that the family must negotiate. Various models were noted in Chapter 6. Another very useful conceptual model has been put forth by J. William Worden, Ph.D., assistant professor of psychology at Harvard Medical School. He has postulated the following *Four Tasks of Mourning*:

Task I: To accept the reality of the loss.
Task II: To experience the pain of grief.
Task III: To adjust to an environment in which the
           deceased is missing.
Task IV: To withdraw emotional energy and
           reinvest it in another relationship.[48]

Worden further writes:

It is essential that the grieving person accomplish these tasks before mourning can be completed. Incomplete grief tasks can impair further growth and development. Although the tasks do not necessarily follow a specific order, there is some ordering suggested in the definitions. For example, you cannot handle the emotional impact of a loss until you first come to terms with the fact that the loss has happened.

Since mourning is a process and not a state, the following tasks require effort, and, following Freud's example, we often speak of a person as doing "grief work." Using Engel's analogy to healing, it is possible for someone to accomplish some of these tasks and not others, and hence have an incomplete bereavement, just as one might have incomplete healing from a wound.[49]

---

[48] All Worden quotes used by permission of Springer Publishing, Inc., New York 10012.

[49] Ibid. Worden, 1982, p. 10.

Only the first two tasks can be dealt with during the initial notification and follow-up process. Thus, the primary goals are to actualize the loss (or overcome denial), and to help those involved begin to experience the pain of their grief. Even so, I have found that keeping all the long-term outcomes desired in mind while working with surviving family members is valuable in shaping the content of our conversations, especially regarding suggestions for their near-future activities.

Supporting the Bereaved

In order to feel competent and secure—feelings you must transmit to those involved with the loss—you must feel sure that you know how to provide appropriate verbal and emotional support. In a study conducted with 366 college students who experienced losses, Weinberg (1985) noted five activities that the students indicated would have been beneficial for them. These activities were ranked in order of importance as follows:

1. verbal sharing
2. providing reassurance
3. giving quiet support
4. engaging in goal setting and referral activities
5. encouraging avoidance (of grief) strategies

The two *least* effective methods of assistance were referral activities and encouragement to avoid the grief experience. Weinberg notes that it was psychological rather than concrete services that the respondents valued most, and that an even smaller percentage of the sample responded favorably to the idea of encouraging people to avoid their loss by "not thinking about it, or by taking medication." In fact, the use of medication was given the lowest value score of any of the items.

Studies of memory and perception have consistently demonstrated that experiences in altered states are difficult to recall. Therefore, with rare exception, the professional who prescribes *extended* medication in an effort to help with coping will actually prolong the pain that must, at some point, be integrated to allow for resolution of the loss. However, for a member of the family whose suffering is particularly acute, a mild sedative may be appropriate to provide a night or two of rest.

In Weinberg's study, noted above, the most meaningful assistance provided by the helper consisted of "verbal sharing" and "reassurance." How can you provide this assistance? Following are suggestions and strategies that may be useful.

Allow Natural Expression

Weinberg (1985) noted that emotional outbursts, although difficult for hospital staff to handle, are part of the natural grieving process. This is especially true immediately after the notification statement has been delivered. As the respondents in her research reported, it was much more valuable for them to express their feelings than to be constrained. To encourage the grieving process, hospital staff must recognize and sanction the need for the expression of a wide range of feelings. It may also be necessary to divert the efforts of a well-meaning family member or friend from hindering these expressions.

Guilt is a natural part of grief. Most people will express such feelings at one time or another. Everyone has "unfinished business" at the time of a loss and must be able to express it. Don't be overly concerned about anxiety over little things, or even more serious feelings of guilt. Simply validate the survivors' feelings and reassure them of their appropriateness.

Therapeutic Viewing of the Body
To facilitate verbal sharing, it is important for the family to view the body. Dr. Elisabeth Kübler-Ross emphasizes this. If the body is not viewed, it may take years longer for the grief to heal, because it is difficult to realize, emotionally, that the person is really dead (Schultz, 1980). In nearly all instances, this is the only way for the family to truly begin the necessary grief process.

Many times, family members will appear to have properly integrated the verbal information given, but it is usually still necessary to see the deceased to fully and firmly ground the knowledge. This is evidenced by the tremendous resurgence of emotions that occurs at the time of the viewing experience.

Verbal Support for the Bereaved

It is difficult to know what to say at a time of a death. The family is usually stunned and silent. Staff members feel uncomfortable, too, not knowing what to say. Dr. Saul Levin, a psychiatrist and grief specialist at the University of California, Davis, Medical Center, encourages the following:

> Break down the walls of silence that surround death. Most of us have a conspiracy of silence about death. We don't know what to say, so we avoid talking about the subject when it happens. . . .
> In fact, a grieving person needs to talk and acknowledge what has happened. The worst thing to say is, "It was meant to be," or "Things could be worse." Usually, the best thing is a simple, "I'm sorry and I'm here to help." Then offer a listening ear for as long as it's needed.[50]

Let me reemphasize: _Your greatest help is to listen_. Even so, I should add that silence is acceptable and needed at times. This is especially true shortly after the death has occurred. It takes time for family members to

---

[50] Levin, S. _UCDMC Staff Newsletter_. Used with permission.

gather their thoughts and to allow themselves to truly experience and *feel* the loss. It may be that they won't want to talk about it until later. Allow for this. Encourage those present to talk when they feel ready and be available to them at that time.

The meaningful silence of allowing the experience to sink in should be distinguished from the uncomfortable silence of not knowing what to say. When it is time to "break down the walls of silence," what do you say?

What Not to Say

Before discussing potential topics to discuss with families in grief, perhaps it would be useful to understand what does *not* help. In working with the bereft, feelings are so tender and exposed that even well-intentioned statements can hamper the grief process.

Two researchers, Davidowitz and Myrick (1984), in an analysis of helping statements for the bereaved, wrote the following:

> The period of bereavement can be filled with sadness, depression, helplessness and desperation. It can also be a time of confusion, guilt, anger, and alienation. When bereaved persons reach out for support and understanding, they need to be received by caring individuals who are sensitive to the depth and complexities of their feelings. Unfortunately, they are often forced to retreat to their world of pain because too many people, through hasty and ineffective statements, attempt to *quickly assuage their grief.*[51]

Richard M. Leliaert (1989), a pastoral counselor concerned about using religious beliefs inappropriately to facilitate healthy grieving, wrote the following:

> Well-intentioned care-givers—family, friends, sometimes bereavement counselors—often shortcut the normal processes of bereavement, especially by statements that are meant to console but actually increase the pain of the bereaved.
> This can be especially true of well-intentioned care-givers with religious convictions. In their desire to console the bereaved, religious persons might make statements like, "Thanks be to God, your husband is with the Lord," or "Jesus' resurrection has robbed death of its sting." Unspoken is the implication that to grieve shows a lack of faith. Spiritual and/or religious beliefs can indeed be consoling, but they can be abused and misused as well.[52]

In his work, Leliaert proceeds to present an excellent treatise on how to *better* present religious concepts to console those who have lost a loved one, allowing them to move from "grief work, to growth work."

---

[51] Reproduced with permission. All rights reserved.

[52] Ibid.

The writing—while primarily for the Judeo-Christian beliefs—is adaptable and appropriate to other beliefs as well.

Erin Linn (1986) has also written a guide on avoiding clichés in comforting the bereaved, citing such statements as, "It was God's will" and, "I know just how you feel." The goal is to help care-givers avoid proscribing someone's natural grief process, forcing them into a "typical" or expected mold. When that happens, people can hide their real feelings, lash out in anger, and in other ways postpone or circumvent their own natural resolution process.

Potential Dialogue Topics

When family members are ready to talk, many topics will surface spontaneously. Some of these are discussed on the following pages. There are also additional concepts you may wish to bring up, to assist with grief resolution. These could be introduced as the need arises.

In general, the concepts suggested below should be introduced only during extended conversation. They are usually appropriate only for use with families without great pathology in evidence. None of the dialogues should be pursued in lieu of, or as a barrier to, other appropriate emotional ventilation efforts. Rather, they should be introduced only to meet the expressed needs of the family members present, to aid in gradual acknowledgement and reconciliation of the death. Sharing memories and feelings is very appropriate at a time of loss, but this is no time for intensive therapy.

You will note that the dialogue topics herein presented do not provide answers to family issues, but rather a forum for verbalizing emotions. The significance of a loss is highly personal and differs with each circumstance. The goal is to facilitate a process in reconciling the death.

Life Telling. Families may fall silent and not know what to say, even when their hearts are crying for expression. The first step in any experience of sharing is for someone to show an interest. Do not broach the topic unless you are willing to invest sufficient time and emotional energy to it—a superficial conversation will not be helpful. If you are willing to provide such time, you may start by saying, "Tell me about (your husband, or son, or daughter, as the case may be)." If the person needs more prompting, you might ask, "Well, how long were you married?" or, "Where was he born?" Other questions might include, "How many children do you have?" or, "Where have you lived?" The idea is to open up the opportunity to talk. Some will talk easily. Others will start slowly and gradually become ready to express themselves.

Regardless of how you start the conversation, this opportunity for sharing will be of immense value to the survivors and will provide opportunities to support them further. Do not be concerned if such discussion leads to tears and painful memories. This is valuable and meaningful, and can be continued to the extent the family members are prepared for it. In this context, you can assess and meet their needs more fully.

Fairness. From such simple discussions as outlined above, more serious thoughts may arise. Survivors may move into discussion of their feelings of loss and begin asking you questions. One thought that often arises is that of pain and fairness. Families consistently describe the loss of a loved one as being incredibly unfair, especially when the deceased was a young and vibrant person. This is a subject that desperately needs validation. Life is *not* fair. Life is a challenge. It is important that the counselor not attempt to philosophically rationalize the loss as being timely. Instead, empathize with the family members in the magnitude of their emotions. Acknowledge the unfairness of their loss. This is an important part of demonstrating some understanding and may empower the counselor to intervene later in other issues.

Owning the Pain. Often family members will look to you to "fix" the pain they feel. Sometimes they may even become insistent that you "do something," especially for another family member who is grieving particularly painfully. At such times, it may be helpful to discuss owning the pain of a loss.

Share with them that pain cannot be accepted in proxy. Help them see that it is important for each person to accept and appropriately manage his or her own pain. Grief is a process. It is not brief, comfortable, or logical. Any efforts by family members or a counselor to abbreviate or force the experience may damage the integrity of the process and effectively prevent its successful resolution.

The Learning Experience. The death of a loved one is a devastating experience. Acknowledge this with each family. Address the very real pain. Allow family members to express their feelings fully, including their anger at the loss and fears for the future. Then, if appropriate, help them to understand that, at the time of a loss, families find themselves at a crossroads or choice-point. They can easily become bitter and cynical; they can choose to risk never caring so much again; or they can labor to accept the loss, gleaning from it insights that may be valuable.

At the time of a loss, this seems painfully meager. Many times families feel that there can be nothing of value to gain from so great a bereavement. Share with them that, in talking with those families who have successfully worked through a death, many emphasize that the experience brought with it important discoveries. Many have developed a greater ability to appreciate and cherish the relationships they still have. One mother who lost a child to a degenerative central nervous system disorder put it this way:

A death will not make you kinder, more loving, or altruistic. You will not compete with Sister Teresa or Billy Graham. But it may make you more sensitive to the needs of others in similar situations. It will not make you less fearful about the health and well-being of your other children. In fact, just the opposite may occur. You may want to wrap your remaining children in cotton batting and place them on a shelf out of harm's way.

But your appreciation of their unique personalities and the quality of your relationships may be sharpened. With his brown eyes and dimples, our middle child is an endearing reminder of Steven. However, we know our charming Andrew is very much his own person. Observing and participating in the normal development of our other children is heightened because Steven's life and death were not normal.[53]

Most families later indicate that the loss experience helped them to develop greater wisdom, restraint, compassion, empathy for others, and an awareness of the "intangibles" of life that truly are of value, both to themselves and to others they love. While no one would choose such an experience in order to deepen these insights, they are of great value and are to be sought after in the wake of the loss. Most persons will readily acknowledge that their loved one would want something positive to come from the loss, whenever possible. At times, this can mobilize families into long-postponed action—to renew family ties, make personal improvements, and further strengthen their feelings for their loved ones.

The Gifts of Love. No one lives a life without having affected others. The warm and choice experiences in memory are special gifts from those we love. They change and strengthen us. They are a permanent part of our lives. We can never live as though the deceased had never been with us, and to that extent, at the very *least,* the person is never far from us.

A discussion of this concept is particularly valuable in helping the bereaved to accept and begin new relationships. Through it, they can see that they are not abandoning a loved one, or replacing him or her with someone else, but are instead increasing the breadth and scope of their caring.

Note: Prior to sharing this perspective it is important that the counselor obtain a feel for the general tenor of the relationships the deceased had with *all* family members. Some relationships—even if they included genuine love and caring—were nevertheless very troubled. In such circumstances, other areas of the experience can be emphasized, thus empowering the family members to move past the loss. A relation-

---

[53] Barnes, Sharon, *Bereavement*, vol. 3, no.3, p. 39. Reproduced by permission of Bereavement Publishing, Inc. All rights reserved.

ship of this nature would also indicate a need for more extensive counseling, and specific follow-up referrals should be made.

The Broken Leaf. For young children, death can be difficult to understand. Many different thoughts can be helpful at this time. One object dialogue that can be useful utilizes a leaf. Any leaf will do. I like to get two—one fresh and alive from a tree or bush, and one brown and dead from beneath it. Show them to the children and let them tell you the difference between the two. Talk about the life cycle of the leaves and ways in which they can get broken off the tree. After sufficient dialogue, turn their attention back to the loss at hand. Help them know that, just like the leaves on the trees, we all someday "stop working." Reassure them that for most of us, this will be a very long time off, so they will feel confident that parents/siblings should be with them for some time to come. Also, remind them that just because someone dies, we do not have to stop loving, or being loved by, them. Love is something we can always give and receive.

The Refillable Ink Pen. Explain this dialogue to a parent first, before using it with a child (generally age five or older), to insure full family support and to modify its content to match family beliefs. Use descriptors with which the parents are comfortable, e.g., grandma goes to "heaven," or "lives in our hearts," or goes to "a beautiful place." In this example, death can be described in the context of an ink pen, chosen because it is readily available to use as a model.

"Roger, let me show you something to help you understand grandma's death a little better. Do you see this ink pen? Let's take this pen and make a mark on our paper, like this. It works just fine, doesn't it?

"Now, suppose we unscrew the pen and see what's inside." Do so, and display the refill cartridge as you proceed. "Look here, Roger, what's this? Yes, this is the cartridge that actually holds the ink. Can you still make a mark with it on the paper? Let's see." Do so again, showing that it still works. "It still works well, only it's kind of hard to hold, isn't it?"

"You know, our bodies are kind of like this ink pen. The outside is what you and I see. But the real part, the part that 'works,' is inside. That's the part that loves and cares and warms our hearts.

"So, while grandma's 'outside' died and will have to be buried or cremated, the 'inside,' or the part of grandma that loves us, is still there and it still works. Some people say this part goes to heaven, some just say it goes to a beautiful place. No matter where it goes, this is the part of grandma that we really love and the part that loves us. And it will always be there, even though we can't see her any more. Now do you understand? Even though we can't see grandma again, she still loves us, and we can still love her. Okay?"

Explaining Cremation to Children. Children at a fairly young age seem to become generally familiar with burial, if only through movies and books, but cremation may require some special explanation. One woman called me saying, "I have a rather precocious five-year-old who is already asking me surprising questions about grandma's death. My mother wanted to be cremated, and I'm just sure my daughter's going to pointedly ask how we got grandma into 'that little box.' What do you think I should say?"

After a great deal of discussion and thought, we settled on the following:

> "You know, honey, after grandma died, we sent her body to some special people at a funeral home. They took grandma's body and helped make it back into the things it came from."
>
> Then, if more questions arise:
>
> "Just like the leaves fall off the trees in autumn, and go back into the things they were made from, so do our bodies. That is what we have here in the box. It's not really dust and ashes, but it looks something like that. Remember, our bodies are only a little part of us, just the part we see. But grandma is still in our hearts and loves us just the same as always, even without this little part of her."

Remember, details should be provided only in small degrees and only as *specifically* requested by the child. Let the child lead you in any such questioning. When children are satisfied, the questions will stop.

The "Magic Wand." A successful approach for use with deaths involving the elderly or chronically and irreversibly ill, where the death may be seen as an escape from pain or struggles, is the "magic wand" concept.[54] This concept is very simple and direct, yet powerful.

You simply ask the following question, "If you had a magic wand and could bring him/her back right now, would you?"

Often, family members will say something like, "Well, he was so sick, and in such pain . . . no, I guess not." In situations where they spontaneously say "Yes," you might ask, "If you did, how would (the deceased) feel about it?" They will nearly always then recognize the circumstances to which they would bring their loved one back and how the deceased might feel about such a return. Consequently, most family members would decline to do so voluntarily and recognize that some good has come in the release from suffering.

After sharing this dialogue, however, it is often helpful to summarize with the comment, "But it doesn't mean we don't miss (the deceased), or hurt at our loss. Am I right?" Universally, they will agree. From this

---

[54] Originally shared by Neil H. Leash, MFCC.

thought stems greater ventilation and expression of feelings, an important part of the grief process.

Reasoning. The question "why" may come up again and again. Families invariably search for some possible reasoning or rationale to explain their loss. Help them to understand that great losses may require a lifetime of vision to even *begin* to understand. To try to completely resolve such a loss today robs us of the learning of tomorrow. Encourage them to allow a perspective to unfold; to never force or wrest meaning before its time. It is a process in which patience is requisite. One bereft individual noted:

> The answers to life's questions will not be revealed to you through grief. In fact, you may have more questions than you've ever had before. But it may make you search your personal philosophy and discover what you really believe. For some, this process hurts too much. Introspection, therapy, and religious scrutiny are painful, but those who make the soul pilgrimage discover inexplicable comfort.[55]

Religious Views. Many families draw upon their religious faith in coping with the loss of a loved one. The counselor should never negate or diminish the value of this response. Sources of deep emotional strength, such as religious conviction, can provide tremendous support to families.

It is important, however, for you to carefully observe all family members and note whether all present possess similar degrees of strength in the expressed belief. While family members generally share similar religious perspectives, occasionally there may be those present who do not possess equal conviction, or may even express greatly divergent views. These family members will need to be allowed their own expressions and to be supported in a manner acceptable to them.

To question their own long-held religious beliefs and philosophies at the time of a loss is normal and should not disturb the survivors. Encourage family members to allow open discussion of such feelings and concerns. Help them to understand that, after expressing their frustrations and fears, people often return to their faith and receive the desired support it was meant to provide. At such times, care-givers should consider calling a hospital chaplain or the family's religious leader to lend support.

Guidelines for Friends of the Bereaved

Often friends and relatives of a grieving survivor will ask what they can do to help. Amy Hillyard Jensen, a twice-bereaved mother, has written a short pamphlet, *Is There Anything I Can Do To Help?*, which has

---

[55]. Barnes, S., *Bereavement*, vol. 3, no.3, p. 39. Reproduced with permission of Bereavement Publishing, Inc. All rights reserved.

numerous valuable suggestions. Copies may be obtained by writing to Medic Publishing Co., P.O. Box 89, Redmond, Washington 98052.

In general, there are three important helping activities that friends and relatives can attend to. The first is simply to listen. We have already discussed the need of bereaved persons to express their feelings. Many grieving persons will want to recount details of a loss again and again. This is normal. However, it takes patience and tolerance to support someone during this phase of grief. Prepare families and friends for this and encourage them to extend themselves.

A second important service relates to further family contacts. Immediately following a death, there are often many telephone calls to be made to friends and relatives near and far. Each will have many questions about the death and the family's plans relating to the funeral. Any assistance a sensitive friend or relative can provide will relieve the immediate family from a substantial burden.

Finally, there are things of a more practical nature that need attention. A death brings with it a multitude of large and small tasks that must be attended to—meeting airplanes, running errands, scheduling meals, and providing housing for relatives coming from a distance. A valuable service can be rendered in assisting with these responsibilities, thus removing undue pressure from those already struggling with grief.

Professional Preparation

Healthy management of grief is critical to a family's resolution of a loss. The manner in which you, the counselor, reconcile yourself to a death will often set the tone for the family. Whether you intend it or not, your feelings will come through in a multitude of ways. Consequently, you cannot provide adequate support to a family if you have major unresolved feelings about death and your role in dealing with it. Consider the following example:

Case Vignette 11.1

It happened the very first time I was on the night shift by myself. We had a call, two women coming in from a bad head-on collision. One was in trauma arrest. Come to find out, she was engaged to one of the doctors from upstairs, a medical resident. She died on the table. So after they've done doing what they're doing—poking her with needles, reintubating her about 20 times (practice for new doctors)—I needed to cut all lines that they put in her, tie them off, and try to clean her up as best I could for viewing. That meant getting the blood off her face and making her look presentable, which was hard to do. After the family's viewing, I had to haul her down to the morgue, though I had never taken a body down there. I threw her on that cold plate and shut the door and knew this was really the end, the coldness of death.   —**Health Aide**[56]

Clearly, a death situation may cause you to feel emotionally vulnerable, and even threatened. Usually, these feelings stem both from unresolved feelings about death itself, and from fear of not being able to meet a bereaved family's needs. In these circumstances, your effectiveness with the survivors will be greatly reduced. Obviously, the first step to take is to resolve your own unsettled feelings about death.

This may require some personal introspection. What *do* you think death is? How *should* you respond to a loss? Do you have a personal philosophy about the meaning and purpose of life?

Speaking for myself, I happen to believe in an after-life. I have always felt comfortable with the idea. Something inside causes me to feel secure that there is a continuation of family life beyond the grave, and that love is an eternally binding tie. Those feelings help me to accept death. Certainly, it is painful. The losses in my own family have always been difficult. Any separation from someone for whom I care deeply may try my emotional strength. But for me, a bright ray of faith provides comfort.

I make that personal statement simply as an example. Your concept of death may be very different from mine. I would not try to press my views on you and certainly would not do so with a grieving family. You must come to your own terms in your own way. The point is that to be effective with others, you must successfully resolve your own feelings first. If you can't handle your own ambivalent feelings, you will find great discomfort in attempting to assist others.

Paul H. Dunn wrote a book entitled *The Birth We Call Death*, in which he details his own philosophy regarding death. You may find it useful as a beginning of this self-examination process. In any event, spend some time pondering and exploring the issues within the context of your own cultural, religious, and/or philosophical beliefs.

Recognizing Your Limits

Even after evaluating and attending to your feelings regarding death, there yet may be some limits to your arena of optimal functioning. These may include the death of someone you know, and death issues that are "too close to home." Usually, the latter category includes situations (1) in which the deceased or families appear similar to your own, (2) where the mechanism of death parallels a prior experience, or (3) when you

---

[56] Richards, E. "The Knife and Gun Club: Scenes from an emergency room." *Life Magazine*, April 1989, p. 54. Quoted with permission.

have experienced a bereavement recently enough to still be grieving. Consider the comments one emergency nurse shared:

> In my life, I am a mother and wife first, a nurse second. Yesterday we had a two-year-old trauma arrest (heart stopped due to traumatic injury) who died. If I had seen that kid, I would have related too much because of my own two-year-old. I could have worked on the kid fine. But after I would have been useless. I would have needed to get away. If I can get away for a few minutes, I can get myself back together and I'll be fine for the rest of the shift.[57]

In situations such as these, if at all possible, someone else should be selected to provide family support and intervention. While you may involve yourself in an ancillary support role, you should not be the family's primary resource. Where situations require your participation, or in any situation where you feel overly burdened by the loss, it is good to involve yourself further in the grief resolution process. Collins (1989), a critical care nurse, writes:

> Death in the intensive care unit (ICU) can be associated with strong emotions of anger, guilt, helplessness, and frustration. To continue to be effective, the critical care nurse must deal with these emotions. One important way to do this is to let oneself grieve with the family. To do so is neither maudlin nor unprofessional, but rather is expressing emotions that need to be shared. Such feelings, if suppressed, do not simply go away, but later emerge as major causes of burnout, fatigue, and job frustration. To handle them by sharing in the grieving process with survivors helps both the nurse and the survivors.[58]

Those who serve in supervisory capacities would do well to allow involved staff these intimate opportunities for grief, when circumstances allow. The return in staff longevity and productivity is well worth the small investment of time.

As mentioned earlier, certain situations of complex or pathological grieving require intervention by a skilled mental health practitioner. In dealing with a family, should you discover such a situation, use caution. Obtain appropriate consultation and support, or promptly refer the family to someone with the skills required to bring the case to a complete and wholesome resolution.

---

[57] Ibid.

[58] Ibid.

Staff Grief and Stress Management

Being a professional health care-giver or first responder of any kind puts you in a compromised position. You are thrust into situations for which you may not be entirely prepared, but in which you must perform efficiently. A natural result of this is that you may accumulate emotional injuries that need to heal. Consider the following example:

Case Vignette 11.2

I always swore I would never let things bother me. But a child, eight months old, died last year, and essentially I was the doctor in charge. The child may or may not have died from something I did or didn't do, but the kid died, and I didn't get the diagnosis right. I saw her about 5:30 in the morning, diagnosed gastroenteritis and sent her home. And two and a half hours later mama awakened to find the kid dead. Right now I feel a ton of bricks is on my heart just because I mentioned it. Back then I was incapacitated for about a month.

—Physician[59]

While the major objective of this book is to assist the professional in helping those who have lost a family member, it bears mention that the helpers themselves can be adversely affected and may need intervention as well. When you find yourself or your co-workers feeling burdened by certain difficult experiences, it is important to seek out an appropriate place to express the issues and resolve them.

In the course of helping families to resolve stress and grief, take special note of the reactions of the staff around you. Place yourself in circumstances that will allow you to assist in resolving complicating scenarios. Here are four suggestions:

1. Take the time to develop a rapport with the emergency response/front-line personnel with whom you work. If they feel that they know you before a problem arises, they are much more likely to approach you with their issues.

2. Circulate with those returning from a recent encounter with a potentially traumatic situation. Share with them whatever comes to mind and practice some reflective listening.

3. Be alert to subtle cues that "something is up" with your personnel. Watch attendance and performance. Don't hastily assume that performance is down because of lack of initiative; find out the underlying cause.

[59] Ibid.

4. Ask timely questions. Don't pry, but don't ignore something that seems out of place, either. Once you have rapport and show your sensitivity, you will earn a reputation as someone who cares. You will find yourself able to bolster the confidence and security of those with whom you work.

While these are certainly not the only ways to become attuned to and resolve budding traumatic-stress issues, by following these suggestions you will discover many of the critical issues facing staff. Your involvement can benefit those in high-stress service and those they serve.

Chapter 12

Delivering a Terminal Diagnosis

> One of my medical school professors was Oliver Wendell Holmes. I have not forgotten his insistence that, while one of the physician's functions is to assist at the coming-in, another is to assist at the going-out.[60]

Your physical examination of the patient has been thorough and complete. The test results are back. Your patient is terminal. Or, perhaps, there is a glimmer of hope, but you know it to be remote. Conveying this knowledge to a vulnerable, frightened human being, and to his or her family, can be one of the most difficult challenges a physician must face.

As you prepare to look into the face of your patient, what do you say? How can you convey your message and still be supportive and involved? How much do you tell? What if the patient does not want to know the news? What if the family does not want the patient to be told? These and other questions are addressed in this chapter.

The Physician's Unavoidable Responsibility

While a great many health-care professionals can potentially be involved in breaking difficult news to patients and their families, delivering news of a terminal illness falls, in most instances, to the physician.

In Chapter 1 of this book, a case is made for considering the designation of someone *other* than a physician to make notifications of death, when it has already occurred. The foundation of that argument rests upon the increasingly impersonal nature of health care in America. In cases of sudden or traumatic death, the pronouncing physician may have had little if any prior contact with the patient or the family and limited

---

[60] Fletcher, W.S. "Doctor, am I terminal?" *The American Journal of Surgery*, vol. 163, 1992, p. 460.

time to gather information beyond that required for immediate medical treatment.

In such cases, other professionals—emergency room social workers, chaplains, coroner's staff, or nurses—may be much more available to the family. Some may possess specialized crisis management skills, and, if involved in the case early on, may also have obtained not only pertinent medical information but other details surrounding the death as well. In such circumstances, they may be in a better position to provide not only the death notification but also the entire "loss context" that is so necessary for a family to come to terms with the reality of a loss.

This can then be followed by both psychological "debriefing" and follow-up emotional and resource referral support. Following or during such an intervention, a physician can easily make brief contact with a family to express condolences and provide further technical medical explanations of the loss as necessary (see Chapters 2 and 5).

However, in the discovery of a terminal diagnosis, the situation is usually much different. The person best informed of all surrounding details, both medical and interpersonal, is likely to be the evaluating physician. Even if there has not been a long-term doctor-patient relationship, it is likely that rapport and a common bond has been developed in the process of sharing the medical investigation and evaluation. Such strengths are of critical importance when the pronouncement of limited life is to be given.

For that reason, throughout this chapter I have made reference to "the physician." However, it should remain clear that the notifying professional could easily be a nurse practitioner in a clinic setting, a genetics counselor in an outpatient facility, or a counseling social worker in a county AIDS testing center. Regardless of the setting of contact, the principles found in this chapter, and elsewhere in the text, remain valid and useful for your application.

The Importance of the Task

The following description is taken from two newspaper accounts of the same event:

Case Vignette 12.1

With her mother terminally ill, six-year old Jackie Johnson told the other children she wanted to be in heaven with the angels. Then she stepped in front of a speeding freight train as her brother, sister, and cousin watched in horror.[61]

---

[61] "Kids struggle with horror of girl's suicide," copyright *USA Today*, June 17, 1993. Reprinted with permission.

> She was on her way to . . . school . . . when they crossed
> some railroad tracks. She fought them off when they told her to
> get off the tracks as a train approached . . .
> The child decided to stand in front of the train . . . "because
> she wanted to be with her mother, who is dying of AIDS," said
> Gloria Wright, a relative who had been caring for the child
> because of her mother's failing health.[62]

While not all untoward events following notification of terminal illness can be avoided, this vignette is an example of the devastating results that can follow, both for the ill person and his or her family. The task of notification deserves careful consideration and preparation.

Preliminary steps

In the discussion with your patient and family members, there are numerous issues that deserve special consideration. Neglecting any of these can potentially leave you or your patient with an obstructed view of either the information that needs to be shared or the meaning of it.

Staging Delivery of the News

Chapter 3 discusses some of the techniques and potential pitfalls in staging discussion of any traumatic or sensitive news with families. In cases of terminal illness, the task can take on even greater importance than in cases of notification of death because it can affect the quality of the time that remains for the patient. Charlton (1992), a physician, notes, "Receiving (the prognosis) is a traumatic event, often vividly remembered, that sets the stage for further care and treatment."

In setting that stage, the following general rules should be observed in nearly every instance:

1. Your primary initial contact should be with the patient, unless he or she is a minor—in which case, contact with a parent or guardian takes precedence.

2. Select an appropriate setting—ideally, a quiet room with sufficient privacy for personal discussion and freedom from prying observation or interruption. It should be a setting where all can be seated and can talk easily. Discussions of this nature should _never_ take place in a hospital corridor, waiting room, recovery room, open ward, or over the telephone.

---

[62] "Donations to help family bury girl who killed self to be 'angel'," _Sacramento Bee_, June 19, 1993.

3. Ample time availability is crucial for thorough discussion and emotional support. You must be prepared, and have the time, to respond to all questions and concerns. The time will vary according to the needs of the patient and family, but usually 30-50 minutes will suffice.

The Potential for Emotional Reactions, Including Yours

Notifying of a terminal illness can be emotionally unsettling, to say the least, for both the patient and the physician. To the patient it may mean, "Medical science can do no more for me; I am hurt, I am frightened, I am threatened." Such feelings can easily be translated into, "YOU, doctor, are at fault! Why did you postpone my biopsy for three weeks? You knew this could have been cancer and that it should have been removed at the earliest possible moment!" or any number of similar rejection monologues.

As a physician, you must consider how to respond to this. Constantly remind yourself that the person is speaking to his or her fear, not actually to you. By so doing, while you may feel threatened, you can maintain your emotional balance and not fall into an escalating dialogue of recrimination and defense.

It also bears mention that professionals, as human beings, are not immune from the human inclination to blame. In the intensity of delivering terminal news, it is to easy to allow negative comments to escape. "I told you to quit smoking!" "It was obvious his drinking was killing him, so why didn't you do something?" "Why did you wait so long to come in? If we had caught this earlier we most likely could have cured it!" What is often really being said at such moments is, "Why are you putting me through telling you this news? I hate it, too!"

Death is the ultimate medical insult—it slaps back at a physician in the face of dedicated efforts to stave it off. Frustration and blame are natural responses but must be guarded against at all costs. The patient and family are already overwhelmed by tragic news and are in great need of sympathy, support, and emotional strength from you.

The Language of Disclosure

As Buckman (1992), a physician, notes, it is essential to "use English, not 'Medspeak'." While this rule may seem obvious, it is violated with enormous frequency. A person who works daily in a highly technical field such as medicine is unlikely to relinquish the familiarity of jargon-laden speech without a concerted effort. To do so is even more difficult because the deliverer of the news is usually, in some measure, a reluctant participant. The language of the profession allows an element of detachment and a demonstration of expertise. However, it is essential to remember that the receiving audience consists of frightened, overwhelmed persons who often suspect the worst even before you open your mouth.

In 1959, Aitken-Swan and Eason investigated patients who had reportedly been informed that they had "curable" cancer. Their findings included the discovery that 19 percent denied having ever been told! It was likely that either euphemisms or technical language had been used, instead of clear and direct communications. The words "malignancy," "metastases," or "invasive tissue," for example, may not mean "cancer" to all listeners. Always adjust your communications to the capacity of the recipients and follow with questions to ensure that they have understood accurately.

Timing Delivery of the News

Concern may occasionally arise about timing the delivery of a terminal diagnosis. Ward (1992), a physician, makes a compelling argument for the telling of impending death early after its diagnosis. He cites the findings of a ten-year study in a burn-center setting. The focus of the study of 39 lethally burned patients was, in part, patient and family reactions to notice of their terminal situation, as compared to those not so notified. The average age of the participants was 52 and average burn size was 78 percent of total body surface area. In the study, 15 patients were told of their impending death, and 24 were not. Those so informed were told early in their treatment, before administration of analgesic or psychotropic medications.

While family members demonstrated a wide variety of responses, the patients were unanimous in welcoming the candor. Ward notes, "All acted forthrightly and purposefully to accomplish goals set according to their own priorities. Rather than anger toward the burn center staff, they showed appreciation for having been told their condition."

Ward states that "once the (prognostic) 'die is cast,' there is no purpose" in delaying the notification. In cases such as a fatal burn where rapid deterioration is expected, delivery of the news should be made within the first hours of admission, when "the patient is awake, can understand, can respond, and can make plans."

The primary goal, at that point, is to allow the dying person to take final control of his or her life. "When awake and alert patients are told that they are going to die soon, there are immediate changes in (their) ambiance and interpersonal relations. It is a difficult line to cross, but they begin to make basic decisions about their lives and the people in them, acting in a calculated, constructive manner. Where children should be placed, where items of value should go, what people should be contacted, and the processes of future planning are addressed. Ironically, the one about to die is the one making the most decisions about the future."[63]

In this situation, demise was imminent and certain, and loss of mental acuity due to medications and injury would likely occur quickly. Early notification, albeit without much onset-to-notification accommodation time, was a gift of immense value to the dying. When in doubt, early truth-telling will nearly always serve you well.

Exploration of What Is Already Known

To properly introduce and discuss your information, it is invariably important to discover what the patient and family already know. Have them summarize their information back to you. Even if you are relatively familiar with previous conversations involving the patient or family, unless you personally (and recently) delivered the information to them yourself, you should question them regarding *their understanding* of what is already known. Failure to do this can easily lead to miscommunication, complicating any relationship with an emotionally ill-prepared patient or family members.

By obtaining a brief summary of their knowledge, you can then more easily clarify any misunderstandings, gauge their immediate emotional states, and assess their capacity for integration of medical facts. You will be able to better choose a "gradient of entry" that is appropriate to their needs. This technique is discusses further in Chapter 3.

Assessment of the Wish to be Informed

No analysis of the staging process would be complete without discussing the assessment of a patient's wish to be—*or not to be*—informed of the diagnosis. Implicit in this discussion is the concept that one does not *insist* that a patient, or family, accept any news that we desire to deliver at the time we desire to deliver it (see also Chapter 3).

There was a time, not long ago, when it was common practice for physicians to withhold diagnostic information. Woodard (1992) cites researchers from the early 1950s and '60s who surveyed physicians, finding that 70-90 percent did not disclose grave illness. She notes that "until the 1970s, most American doctors subscribed to the view that patients should not be informed about the diagnosis of cancer." Charlton (1992) also cites data, obtained from numerous studies completed during the past 40 years, demonstrating an early reluctance to disclose diagnosis and prognosis, progressing toward an increasing wish by patients, families and physicians for more openness. However, as he further notes, "The

---

[63] Ward, C.G. "The die is cast: Telling patients they are going to die," *Journal of Burn Care and Rehabilitation,* vol. 13, 1992, pp. 272-274.

important issue is not what most patients or doctors think, but what the particular patient in the particular circumstances wants at that time."

Few topics, in the context of terminal illness or other traumatic news, engender so much conflict in the medical community as the duty to tell—the duty to truth. One writer (Higgs, 1985), stresses strongly the need for complete truth and disclosure. He notes in support of this view, "If truth is the first casualty, trust is the second." Another, an ethicist (Jackson, 1991), argues that truth-telling is by no means absolutely clear in all circumstances. She gives examples of "child patients or dying patients, or depressed patients" in her examination of when incomplete disclosure or morally defensible deception may be considered.

Jackson discusses differences between benevolent deception, evasion, and lying versus intentional deception, "being economical with the truth," or "merely refraining from correcting a misunderstanding." She concludes by suggesting that deception in some cases may be realistically expedient, and that, "While doctors, generally speaking, should have no truck with lying, deliberate deception need not in general pose a threat to trust."

This having been said, there is a middle ground, embodying both duty to truth and avoidance of "brutal truth."

"Offering" Truth

One physician/clinical ethicist, provides a profound discussion of this issue in an article titled "Offering Truth."[64] As the title implies, the key concept put forth is that truth can always be _offered_, without brutalizing someone with it.

A family was cited who had been adamantly opposed to disclosure to their 70-year-old mother that her condition was terminal. The patient had "widespread metastatic seedings in the pleura and pericardium from an unknown primary tumor." All arguments by medical staff that the patient had a "right to know" had been to no avail. Legal action had been threatened by the family, and they had offered to "sign any document" waiving any liability incurred by not notifying the patient of her status. At this point the clinical ethicist was consulted, and the following concepts and steps were agreed upon:

1. A patient's knowledge of diagnosis and prognosis is not all-or-nothing. It exists along a continuum, anchored at one end by the purely theoretical "absolute ignorance" and at the other end by the unattainable "total enlightenment."
2. While the patient has a _right_ to know, she does not have a _duty_ to know. We would not force this information upon her—indeed, we cannot.

---

[64] B. Freedman. "Offering Truth," _Archives of Internal Medicine,_ vol. 153, pp. 572-575, copyright 1993, American Medical Association.

Patients who do not want to know will sometimes deny ever having been told, however forthrightly they have been spoken to.

3. Of greatest importance is the *opportunity* to know that further information exists, which information can then be accessed by the patient *to the degree he or she desires it.* The most important step is to ask questions of the patient and then listen closely to the responses. Or to generate a dynamic within which the patient is speaking and the physician responding, rather than vice versa. Only then can the pace of conversation and level of information be controlled by the patient.[65]

In the example cited, the following dialogue then ensued:

Case Vignette 12.2

The patient was found awake and reasonably alert. She was told that she had an infection that was now under control, but that she remained very ill, as she herself could tell from her weakness. Did she have any questions she wanted to ask; did she want to talk?

She did not. We repeated that she remained very ill and asked if she understood that—she did. Some patients, it was explained to her, want to know all about their disease, its name, prognosis, treatment choices, famous people who have had the disease, etc.—while others do not want to know so much, and some want to leave all of the decisions in the hands of their family and physicians. What would she like? What kind of patient is she? She whispered to her daughter that she wanted to leave it alone for now.

That seemed to be her final word. We repeated to her that treatment choices would need to be made shortly. She was told that we would respect her desire, but that if she changed her mind we could talk at any time; and that, in any event, she must understand that we would stay by her and see to her comfort in all possible ways. She signified that she understood and said that we should deal with her children. We understood this as explicitly authorizing her children to speak for her with respect to treatment decisions.[66]

Informed Consent

Another argument for complete disclosure to a patient has been that of informed consent. How can a patient legally and morally accept any treatment without full knowledge of the diagnosis and expected prognosis? The law of informed consent has its roots in the concept of self-determination, put forth in a Supreme Court opinion by Cardosa in 1914: "Every human being of adult years and sound mind has a right to

---

[65] Ibid.

[66] Ibid.

determine what shall be done with his own body."[67] Although specific rules of informed consent are based on the laws of the state in which the physician practices, the generic elements of the law include the following:

(1) A description of the patient's condition and the treatment being recommended;
(2) The risks of the recommended treatment (including the seriousness and probability of the risks);
(3) The benefits of the recommended treatment; and
(4) The discussion of alternative treatment(s)—including the alternative of no treatment—as well as the risks and benefits associated with the alternatives.[68]

Cotsonas, a medical-legal attorney, then continues, "For a plaintiff to prevail in an informed consent lawsuit, he or she must persuade a jury of four key allegations:

(1) The physician had a duty to disclose information;
(2) The physician failed to disclose information that should have been disclosed;
(3) The treatment resulted in injury to the patient; and
(4) The patient would not have consented to the treatment had the patient been told the undisclosed information.

The overriding concern, however, should be the patient's right to control all aspects of the information process. As Freedman (1982) notes, "A patient's right to information vests in the patient, to exercise as he or she desires; so that a patient's right to information is respected no less when the patient chooses to be relatively uninformed than when full information is demanded."[69] With proper management of the process, no persons need remain in the traumatic situation of either being denied the information they desire, or having it thrust upon them in spite of their contrary wishes. Physicians must be sensitive to, and prepared to accommodate, both possibilities.

Delivery of the News

Buckman (1992) notes, "An expert in breaking bad news is not someone who gets it right every time—she or he is merely someone who gets it wrong less often, and who is less flustered when things do not go

---

[67] Taub, S. "Cancer and the law of informed consent." _Journal of the American Medical Record Association_, vol. 54, 1989, pp. 30-35.

[68] Cotsonas, 1992.

[69] Cobbs vs. Grant, 502 P2d 1 (Cal 1972): "A medical doctor need not make disclosure of risks when the patient requests that he not be so informed." See also, Reibl vs. Hughes 2SCR 880 (1980).

smoothly." His book, *How to Break Bad News*, is an excellent text for those who desire more detailed information than is provided here. For our purposes, the salient points of various authors are presented for examination and adaptation by the practitioner.

Key Concepts

In a study in which 32 doctors were interviewed regarding their practice of truth-telling in the care of dying patients, three basic elements were identified (Miyaji, 1993): "telling what patients want to know," "telling what patients need to know," and "translating information into terms that patients can take." The styles were found to be supported by five basic normative principles: respect for the truth, patients' rights, doctors' duty to inform, preservation of hope, and individual contracts between patients and doctors.

Practical Application

In concert (or at times in conflict) with these principles, another physician (Brewin, 1991) describes three observed ways by which the news is delivered: "the blunt and unfeeling way," "the kind and sad way," and "the understanding and positive way." The latter, of course, is preferred.

The "essential ingredients" noted for the "understanding and positive way" are "flexibility, based on feedback," and "positive thinking, re-assurance, and planning for the immediate future, all blended with the bad news, not just saved for later." His model illustrates the combining of bad news with hope and forward thinking, to any degree possible. It differs from the delivery of the news of an already-transpired death primarily in that it *can* offer hope, a critical ingredient in any patient's battle with deteriorating health.

Buckman, cited above, provides a six-step protocol, embodying elements of the preparation work described earlier and progressing beyond:

1. Getting started; getting the physical context right. In this step the writer encourages careful selection of an appropriate physical setting.

2. Finding out how much the patient knows.

3. Finding out how much the patient *wants* to know.

4. Sharing the information (aligning and educating). In preparation for this step the physician is encouraged to "decide on your objectives." Essential elements include all aspects of "diagnosis, treatment plan, prognosis, (and avenues) of support." Of particular note: "It is not essential to state your own agenda, but it is essential to have one (or at least part of one)." "Aligning" is described as starting where the patient is (in views and beliefs about the illness), and "educating" is the process of bringing him or her "closer to the medical facts," to the degree necessary.

5. Responding to the patient's feelings. While often the most difficult step for the person delivering the news, empathetic, genuine response to a patient's reactions "is the part of the interview that requires your most sustained and continued concentration." Without this, you cannot fully align with and support your patient.

6. Planning and follow-through. This is a critical stage in the delivery of terminal news and one often overlooked or underrated. It is in this stage that the physician reaffirms commitment—a willingness to "stand by" and fight for the patient, as long as he or she so desires. Or, even at the rejection of the recommended aggressive management plan, it is here that the physician must demonstrate a willingness to supply all comfort measures, with a continued commitment throughout the dying process. This is addressed further below, in the section entitled "Necessary Follow-Up."

Let There Be Hope

In pursuing these methods of delivery, the basic principles of the "Sequential Notification Technique" (See Chapter 3) still apply, but, as so aptly emphasized by Brewin, its application can now be bolstered by hope. For example, he encourages delivery statements such as, "I'm afraid the tests show . . . ," then continuing with emphasis and without any pause after giving the bad news, "But I'm glad to say that the position is at least more hopeful than some cases we see," or, "the liver seems normal and healthy, which is a relief." Encouraged are use of such words as "normal" and "healthy," further emotionally empowering the recipient of the news. Setting the stage for available joint patient-physician efforts is also seen as valuable. For example, "At least we know what we're up against and what has to be done (or what the options are)," all pointing to continued commitment and hope.

Use of Humor in Notification

With a patient well known to you, humor is not entirely ruled out in your communications. One physician (Herring, 1993) stated, "Though death is inevitable, Americans seem to have chosen to make it an option." He continued by alluding to our ever-serious manner in dealing with the inevitable. Sharing his use of humor in disclosing a terminal diagnosis, he describes a "once golf-playing patient" as someone he knew well, and he thus felt assured of a positive response when he said, "Russ, I hope there's golf in heaven because I think you have a tee (date) in a few days." The patient then replied, squeezing his hand, "I hope, Doc, that you won't be my partner!"

Another patient, visited at home, was a woman wasting away from a colon tumor, and down to 80 lbs. He felt he should tell her that she would likely die in a short time. Having just learned that she had recently had her hair done by a beautician neighbor, he said, "Helen, your hair is gorgeous! In a few days you will be the most beautiful woman in heaven." Her reply was both enjoyable and telling: "Don't heaven me, young man. I did this for you, since I knew this would be our last date, and if you hadn't noticed, I'd have punched you in the nose." Clearly, in the right circumstances and utilizing your own personality and what you know about your patient, humor can be used to maintain a warm relationship. When handled sensitively, this should boost the coping skills that *both of you* will need at this difficult time.

Responses and Family Perspectives

In one study, parents of 24 children with severe developmental disabilities were interviewed regarding their experiences in receiving the "bad news"—learning of and about the diagnoses of their children. From this, researchers identified nine main areas of parental concern. I have summarized critical points important to the families, listing the eight which are obviously applicable to the delivery of a terminal condition.[70]

1. Communication: clear, direct, understandable; positive as well as negative (information); future questions anticipated; information about resources provided.

2. Diagnostician (notifier): familiar person; information delivered consistent with other professionals involved.

3. Affect: able to display feeling of caring, compassion; equal vs. superior deportment; seems comfortable.

4. Pacing: information delivered gradually, adjusted to receiving family; sufficient time provided.

5. When: told as soon as possible, but only after diagnosis is certain.

6. Where: appropriate setting.

7. Support: told with supportive friend/family present.

8. Process vs. Content: expect hearing always to be hard.

Another study (Peteet, 1991) also captured similar information: "Patients said that being told with hope, information, and caring, and with respect for their privacy and wishes to have a supportive person present were particularly helpful."

---

[70] Gloria L. Krahn, et al, "Are There Good Ways to Give Bad News?" *Pediatrics,* vol. 91, no. 3, March 1993. Used with permission.

Being familiar with and sensitive to the needs of those who must manage the news you deliver, regardless of your method of delivery, can help you immensely in successfully helping them over this most difficult first hurdle.

"So, Doctor, How Much Time Do I Have?"

Charlton (1992) states, "This is an impossible question; the time left can rarely be quantified (and estimates will invariably be wrong), so the doctor should concentrate on the good quality of life that exists at present." Langlands (1991) suggests that the discussion of prognosis in terms of finite time "is appropriate only when the prognosis is apparently measured in a few days to a few weeks," noting that precise estimates for longer periods cannot be made with any surety. He suggests, instead, that longer periods of prognostic time be given in terms of "median survival" rates—for example, "You have a 50/50 chance of living another five years." With this method, the patient is able to adapt his or her own personal philosophy to the situation—"I'll beat the odds," or, "I may not be here in a few years, so I'll make the best of my life now." If the patient survives longer or shorter than anticipated, the family is less likely to be surprised or upset with the physician.

Familiarity with various patient-engaging responses may be enormously helpful at this time. For example, Brewin (1991) notes responses such as, "Statistically, it looks bad . . . (but) some people, against all the odds, do amazingly well," or, "The situation is serious, but far from hopeless—you have a chance of doing well." He also encourages "indirect reassurance," such as, "What will you do for your holiday next year if you are fit enough?"

Another physician (Fletcher, 1992) mentions a mentor who would frequently turn the question back to the patient saying, "How long do you want to live?" He notes, "The answers were amazingly candid, such as 'until after Christmas' or 'until after my son John's graduation in June.' The answers were helpful in being able to reassure the patients, or to gently tell them that their aspirations for life probably were not realistic."

Comments on Denial

Except in circumstances where the actual death event has already occurred, or where highly recommended treatment options are obviously being ignored, denial is not the pathological demon we often see it to be. If a patient flatly states, "God is going to heal me!" who are we to argue? Even expressions such as, "It's not a tumor, it's just tenderness from a pulled muscle," are not _prima facie_ problematic. Remember, your patient is dying. The goal is not to get patients to move into our own comfort zone of acceptable recognition and grief, but to allow autonomy and self direction—to maximize _their_ views of happiness for their remaining days. If denial serves this purpose, barring any other difficulties, it should be accommodated.

This does not mean that the physician must act in full complicity with the patient or family. He or she can still maintain a professional expression of belief without being confrontational or demanding. A gentle smile and expression of, "You never know, miracles can happen," can go a long way in finding some common ground for both parties.

Cultural Issues

The cultural background and beliefs of the patient and family must also be considered. Charlton (1992) cites studies in seven nations, with responses from both patients and the general public, expressing their views on whether or not they would want to be told of a terminal diagnosis. From this research, it is clear that there is great variety in how much disclosure is appropriate.

Miyaji (1993), a physician from Japan, citing research and personal experience, notes that most Japanese patients and doctors elect not to disclose the terminal nature of a disease.

While you cannot know all the traditions and wishes of all patients with whom you may interact, your recognition that someone is from a different social or religious background should be an indication that further inquiry is needed. Ask questions in the beginning, such as, "How do traditional Sikhs view hospitals and illness?" and then progress toward more specific questions. For example, you might ask, "Do people share much about their sicknesses, even in the family?" or "If someone you knew were very sick, would they want you to know and talk with them about it?" You need not be a multicultural expert to show sensitivity toward those with whom you interact.

Therapeutic Privilege

When the patient is a child, elderly, psychologically compromised, or mentally infirm, many physicians express reluctance to reveal the diagnosis. Often cited in such situations is the legally recognized concept of "therapeutic privilege." This concept allows physicians to limit a complete disclosure if such disclosure might be found "counter-therapeutic." (Goldberg, 1984)

However, caution must be urged in choosing to exercise this privilege. My experience with patients has been that they almost invariably suspect, and occasionally already know, the very information from which we try to shield them. Even when cognitively infirm or in some other way compromised, every responsive human being is aware of the surrounding environment and can sense changes in it. He or she can feel the change in responses from visiting family and friends and will usually want to know what has happened and why. No one can shield us from the feelings in the hearts of those we love and who truly love us.

When such changes are felt, it may be important to offer at least a cursory revelation of the associated facts. Understanding the reasons for environmental change can bring a return of some measure of the peace and normalcy that are so important at a time of devastating illness. Finally, it has been found that children (and, it follows, those of similar capacity) who were informed of their diagnosis early after its discovery exhibited better long-term adjustment than peers who were not so told (Slavin, 1982). Openness, candor, and caring are far better tools than evasion and secrecy.

Suicide Management

In times of great stress—such as upon the delivery of difficult news—a person (likely someone already experiencing significant preexisting stress) may possibly become suicidal. This is not common, but if you harbor even mild suspicion of such an outcome, it should not be ignored.

Gently but directly inquire of the patient, "Is this news so overwhelming to you that you are thinking of hurting yourself?" While this may seem blunt or intrusive, particularly when no dramatic suicidal symptoms are seen, it remains a critical question to be asked. Patients generally will recognize the appropriateness of the question and will respond directly. Should continued concern remain, a competent professional with skills in suicide management should be engaged for prompt follow-up. If you must provide this requisite intervention, the guidelines in Chapter Eight may be useful to review.

Necessary Follow-up

One physician notes, "Professionals who rely on one interview (to discuss a terminal diagnosis) are likely to find that communication has failed" (Charlton, 1992). The challenge of managing the impact of the news will invariably take the patient time to absorb, and reinforcement and clarification will be necessary to accommodate and address the situation meaningfully. To this end, follow-up discussions, making written information available to patients and families, and facilitating contact with other patients with similar conditions can be enormously valuable.

The Treatment Plan

One of the most useful tools for a physician at such a time is joint discussion with the patient about a recommended long-term treatment plan, specifically including the patient's end-stage wishes. Such a discussion should take place _early_ after a terminal diagnosis, before the patient becomes physically and emotionally weakened. Deferring to a later time only increases the chance that the patient will be unduly upset by the topic, recognizing its nearness, and that progression of the illness will outpace the scope of interim preparations.

Dialogue should be in clear-yet-gentle terms, about the usual progression of the disease and the concerns that are likely to arise. This communication should be sought with the patient at an appropriate time and place, with the primary goal being to learn of his or her wishes in the event of specific likely situations.

The following dialogue is an example:

Case Vignette 12.3

Doc: "Well, Harold, your emphysema seems to be progressing more slowly than it has in the past. That's great news! So, how are you feeling?"

Harold: "Really pretty good, doc. I've been resting and eating better for the past week, and haven't needed my oxygen as much during the day. All in all, I guess I'm doing pretty well."

Doc: (Pause) "You know, there's something I've been meaning to talk with you about. Maybe we could take a few minutes now. Would that be all right?"

Harold: "Sure, go ahead."

Doc: "Harold, you have been doing much better with these latest breathing medications and you have been taking better care of yourself. We may have this thing in check for a good length of time in the future, perhaps even a few years. But, someday it's going to catch up with us, and I want to make sure I follow your wishes when it does. Do you follow what I'm saying?"

Harold: "I think so."

Doc: "One of the typical treatment possibilities with your illness is that you could be placed on a breathing machine if you came in with very bad lung function. How do you feel about the possibility of our using a machine like this?"

Harold: "Well, does it hurt?"

Doc: "No, not really. The most uncomfortable part is putting the tube into your airway, but we always put people under briefly with medications when we place it. Beyond that, the most difficult part for most people is that they can't talk once the tube is in, until it is removed, and some describe feeling panicky when they find that they can't breathe normally. We can't help much with the talking, although you can write notes, but we can give you some anxiety medications if you feel stressed when you first get on the machine."

Harold: "How long might I be on this machine?"

Doc: "It's hard to say. With decreased lung function like yours, sometimes it takes a very long time to wean people off the machine. It's also possible, if your lungs have really deteriorated, or if pneumonia causes extensive damage, that we may not be able to get you back off the machine."

Harold: "You know, Doc, I've seen movies with people on machines like that, and I don't know that I want to be on one. I think I'd rather just be 'natural.' I just don't want to suffer or be a long time dying."

Doc: "No, we won't let you suffer. We can give you medicines to help you sleep and relax, if nothing else can be done. Harold, why don't you give this some thought, talk with your wife about it, and we'll talk again at our next visit.

"I only ask about it now because, if you came in here in respiratory distress and were kind of 'out of it,' well, I'd have to put you on the machine anyway, and I wouldn't even know for sure what you wanted. You don't have to decide now, just think about it and we'll talk again. Oh, and remember, you can always change your mind later. I'll do whatever you want and need. I just want to get a feel for what your wishes might be."

Some may argue that this conversation should be put off until the patient actually presents in need, and then to engage the resources available with the consent of either the patient or the family. However, my experience has been that patients frequently are not able to speak lucidly for themselves at such a time, and that family members, in the stress of the moment, almost invariably consent to aggressive intervention, in fear of the patient's immediate death if they don't.

Delaying the conversation makes it less likely that the wishes of the patient can be honored when the need arises. The discussion may make both of you uncomfortable, but by knowing in advance the common eventualities of a well-known disease process, the patient will be better able to make an informed decision.

Treatment Plan "Evolution"

Once agreed upon, the end-stage treatment plan must be allowed to evolve and change at any time. What a given patient wants early on in the disease process may change with time and with exposure to the effects of the illness and the medical interventions. Regular discussion and flexibility are both necessary to ensure that medical practice matches the patient's desires.

Case Vignette 12.4

A 61-year-old man with chronic obstructive pulmonary disease presented in the ICU in acute respiratory distress. His illness had been long and progressive. Many months earlier, he had refused mechanical life support, but he had continued to present with some frequency for medical management of his illness. He was now extremely emaciated and vulnerable to respiratory illness.

After three acute pulmonary episodes in as many days, he felt he didn't have much more time to live, and had resolved to "let the next episode take me." When it struck, however, it became apparent that his physician and he had not thoroughly discussed this change in plan, as the orders still read for various treatments to be given, instead of comfort measures only.

The patient removed his wedding ring, handed it to his wife, and gasped, "This is it." He then indicated he wanted something to make him comfortable. This necessitated contact with the physician for morphine orders. The resident on call was summoned and immediately assessed that morphine would compromise the patient's respiratory functions further, in effect precipitating his death. She was uncomfortable with this, and bluntly asked, "Are you ready to die tonight?" When the patient nodded "Yes," she seemed caught off-guard and uncertain how to proceed.

The primary-care physician was then called and arrived some 20 minutes later. By now, the patient was grey and fatigued from his respiratory efforts. Supported on one side by his wife, with tears streaming down her cheeks, and on the other by me, the patient continued to indicate his wishes for comfort medications. His wife had by then begun to state, "This is cruel, give him something and stop this suffering."

Instead, however, the primary-care doctor elected to try "just one more aggressive pulmonary treatment." This was temporarily success-ful. Over the next six days, successive crisis treatments were given, until finally the patient expired against all efforts.

Much of the trauma of these events could have been avoided with clear communication between the patient and his physician prior to critical onset of his chronic illness. With thorough discussion, the patient and physician could have reached an accommodation for all final eventualities. Appropriate comfort measures might have been much more in keeping with his wishes.

Accepting the Patient's Choices

As noted earlier, it is not uncommon for a physician to also feel great distress at the discovery of a terminal diagnosis. For healing profes-sionals, the feeling that "I must do something" can be quite strong. The need to have *the* answer, to provide the needed treatment and resolve the problem is acute. This may require some letting go. Giving the patient the right to lead, after having been fully informed, is difficult but essential.

I recall a discussion with a 54-year-old man who had returned to the hospital with a recurrent malignant brain tumor. This was to have been his third tumor debulking. He stated, "It's just like cutting the grass. They cut it out and it comes back. I'm tired of it, and I just don't want any more surgery." Instead of accepting the recommended treatment, he opted to let the tumor run its course and accept the consequences.

Our discussion then turned to his hopes and plans for the time he had left. I was surprised at how clear his goals were—how much thought he had actually given to this decision. It was clear that he knew what he wanted.

For his physician, however, this was no small challenge. It wasn't until a palliative-care plan had been formulated that the he felt more comfortable. Indeed, this was an excellent coping strategy. As a physician, when all curative measures have failed, turn your attention to the new treatment course and you can again feel and be empowered to make active contributions to your patient's life.

Eighteen days later, this patient died comfortably in his home. Hospice nursing and pain medication administration by an infusion pump had been arranged. He slipped away quietly in his sleep. In the preceding days, he had invited all his family, including those from out of state, to his home where he and his wife had arranged to have personal time with each of their several grandchildren.

One of his fondest wishes had been to have "cold beer and pizza just one more time." Therefore, the family rented a pizza parlor and joined him in this event. His final days were as he had hoped and in concert with the medical plans made previously with his physician.

Advance Directives

An excellent way to encourage patients and families to begin considering their wishes for terminal care is via preparation of an _advance directive_. These legally binding statements of a patient's health care wishes are called by various titles depending on the state in which you live, including a Living Will, a Physician's Directive, or a Durable Power of Attorney for Health Care. (Sometimes a Living Will, describing the person's general wishes, may be supplemented by a Durable Power of Attorney, designating specific decisions to another person if the patient is unable to speak for him or herself.)

The documents usually provide for the following: the appointment of a health-care agent for surrogate decision-making (including an optional individual if the primary agent is unavailable or becomes incapacitated); a granting of specific authority to the agent(s) in keeping with the legal authority accorded the instrument in the state of application; a statement of medical treatments desired and any limitations identified by the patient (e.g., "no mechanical life support measures," or, "application of all life-sustaining measures except in the event they will serve only to prolong the moment of my death."); and, in some cases, the document may address organ and tissue donation, as well as disposition of remains.

Having a surrogate decision-maker appointed and possessing some knowledge of the patient's wishes can spare the family and the physician much concern and anxiety. Few challenges are greater for those involved than trying to decide on a treatment course without having had specific discussion and documentation of a patient's personal wishes.

Do Not Resuscitate (DNR) Orders

Subsequent to completion of the advance directive, another important element of the palliative-care plan, *when all hope is truly exhausted*, should be consideration of DNR orders. This step is often overlooked or deferred, and even the seasoned practitioner may delay broaching the subject until literally death-precipitating changes already exist. However, discussion of DNR orders can emotionally prepare a family for an impending loss.

It is easy for families to hope against hope and to miss the final stages of gradual decline, masked as they may be by coma and chemical or mechanical supports. Thus, it is not uncommon for a family to be caught off guard when culminating events finally coalesce and death occurs. If, however, the physician approaches the patient or family when these culminating factors are looming, and discusses plans for a DNR status, all then can make personal preparations for accepting the death. An example of a dialogue with a family is provided below.

Case Vignette 12.5

"Mrs. V., in situations where a patient is terminally ill and then begins to experience life-threatening medical changes, such as when his heart or breathing stops, or when blood pressure begins to fall dramatically in a recurring fashion, it is a signal that the body is trying to let go. We find that if we perform CPR (define if necessary) or begin some other aggressive medical treatment, we only prolong an inevitable event.

"With John, we have done all that is humanly possible to extend his life, and now nature is in charge. I think it may not be long before your husband will begin to experience some of these changes. Anticipating this with him, I am now recommending that orders be written to take no aggressive action should his heart, breathing, or blood pressure fail. Do you understand and feel comfortable with this decision?"

While this dialogue is likely to lead to some further questions, clarification and family education, it is surprising how clearly and easily the necessary answers unfold. To avoid this dialogue is to potentially compromise the patient's and family's wishes to whim of circumstance, leaving them no opportunity to see your knowledge of impending death, and leaving them unaware and unprepared. While the family may initially express reluctance and want more time to further consider the recommendation, with few exceptions, when properly prepared they will understand and accept the proposal. In cases where reluctance persists long, the following may help:

"I can understand your desire to prolong your husband's life as long as possible. We all want our family with us for as long a time as we can have them. But there is something else we have to consider. Suppose that we somehow bring John back—what happens then? We've now done CPR and given him some powerful medications; perhaps we've used the "shock paddles" to shock his heart back into action, or put him on a breathing machine to keep him alive longer. Now what? We still know that John is dying, and he will die shortly no matter what we do.

"Death is never easy. However, the moment of passing is usually remarkably calm. In most instances, the patient is unconscious and peaceful at that time. But _getting_ there is quite another thing. There is the fatigue of struggling to breathe and respond, and the labor of hanging on. While that is a natural and expected part of the process of leaving this life, it is not easy. It doesn't seem fair that we put John through this longer than is necessary, when we can't hope for anything more than just putting him through it all over again. What do you think? What would John want?"

Gentle, insightful dialogue such as this can gradually help family members to turn from their own personal fears and feelings of loss to the feelings, concerns, and fears of the patient. With rare exception, the family will begin to see beyond themselves and turn their thoughts and hearts to letting go.

Hospice

For patients and their families who recognize that there is nothing more for curative medicine to offer, there is hospice. The general intent of most hospice programs is to maximize a patient's _in-home_ time with family members, and, as one program notes, "to enable the patient to live in dignity through symptom control, pain relief, and emotional support." Some persons want very much to remain at home up to and even including the time of death. In such situations, hospice programs can provide medical staff, counseling, care-giver respite services, and a wide range of other support services. Typically limited to persons with prognoses of from 6 to 12 months, hospice programs deal with those who know they are dying and who have elected not to seek any further aggressive medical treatment beyond comfort care.

Because most hospice programs have waiting lists, prompt referral— _after_ patient preparation and understanding of program purposes have been made clear—is important. I have often heard family members state, "I just wish we could have become involved in the hospice program earlier—they have provided so much support." Prompt patient education and program contact, when prognostic criteria have been met, can be a valuable gift for a physician to give.

Extrapolation of Techniques

An interesting corollary to the rules for delivery of "bad" news was discussed in a brief column entitled "Ways of giving good news"

(Wofford, 1991). Drawing from similar principles as those outlined in this chapter, the writer noted that even the receipt of "good" news can be stressful at a difficult and tense time. For example, the author notes that patients with "persistent symptoms" may be "disappointed at not being able to document their suffering by a diagnostic test." In that event, "the explanation of how time, alternative tests, a repeat test, and empirical therapy fit into the plan should be presented." In short, mastering the skills for delivery of "bad" news can also enhance your ability to deliver "good" news.

The management techniques described in this chapter can have broad applicability in a variety of other settings and can continue to serve you well as you develop them further. Notice of terminal illness is not unlike the delivery of any other traumatic news, be it chronic disease, disfigurement, infertility, disability, or actual death. Similar principles apply and should be regularly used.

Medical Training

Numerous researchers and physicians point to the need for further training in the area of terminal care management for all medical professionals.[71] Several emphasize this need both at the undergraduate and postgraduate levels, with one suggesting ongoing education.

For all involved—including families and medical staff—dealing with the news of impending death is challenging and difficult. Knowing that the time is not far off does not necessarily make it easier. No single formula can provide all the answers for all situations, so learning how to better manage and cope with death and loss is an ongoing process. My hope is that this book will contribute to that process.

---

[71] Charlton, R.C. "Breaking bad news," *The Medical Journal of Australia*, 1992; 157:615-621.

Graham, J.R. "Touching and imparting of bad news," *Lancet*, 1991; 337: 1608-1609.

Graham, S.B. "When babies die: death and the education of obstetrical residents," *Med Teacher*, 1991; 13: 171-175.

Holdaway, J. "The management of dying patients in New Zealand Coronary care units," *New Zealand Medical Journal*, 1985; 98: 639-641.

Souhami, R.L. "Teaching what to say about cancer," *Lancet*, 1978; 2: 935-936.

Sykes, N. "Medical students' fears about breaking bad news" (letter), *Lancet*, 1989; 2:564.

Case Vignette 12.6

A Family's Plea

My husband had had a pain below his chest for several weeks and finally went to see his GP. At first the doctor thought that he had pulled a muscle, but on a second visit took a blood test. The doctor then decided that my husband should go to a specialist at our local hospital, and he was subsequently taken in for a biopsy.

The specialist then told my husband that he had liver cancer and nothing could be done for him. He died ten weeks later. I regret that the specialist told my husband without first telling me or asking me to be present and that he was so blunt about it. I also felt it negative to give no treatment of any kind, as I feel there are many alternative treatments that could have been tried and that might have given hope. Soon after my husband told me the result of his biopsy, a friend advised me to get in touch with Macmillan* nurses. I went and asked my GP how to contact them and he told me they would not be needed yet and did not seem to know where they were based. I then rang a cancer charity in Edinburgh who told me that they were in the same hospital where the specialist was based and had a part-time cancer doctor working with them.

I got in touch and from that time their support was invaluable. They are, in fact, not just nurses but specialists in the treatment of cancer and also counselors. The nurse who called at the house regularly soon realised that my husband was in far more pain than he would admit to the doctor and arranged for him to have increased painkillers. When later he was given drugs to combat sickness, constipation, etc., she was able to tell me whether the way he reacted to them was normal. She gave me her telephone number, and I was able to ring her at home any time I needed advice. I find it sad to think that the specialist does not send his patients along the passage to see the Macmillan nurses as soon as he has had to tell them that they have terminal cancer. The doctors appear not to want to recognise that these nurses can help the patients and families more than they can.

My husband did not need much nursing until the last week. Although he might have been a little more comfortable with a special bed, bed pans, etc., in a hospital, I am sure the fact that we could be with him most of the time in a normal way, and not as a hospital visit, made up for that. I was able to sleep in the same bed with him right until the day he died.

The world makes us feel that dying is unacceptable. Those who live to a great age are congratulated so that conversely those who do not are almost regarded as failures. . .[72]

* Similar to Visiting Nurses in the U.S.

---

[72] Adapted from a letter to _The Natural Death Centre_, as printed in _The Natural Death Handbook_, 1993, London: Virgin Books.

Part III

Research Presentation

Chapter 13

Formal Research Examined

Introduction

One research participant wrote about her feelings regarding the loss of her son and the emotional trauma she experienced from the manner in which she was notified of his death. She noted the following:

> My son was killed two years ago, in another state—a gunshot wound to the face. When I first talked to the physician I was told that he was on a respirator, he was not in any pain, and if pain occurred they would be able to control it. I was also told he was seen by a neurosurgeon, and that it had been decided they would not operate to remove the bullet at that time.
>
> I was also told that his pupils were fixed and dilated.
>
> I am a nurse and have worked in an emergency room for more than four years. However, because this was my own child, I did not grasp the fact that he was [brain] dead. I was also asked about organ donation, and I told the physician I did not want to make a decision at that time.
>
> Two hours later I was phoned again by the physician, asking me to make a decision about organ donation. I told him I did not want to make a decision about it unless my son died [brain-death]. He responded, "Lady, he is already dead; he's been dead for four hours."
>
> Why didn't he tell me this at first? I was tempted to tell him what to do, to and with himself! But as a nurse I did want to help someone else if my son was dead, so I gave him my permission for organ donation over the phone, with another nurse listening, as a witness.
>
> I would prefer a chaplain or a nurse tell me if another member of my family dies.[73]

Much has been written about death and dying, and the associated grieving processes necessary. However, very little has been written in the form of guidelines for the professional who is managing the initial notification of the death. The social and psychological aspects of post-notification grief are detailed to the point of redundancy, but where are the suggestions and guidelines for those primarily responsible for

---

[73] Research participant, 1988.

initiating this difficult and important process we call grieving? Would it not seem important that the process be begun properly? Which of the many elements involved are the most critical?

Several questions need to be addressed. Should notification be made by phone if the family is located some distance from the hospital? How far *is* "far" when you must decide whether to call family members in for notification and to view the body, or to tell them on the phone? If next of kin obviously live too far away to come to the hospital, should local law enforcement personnel be requested to assist by going to the family's home to personalize the notification, rather than deliver the notification by phone? Would the contact with an officer in uniform unduly upset the family further?

How do you find out if the person you reach by phone is home alone, or even able to come in, without the questions leading to a premature notification? Should notification be made late at night to ensure that the family is notified promptly? Would the family be hostile if the notification were delayed, leading them to believe that information was being withheld from them for some reason? Who should be responsible for notification and making these decisions? And, finally, what is an acceptable protocol for the verbal process itself?

After observing hundreds of death notifications in the course of my profession—many of which were far from ideal—I became moved to study what families wanted and needed at this delicate time, to provide the answers to these questions.

Assumptions

In this work, I assumed that: 1) most people are stable and fairly well adjusted, 2) the bearer of the news will be able to evaluate a family's needs and be able to tailor the discussion accordingly, and 3) the most important time to assist family members with a crisis is at the time they are experiencing it most acutely.

Research Format

Design

The research design employed to study the subject was a survey. I chose this approach because of the minimal information available in the literature about staging and making notification of unexpected death. Consequently, the research design required an exploratory format, delving into many areas not previously studied.

Content

In addition to the questions relating to death notification, subjects were asked to provide demographic and personal history data, including: a) age, b) gender, c) ethnicity, d) gross total family income, e) education completed, and f) previous experience with the loss of an immediate family member.

Research Subjects

The survey was given during 1988 to 400 people, all in the Sacramento, California area: 200 health care professionals exposed to traumatic injury and death on a daily basis, 100 college students in a Death and Dying course, and 100 family members and friends of someone traumatically injured, or taken suddenly seriously ill. This latter group provided the perspective of people intimately involved with the issue at hand. To ensure that the sample surveyed was representative of the population seen in the Trauma Center, the participants were limited to families and friends of patients admitted to the hospital via the Emergency Room at the University of California, Davis, Medical Center, Sacramento. There was no direct patient contact; only those accompanying the patient(s) were approached. Of these, only those 18 years old and older were permitted to answer the questionnaire. Families and friends who were approached were contacted either in the Emergency Room waiting area or in the various floor or intensive care waiting areas of the hospital.

Special consideration was given to this family/friends group, in that the survey was administered only after it had been determined that the patient would indeed survive the injury or illness. This criterion ensured both that the family and/or friends were not unduly upset by exposure to the questionnaire's content, and that they would be free of the distracted, shock-state thought patterns associated with the initial news.

After they completed the questionnaire, all subjects were assessed to ensure that there were no adverse reactions to the content of the survey. Any concerns were promptly addressed and resolved.

Weaknesses

Ideally, the survey should have been administered directly to families who had actually experienced a sudden death in recent weeks so that answers reflected their factual, personal experience. However, because of concern about the additional emotional distress such administration might produce and possible bias (due to a previously experienced method of notification), it was decided to select the subjects as detailed here. Further, it would have been helpful to have obtained a more thorough family death history for each subject than time allowed.

Although these weaknesses are worthy of note, they should not significantly jeopardize the research results. To a large extent, the anecdotal reports I have included throughout this text give personal verification to the statistical analysis.

Analysis of the Data[74]

Demographic Commentary

After analysis of the data, it became clear that certain points should be noted regarding the sample participants.

The group includes disproportional representation by women (73.7%) and Caucasians (79.5%). Health professions continue to be dominated by Caucasian women, and women have begun to represent a significantly larger portion of those attending colleges and universities.

In addition, the sample sizes of the other ethnic groups were uncomfortably small. Although no single group numbered fewer than 20 people, larger samples of the ethnic groups would have been preferable, and the validity ascribed to these findings should be weighed accordingly.

Other variables—age, income, education, and death history—appear to be well represented and should offer a high degree of validity for a general population.

Table I

Demographic data for all groups combined:[75]

Age:	Average = 31.8 years Range = 18 to 70 years of age
Gender:	Male = 26.3% Female = 73.7%
Ethnic origin:	White = 79.5% African-American = 6.6% Hispanic = 5.3% Asian = 5.8% Other = 2.8%
Income:	Average = $35,000 Range = < $15,000 to > $55,000+
Education:	Average = 6.853 (or 2.8 years of college)

---

[74] Research findings are reported here in a reader-friendly format. Anyone seeking further academic and scholarly details may contact the author through the publisher.

[75] When totals do not equal 100% for any category, the remaining fraction should be attributed to participants' unanswered items.

Death history:

A. Loss of immediate family member:
Yes = 61.1%[76]
No = 38.9%

(of those who answered yes to "A," above)
B. Lived in your home at the time of death:
Yes = 34.0%
No = 66.0%

(of those who answered yes to "A," above)
C. Was the death "expected"?
Yes = 43.3%
No = 56.7%

Bellwether Groups

In the brief analysis that follows, reference is occasionally made to three "bellwether" groups, the views of which provide unique perspectives on the data. They are identified as:

A. The **combined group**. This is the total sample, 400 participants.

B. The **unexpected death group**, defined as those participants who had previously experienced the *unexpected* death of an immediate family member ("immediate" = parent, sibling, child, or spouse). There were 135 participants in this category.

C. The **family/friend group**, defined as family/friends who were surveyed at the hospital at the time their loved-one was being attended to in the emergency room or intensive care unit, total of 100.

From these groups, we can draw inferences better illuminating how one should proceed with a notification, matching its timing, staging, and manner of delivery to the family's wishes.

---

[76] The young group of students had experienced fewer deaths than the other two groups.

Survey Opinions

There were 15 specific questions asked of all participants. In this section the general consensus of opinion is presented for each, with commentary.

Part I. For this section, assume only the following:

Someone in your family has experienced a sudden injury or illness. An ambulance has transported him/her to the hospital Emergency Room. All treatment efforts there have failed, and your family member was pronounced dead at the hospital.
A staff person has spoken with everyone involved with the medical treatment, and has a clear description of the major events leading to the death. Your phone number has been found with his/her belongings.

Please answer the following: (circle your answers)

1. Upon the death of a family member, I should be contacted immediately, regardless of how late at night it is.

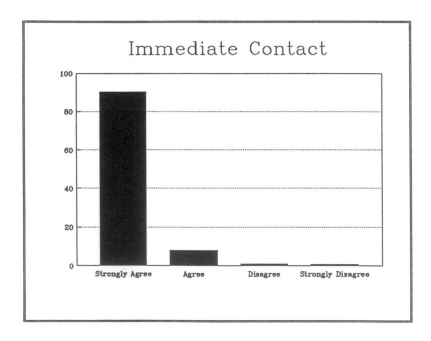

Strongly Agree	Agree	Disagree	Strongly Disagree
90.3%	8.0%	1.0%	0.7%

This revealed the single most universally agreed-upon factor in the staging process of a notification. All groups *strongly agreed* that they should be contacted immediately—90.3%. While those 65 years of age or older only selected *strongly agree* by a margin of 78.9%, the remaining 21.1% responded that they *agreed* with this statement. Thus it appears that immediate family contact would be universally appropriate in the absence of other mitigating circumstances.

2. I should not be told about the death of my family member until I arrive at the hospital.

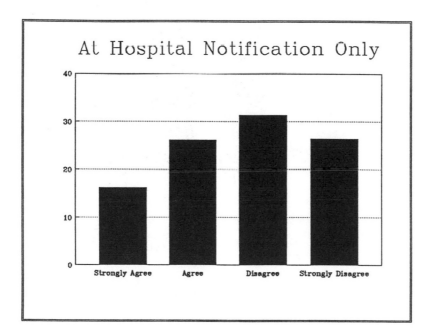

Strongly Agree	Agree	Disagree	Strongly Disagree
16.6%	25.3%	31.2%	26.9%

The consensus *disagreed* or *strongly disagreed* with this statement but only by a combined margin of 57.6%. With ambiguity on the part of the respondents, this leaves room for interpretation by the professional making the notification as to when and where the statement should be made. Examples of the inconsistency in answers: those over 65 tied between *strongly agree* and *strongly disagree,* and the Family/Friend bellwether group tied between *strongly agree* and *disagree*.

3. I should be told only that information which I specifically request.

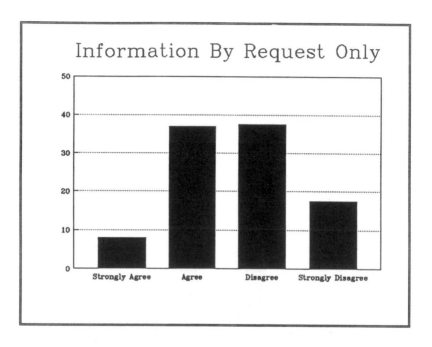

Information By Request Only

Strongly Agree	Agree	Disagree	Strongly Disagree
7.9%	37.0%	37.5%	17.6%

Again, the consensus *disagreed* with this statement but only by a narrow margin: *disagree* = 37.5%, and *agree* = 37.0%. Even summing the selections of *strongly disagree* and *disagree* provided a response of only 55.5%, and all three bellwether groups were near ties between *agree* and *disagree*. Given this recurrent ambiguity, it would appear that participants want professionals to use their judgment in disclosing traumatic details of the death.

4. The caller should voluntarily give all available information about the death without requiring that I specifically request it.

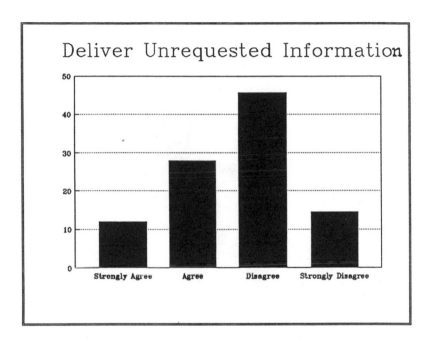

Strongly Agree	Agree	Disagree	Strongly Disagree
11.7%	27.9%	45.7%	14.7%

Considering the response to item three, it would seem that a greater portion of the subjects would agree with this statement. However, that was not the case. Consensus *disagreed* with this statement, as well, and did so by a wide margin: *disagree* = 45.7%, *agree* = 27.9%. Although young people voiced a greater interest in full disclosure of information, the response to this item clearly indicates that the notifier should use sensitivity in imparting the details of injury and death.

5. I am to be notified of the death by phone, and the caller discovers that I am home alone. The notification should then be delayed until I am able to contact someone to come and be with me.

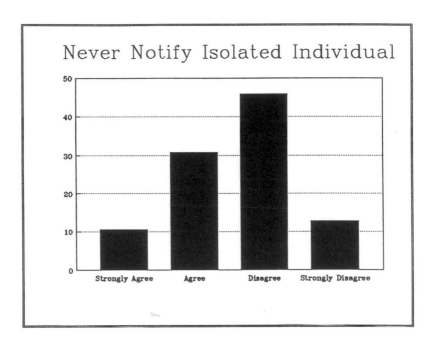

Strongly Agree	Agree	Disagree	Strongly Disagree
10.4%	30.9%	45.9%	12.8%

The most frequent response to this item (45.9%) *disagreed* with the statement. The most noticeable exception to this was the over-65 age-group, 42% of whom *strongly agreed* with the statement. One could speculate that elders were concerned regarding their own health and physical ability to deal well with the news. It should be noted, however, that the next most common selection, at 36.8%, was not *agree* but *disagree*, and that the Unexpected Death group survivors selected *disagree* and *strongly disagree* by a combined margin of 71%.

6. Upon the death of a family member, the hospital should contact local law enforcement authorities and have an officer come to my home to make a face-to-face notification of the death.

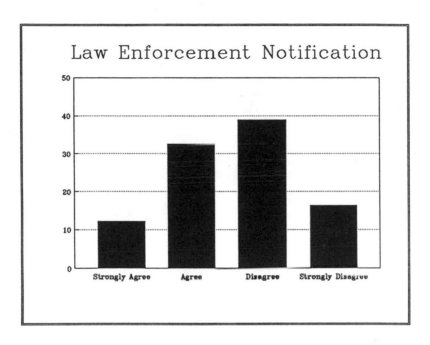

Strongly Agree	Agree	Disagree	Strongly Disagree
11.5%	32.6%	38.9%	17.0%

By a rather narrow measure, the subjects *disagreed* (38.9%) with this statement, versus 32.6% for those who *agreed*. It should be noted, however, that two bellwether groups (Unexpected Death and Family/ Friends groups) selected the *agree* response somewhat more than the other choices (34.4% and 34.3%, respectively). Certainly under some circumstances, a face-to-face notification is required—for example, when only minor children are available for contact; often, law enforcement staff are the only means of providing such a notification. The narrow margin of opinion in the overall group clearly demonstrates some reticence on the part of the public to have such officers make notification, when not otherwise constrained to do so.

Part II: For this section, assume <u>only</u> the following:

You receive a telephone call from the hospital, and the caller states:

"Hello. This is (caller's name) from the hospital. Is this (your name)?"
You respond, "Yes."
"Your (family member) was brought here with (an injury or illness), and we would like you to come to the hospital if you could." You ask how (s)he is doing.
"Well, I haven't had an opportunity to speak with his/her physician yet. When you arrive I will locate the doctor and we can tell you more then."
"Is (s)he alive?" you ask.
"(S)he is in the Emergency Room now. We'll be able to tell you more when you get here."
"O.K.," you respond, "I'll be right there."

Please circle your answers.

7. If you later discovered that the caller already knew that your family member was dead, would you be angry that (s)he didn't tell you then?

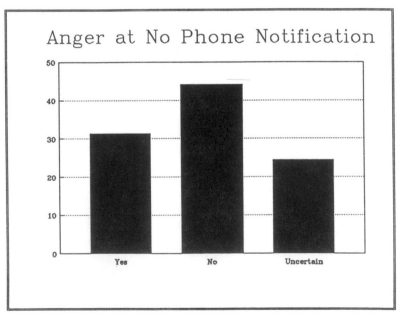

Yes	No	Uncertain
31.3%	44.2%	24.5%

The majority of the respondents stated they would *not* be angry. Only the college students, responded with a *yes,* and this by a margin of only 3% over the *no* selection, their second most common response. In practice, it would appear that families can understand a delay in the actual notification. In my experience I have never had a family become angry if my prior knowledge of the death came up in conversation.

8. You must travel some distance to reach the hospital. You would prefer to be told of the death over the phone if the travel time was greater than: (circle one answer)

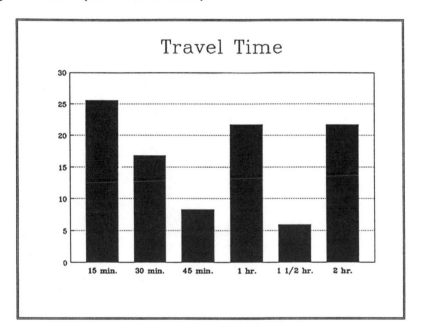

Travel Time

15 min.	30 min.	45 min.	1 hr.	1½ hrs.	2 hrs.
25.7%	17.4%	7.7%	21.7%	5.8%	21.7%

There was a great variety in these answers. Most responses clustered about the *15 minute* (25.7%), *1 hour* (21.7%), and *2 hour* (21.7%) responses, with the most frequent choice being *15 minutes.* Ironically, the under-25 age group that had expressed a slight preference for full telephone disclosure in question four was more willing to wait two hours for death notification in this scenario. The *2-hour* response was also selected somewhat more frequently by those over 65 but not by a large margin. In essence, it appears that most were unsure how they felt, but generally did not want to be left in ignorance for too long.

Upon questioning participants following the administration of the questionnaire, most *15-minute* respondents stated they would rather have been told over the phone, and most *2-hour* respondents *never* wanted to be told over the phone.

9. When you arrive at the hospital, you are shown to a private room. Here you are to be told of the death. Who would you choose to tell you: (circle one answer)

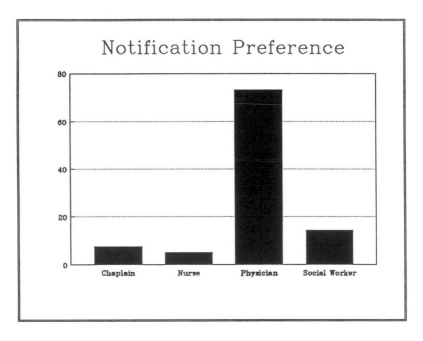

Chaplain	**Nurse**	**Physician**	**Social Worker**
8.0%	4.6%	73.3%	14.1%

There was tremendous preference for the *physician* to notify. This was by a very wide margin of 73.3% to 14.1% in all groups. However, in talking with participants after the survey, most indicated that this selection was based on their desire to meet the physician and be told the medical facts surrounding the death, and was not to indicate that notification should be made by physicians only.

The next most common person selected was the *social worker*, who was selected as second-place choice 26 of 30 times. Surely this would indicate a favorable response to having a social worker present at or making the notification. Of course, it may also reflect, to some degree, my participation in administration of the questionnaire.

10. Would you like to view the body at this time?

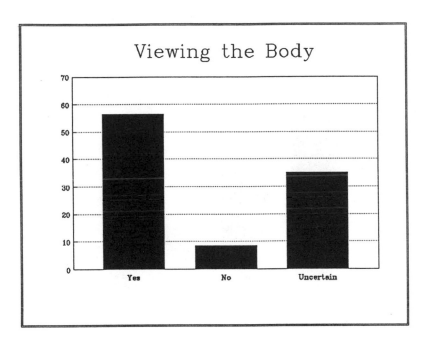

Yes	No	Uncertain
56.5%	8.5%	35.0%

Participants also responded to this question with a strong desire to view the body—*yes* = 56.5%, *uncertain* = 35.0%. The only exception was the 65 and older age-group, who tied their *yes* response with *uncertain*. Following administration of the questionnaire, with rare exception, those who expressed reservation about viewing did so with the comment, "It depends on the condition of the body." Therefore, it would seem that, if properly prepared, most people would want to view the deceased.

11. Upon the death of a family member, how likely is it that you would give permission for organ/tissue donation?

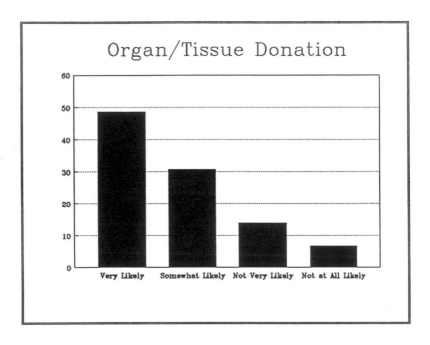

Very likely	Somewhat likely	Not very likely	Not at all likely
48.6%	30.8%	13.2%	7.4%

Respondents selected *very likely* and *somewhat likely* by a margin of 79.4%. Generally speaking, most people responded very favorably to the question. Notable exceptions were the following groups: *not very likely* = males, 21.0%, and Asians, 28.6%.

Part III: Please rank the elements of notification noted here in their order of importance to you, one (1) being the most important and four (4) being the least important.

12. How you were told (carefully vs. bluntly). ____

    1 = 50.0%   2 = 27.5%   3 = 13.0%   4 = 9.5%

13. Where you were told (at home, hospital, etc). ____

    1 = 5.1%   2 = 18.2%   3 = 35.2%   4 = 41.5%

14. When you were told (how quickly you were notified). ____

    1 = 42.0%   2 = 35.0%   3 = 15.7%   4 = 7.3%

15. By whom you were told (physician, chaplain, etc.). ____

    1 = 5.1%   2 = 19.0%   3 = 34.2%   4 = 41.7%

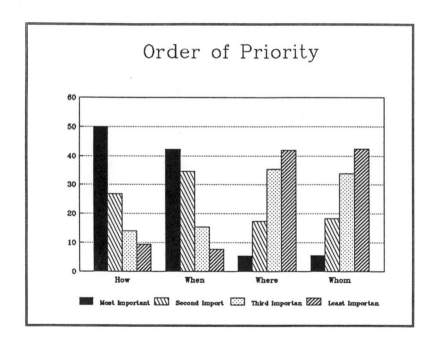

How people were notified was the ***most important*** variable. Demographically, the only substantial subgroup which did not pick this as the most important were those in the 45-54 age range, who selected it as the second most important factor in notification.

When was clearly the ***second*** most important variable by a generous margin. Again, the only exception were those 45-54 in age who selected this variable as first in importance to them.

Where people were told was ranked as the ***third*** most important element of the four, narrowly edging out the selection of who made the notification.

With mixed results, ***by whom*** was chosen to be the ***least important*** to the family, although the next most frequent choice placed it third.

Research Summary

As the data were analyzed and grouped, they showed a definite profile of public opinion. This information, combined with the perspective of practical experience, was used to identify an optimum method for the notification process.

In reviewing the results obtained, it was noted that certain groups differed from the norm more often than others, particularly: age under 25 and over 65, and, to a smaller degree, those of highest and lowest income and education. Although not represented by substantial number in the participant population, Asians, African-Americans, and Hispanic persons also seemed to hold differing views. It may be useful, at some future date, to more fully research these groups to identify specific profiles that could assist in tempering the emotional stress of the notification process for each.

Conclusion

The need for information and expertise in death notification is a serious one: Just one unpleasant "case vignette" is one too many. It is my hope that *Death Notification* will fill the void in professional literature and training, providing authoritative information backed by sensitive and thorough research.

Appendices

Appendix A

Telephone Contact Checklist[77]

Patient name: **Birthdate:**   **Age:**   **Sex:**

Relative name:
Tel:
Relationship:

Relative's name:
Tel:
Relationship:

Presenting problem:

Time of onset:

Time of arrival:

> **Data from family:**
>
> Medication allergies?
>
> Current medications?
>
> Medical history?

Condition: ___Critical   ___Serious   ___Fair   ___Good

Vital signs

Consciousness:
___ awake, alert
___ awake, groggy
___ semiconscious, confused
___ unconscious but follows simple commands
___ unconscious but responds to stimuli
___ unconscious, unresponsive

Breathing:
___ normal
___ rapid/slow, labored
___ requires oxygen
___ assisted by respirator
___ dependent on respirator

Pulse:
___ normal
___ slower/faster than normal
___ erratic and uneven

Blood pressure:
___ normal and stable
___ lower/higher than normal
___ fluctuating and unstable

Suspected injury sights:

Intact areas/functions:

Comfort/discomfort:

Visual description:

---

[77] Adapted from "Telephone Notification of Relatives of Emergency and Critical Care Patients," Mark Robinson, MSW, *Annals of Emergency Medicine*, November 1982. Used with permission.

Appendix B

Tissue Donation Protocol

Donation
The opportunity for donating eye and other tissues should be offered to a deceased's next-of-kin in accordance with your hospital's policy. Eye and tissue donation can take place from 6 to 12 hours after death, even up to 24 hours following cardiopulmonary arrest (asystole), depending on the circumstances.

If next-of-kin find whole eye donation objectionable, corneal tissue donation can be offered as an alternative. Explain that the cornea is a small (11.5 mm in diameter by 1 mm thick) piece of tissue that sits on the front of the eye like a watch crystal. This tissue alone can be excised, leaving the remainder of the eye intact.

Consent
Once verbal consent is given, have next-of-kin sign a permission form that must be witnessed and signed by two other people (family members and/or hospital staff). Specify in writing *whole eye* or *cornea only* donation, as well as all other tissues to be donated, for example, tendons or cartilage.

Contact Information
Have available a copy of the signed consent form. Most eye and tissue banks are required to have the signed consent accompany every tissue donation. When calling a tissue bank about a donation, you should report the following:

    — Hospital name
    — Caller's name and telephone number
    — Name and age of donor
    — Time and cause of death
    — Whether the donor is on a ventilator
    — Tissue for donation authorized on the consent form
    — Location of the donor's chart and body
    — Contact person's name, if other than caller

Most tissue banks will obtain the donor's complete medical history from the referring physician or nurse. Tissue bank staff may also need to contact the family about past medical and social history, so a telephone number where family may be reached is vital.

Medical Preparation

Two (2) red-top tubes of the donor's blood are required for necessary testing. Usually tissue bank staff will draw this when the tissue is procured. If the donor has received blood transfusions within the last 48 hours, however, a pretransfusion blood sample may be required (often found in the hospital's own blood bank for transfusion blood-typing).

If blood has already been obtained, please label the tube with the donor's name and tape it to the donor's ankle.

Donor Preparation

It is recommended that the following preparations of the donor be made:

— Elevate the head
— Apply Neosporin Ophthalmic solution, sterile saline, balanced salt solution (BBS), gtt OU, or Lacrilube ointment OU, (to the eyes)
— If necessary, lightly tape the eyes shut with paper tape
— Place ice packs over both lids (latex gloves filled with chipped ice work well)
— Refrigerate the body as soon as possible

The tissue bank will usually notify your hospital of the approximate time for tissue retrieval. They always act as quickly as possible to prevent any delay in funeral arrangements. A thoughtful letter will typically be sent to hospital staff and family members, thanking them for the donation.

Eye and Tissue Donor Criteria[78]

Always call your local tissue bank for case-specific criteria and individual evaluation for _any_ donation. In general, however, the medical history should _not_ include: AIDS or high risk for HIV as defined by the Center for Disease Control; viral or bacterial encephalopathies such as rabies or meningitis; hepatitis; certain malignancies (see below); sepsis (bacterial, viral, or fungal); neuroencephalomyelopathy; or any disease of unknown etiology. Additional tissue-specific criteria include the following:

---

[78] Sierra Regional Eye and Tissue Bank, 1700 Alhambra Blvd., Suite 112, Sacramento, CA 95816.

Tissue: Bone
  Recovery time: Up to 24 hours
  Tissue specific medical contraindications: Autoimmune disorders, toxic
    exposure, all malignancies except basal cell cancer of skin

Tissue: Cartilage
  Recovery time: Up to 24 hours
  Tissue specific medical contraindications: Same as for bone, plus
    Herpes Zoster

Tissue: Dura Mater
  Recovery time: Up to 24 hours
  Tissue specific medical contraindications: Same as for bone

Tissue: Eye or Corneas
  Recovery time: Up to 12 hours
  Tissue specific medical contraindications: Only the following malig-
    nancies—leukemias, lymphomas, carcinomas metastatic to the
    brain, retinoblastoma, history of disease or eye surgery to
    anterior segment, such as cataract

Tissue: Ear ossicles
  Recovery time: Up to 24 hours
  Tissue specific medical contraindications: Same as for bone

Tissue: Facia lata
  Recovery time: Up to 24 hours
  Tissue specific medical contraindications: Same as for bone

Tissue: Heart valves
  Recovery time: Up to 12 hours
  Tissue specific medical contraindications: Same as for bone, plus
    significant chest wall injury, history of rheumatic fever, significant
    valvular heart diseases

Tissue: Saphenous veins
  Recovery time: Up to 12 hours
  Tissue specific medical contraindications: Same as for bone, plus
    atherosclerosis, trauma to the vessel(s), circulatory disorders,
    donor weight less than 100 pounds

Tissue: Skin
  Recovery time: Up to 12 hours
  Tissue specific medical contraindications: Same as for bone, plus
    donor weight less than 120 pounds, any malignancies of skin

Appendix C

Organic Donation Protocol

Criteria:

— Ages 0 to 70 years (Age-limiting criteria have changed rapidly in recent years, and this is expected to continue. Call a procurement agency for individual evaluation.)
— Maintain circulation to organs, and blood oxygen saturation
— Maintain an intact heart beat
— Brain death of known etiology
— Absence of HIV

Physician's goals for donor management:[79]

— Maintain systolic blood pressure of 90 mmHg or greater.
— For systolic blood pressure below 90, treat first with vigorous hydration using lactated Ringers (other crystalloid or colloid solution can be used at the physician's discretion).
— If hypotension continues after aggressive fluid therapy, begin Dopamine (400mg in 250cc's N/S), titrate to maintain blood pressure greater than 90mmHg systolic.
— If hematocrit is less than 30%, transfuse with one unit packed red blood cells.
— Urine output greater than 300cc's/hr usually indicates diabetes insipidus. Replace urine output cc/cc with lactated Ringers. Titrate pitressin (1-10 units) for UOP. May also use DDAVP IV (1-2 mcgs/hr.).
— After correction of volume depletion and hypotension, if donor is anuric or oliguric (adults, less than 30cc/hr; peds, less than 1cc/kg/hr) administer Lasix 10-40 mg IV.
— Body temperature must be maintained at greater than 33 degrees centigrade, rectal.

---

[79] Golden State Transplant Services, 1625 Stockton Blvd., Sacramento, CA 95816 (916)457-7672

Appendix D

Legal Next-of-kin Determination

For legal decisions made on behalf of a decedent, written permission must be obtained from the legal next-of-kin. These criteria become effective in executing the following:

—Decisions regarding application of life-saving measures
—Discontinuance of life-support systems
—Authorization for organ and tissue donation
—Release of a body to a funeral home or cremation facility
—Other circumstances may also apply.

The legal next-of-kin has been defined, in order of priority, as:[80]

1. Surviving spouse
2. Oldest adult son or daughter
3. Adult guardian of the eldest minor child
4. Either parent
5. Adult brother or sister
6. A guardian or conservator of the decedent at the time of the decedent's death
7. Any other person entitled by law to control disposition of the remains of the deceased.

---

[80] Decedent Affairs Department, UC Davis Medical Center, 2315 Stockton Blvd., Sacramento, CA 95817.

Appendix E

Organ and Tissue Donor Designation in the Absence of Legal Next-of-kin

Diligent Search Protocol

In cases where legal next-of-kin cannot be found in a timely manner, it is possible in most states to make an individual an organ donor without the consent of his or her family. This is done by following a "diligent search" protocol. While this is rarely done, I have seen it successfully carried out, and families have responded well to the exercise of this option. Of course, it is extremely important that you take adequate time to explain all the mitigating factors and location efforts to the family to ensure a good response.

The Golden State Transplant Services agency (GSTS) has provided the following guidelines for use in California. Procedures may differ in other states.

Background

The California Uniform Anatomical Gift Act, Health and Safety Code §7151.5 (West Supp. 1984) describes the manner in which individuals are authorized to make gifts if the person has not made a gift of his body pursuant to the act. The persons who are authorized, in order of priority stated, when persons in prior classes are not available at the time of death, and in the absence of actual notice of contrary indications by the patient or actual notice of opposition by a member of the same class or a prior class, may give all or any part of a deceased patient's body for any purpose specified in other sections of the code:

1. The spouse
2. An adult son or daughter
3. Adult guardian of the eldest minor child
4. Either parent
5. An adult brother or sister
6. A guardian or conservator of the patient at the time of the patient's death

7. Any other person authorized or under obligation to dispose of the patient's body, including an attorney in fact appointed by the patient pursuant to a Durable Power of Attorney.

Section 7151.5 (West Supp. 1984) describes the steps to be taken to determine the nonavailability of persons authorized or under obligation to dispose of the body. If the hospital should make a determination that all of the persons authorized or obliged to dispose of the body are not available, a donation of all or part of the patient's body may still be made. Such a determination of nonavailability shall be made only by a hospital which is accredited by the Joint Commission on Accreditation of Healthcare Organizations (JCAHO).

The hospital shall certify nonavailability and shall authorize and specify the removal and donation of body parts. Such search shall include a check of local police Missing Persons records, examination of personal effects, and the questioning of any persons visiting the decedent before his death in a hospital, accompanying the decedents body, or reporting the death, in order to obtain information which might lead to the location of any persons who might be authorized to consent for such donation.

The search may begin prior to death, but determination of non-availability may not be made until the search has been underway for at least 24 hours, except if corneal material is to be recovered. The decision should be made by the hospital administration. Any such determination of nonavailability shall be made only after examination of all evidence leads to the conclusion that no relatives are available. Any such determination shall be subject to a review by such office as is designated by the board of supervisors of the county where the death occurred.

Procedure[81]

1. Upon notification of a potential donor, where there is no party available to give permission for a donation, the GSTS (or tissue bank) procurement coordinator shall determine from the hospital staff if a diligent search is underway to find family or other persons authorized to dispose of the body pursuant to §7151.5 of the California Health and Safety Code, as well as the length of time the search has been underway.

2. Following evaluation and acceptance of the patient as an organ donor, the GSTS (or tissue bank) procurement coordinator shall contact the administrator on call to request implementation of s/s 7151.6 of the California Health and Safety Code to allow organ and tissue donation.

---

[81] California Health and Safety Codes 7150-7157. California Hospital Association Memorandum, December 19, 1985, Hospital Protocol for Identifying Potential Organ and Tissue Donors.

3. The GSTS (or tissue bank) procurement coordinator will follow the customary procedure for organ and tissue donations at the hospital, including obtaining permission from the coroner for donation in all appropriate cases.

4. If approval for the donation is to be given by the hospital administrator on call, documentation shall be placed in the medical record of all attempts to determine availability of someone authorized to dispose of the body and the name of the hospital administrator granting permission for the donation.

Appendix F

Religious Views
On Organ Donation and Transplants

Amish: The Amish consent to transplantation if they know it is for the health and welfare of the transplant recipient. They are reluctant to donate their organs if the transplant outcome is known to be questionable.

Buddhism: Buddhists believe organ donation is a matter that should be left to an individual's conscience. There is no written resolution on the issue; however, Rev. Gyomay Masao, president and founder of The Buddhist Temple of Chicago and a practicing minister, says, "We honor those people who donate their bodies and organs to the advancement of medical science and to saving lives."

Catholicism: Catholics view organ donation as an act of charity, fraternal love, and self-sacrifice. Transplants are ethically and morally acceptable to the Vatican. Pope John Paul II has expressed considerable concern about donors' psychological and physical integrity, but he has not taken any position against organ transplants.

The Church of Christ Scientist: Christian Scientists do not take a specific position on transplants or organ donation. Christian Scientists normally rely on spiritual, rather than medical, means for healing. The question of organ donation is left to the individual church member.

Gypsies: Gypsies, on the whole, are against organ donation. Although they have no formal resolution, their opposition is associated with their belief about the after-life. Gypsies believe that for one year after a person dies, the soul retraces its steps. All of the body parts must be intact because the soul maintains a physical shape.

Hinduism: Hindus are not prohibited by religious law from donating their organs, according to the Hindu Temple Society of North America. This act is an individual decision.

Islam: In 1983, the Moslem Religious Council initially rejected organ donation by followers of Islam, but it has reversed its position, provided donors consent in writing prior to their death. The organs of Moslem donors must be transplanted immediately and should not be stored in organ banks.

Jehovah's Witnesses: According to the Watch Tower Society, the legal corporation for the religion, Jehovah's Witnesses do not encourage organ donation but believe it is a matter best left to an individual's conscience. All organs and tissue, however, must be completely drained of blood before transplant.

Judaism: Judaism teaches that saving a human life takes precedence over maintaining the sanctity of the human body. A direct transplant is preferred. According to Moses Tendler, Ph.D., an orthodox rabbi, "If one is in the position to save another's life, it's obligatory to do so, even if the donor never knows who the beneficiary will be."

Mormons: The Church of Jesus Christ of Latter-day Saints considers the decision to donate organs a personal one. Jerry Cahill, director of public affairs for the Mormon Church, says, "Mormons must individually weigh the advantages and disadvantages of transplantation and choose the one that will bring them peace and comfort. The Church does not interpose any objection to an individual decision in favor of organ and tissue donation."

Protestantism: Protestants encourage and endorse organ donation. The Protestant faith respects an individual's conscience and a person's right to make decisions regarding his or her own body. Rev. James W. Rassbach of the Board of Communication Services, Missouri-Synod, says, "We accept and believe that our Lord Jesus Christ came to give life and came to give it in abundance. Organ donations enable more abundant life, alleviate pain and suffering, and are an expression of love in times of tragedy." (Goss, 1987)

Appendix G

Media/Information Release Protocol[82]

<hr>

Introduction

Most patient-identifiable information is confidential and should not be released except as authorized by law or with the written consent of the patient or the patient's authorized representative. Particular care must be taken when the patient is a psychiatric or drug- or alcohol-abuse patient, because state laws and federal regulations prohibit the release of information about such patients to the public.

With the exception of the psychiatric or drug- or alcohol-abuse patients and other patients identified below, the items of information enumerated in section B may generally be released to the news media and public.

Please see Attachment 1 for guidelines on disclosures by type of injury, including the limitations on disclosures in battered/neglected child cases.

General Policy and Procedure

A. "No-information" Patients

If a patient is a "no-information" patient, then the information identified in section B should not be released, as in the following cases:

> 1. The patient or his or her authorized representative, requests that no information be released to the public (by means of a "Request to Withhold Public Release of Information" form).

> 2. The patient is a psychiatric, drug- or alcohol-abuse patient. This includes prisoner patients identified as psychiatric, drug- or alcohol-abuse patients. No arraignment coverage by media will be granted for these cases.

<hr>

[82]. Policy adapted from the University of California, Davis, Medical Center (Copyright, Regents of the University of California). Used by permission. Intended for informational use only. Consult a legal-risk management department for your state and facility's current protocol.

3. The patient is subject to a blackout request by a law enforcement or correctional agency for the protection of the patient and/or hospital staff. Blackout request patients generally fall into two subgroups:

a. Arrestees, prisoners, and inmates of other correctional facilities: No information may be made available to the public. Inquiries about such patients shall be referred to the agency having jurisdiction of the inmate.

b. Informers, alleged crime victims, suspects not under arrest and other persons in whom law enforcement agencies assert an interest: No information may be released to the public unless the patient, or his or her authorized representative, countermands the agency's blackout request.

B. Guidelines for Releasing Information—General Patients

The following information about patients (except for patients identified in section A) may be released to the public, including the news media, by hospital staff:

1. Name, city of residence, age, sex.

2. General reason for admission.

3. Patient's general condition. The patient's condition should be expressed in accordance with the criteria set out in Attachment 1, avoiding expressions involving medical judgment.

4. General nature of injuries. A brief general statement may be made as to how the incident allegedly occurred (i.e., auto accident, explosion), but no details should be given. It should not be stated or implied in any way that the injury was self-inflicted or that a patient was intoxicated. No statement may be made that a suicide or an attempted suicide has occurred. Except as otherwise provided in Attachment 1, the type and location of an injury may be given.

C. Photographs, Interviews, and News Media Requests for Additional Medical Information

The consent to photograph and/or interview a patient or to release detailed medical information concerning a patient must be in writing and signed by the patient, or, if the patient is a minor or incompetent, by the authorized representative. In addition, the medical opinion of the attending physician, that the patient's condition will not be jeopardized if photos are taken or interviews conducted, must be obtained.

D. Persons Responsible for Releasing Information

The hospital public affairs department is responsible for coordinating the release of patient information, including condition reports, to the news media between 8 A.M. and 5 P.M. The nursing supervisor will respond between 5 P.M. and 8 A.M. on weekdays. At all other times, on-call personnel in the public affairs department may be reached through telecommunications or the administrative officer of the day (AOD).

Certain cases will be referred to outside agencies (or other departments):

1. Coroner's cases: Requests for details other than routine information (all violent, sudden, or unusual deaths, and deaths suspected to be caused by criminal means) shall be referred to the coroner.

2. Crime victims and persons, other than arrestees, inmates, or prisoners who are subject to law enforcement blackout requests: When a patient is brought to the hospital for treatment by a law enforcement agency, even though not under the jurisdiction of the agency (e.g., informer, crime suspect not under arrest, alleged crime victim), a request for an information blackout for the protection of the patient and/or hospital staff may be signed by the agency representative. It remains in effect until the patient or his or her representative is able to sign the "Request to Withhold Public Release of Information" form. If the patient or his or her representative does not wish the information blackout continued, a new form must be signed requesting that the blackout be discontinued. All inquiries about the patient shall be referred directly to the hospital security department.

3. Prisoner patients: All inquiries about patients from the prison should be referred to the chief medical officer at the prison. All inquiries about patients who may be in the custody of the county sheriff's department should be referred to the medical detention ward. Even information regarding the patient's presence in the hospital shall be withheld if he/she is the subject of an information blackout.

a. Public arraignments held at the hospital must be conducted in conference rooms away from in-patient care units whenever possible. If the patient is too ill to be moved, and media coverage has been requested, a pool situation will be arranged by the media with the consent of the attending physician. One television camera, one print camera, and one reporter from each medium will be allowed.

b. Prisoner patients are identified by a pound symbol (#) on the hospital information system.

4. Juvenile inmates—CYA (Calif. Youth Authority): Inquiries about juveniles under California Youth Authority detention shall be referred to the Department of Youth Authority, Northern Reception Center.

E. Requests by a Patient or Next-of-kin to Restrict Release of Basic Information

1. Notice to patients of their right to restrict the release of information to the public (including the news media) is made through the Terms and Conditions of Service forms, although the patient's prior consent to the release of the basic information identified in section B is not required. Basic information should be released until and unless the patient or his or her representative completes and signs a "Request to Withhold Public Release of Information" form. (Except that "No-information" status is automatic for psychiatric and drug abuse patients and certain other patients identified in section A.)

2. It is the responsibility of the nursing department, upon receipt of a signed request to withhold public release of information, to immediately notify the patient identification section of the medical records department, telecommunications, hospital public affairs, nursing services, emergency room registration, bed control, and the front information desk.

3. The telecommunications department will call patient identification and ask that an asterisk (*) be placed next to the patient's name in the hospital information system. The asterisk identifies a "no-information" patient on the computer system.

4. To remove a restriction on the release of information, the patient must sign a second form authorizing release of the information. The telecommunications department will ask patient identification to remove the asterisk.

Attachment 1

Patient's General Condition:

1. *Treated and released.* Patient was treated and sent home.

2. *Good.* Vital signs are stable and within normal limits. Patient is conscious and comfortable. Indicators are excellent.

3. *Fair.* Vital signs are stable and within normal limits. Patient is conscious, but may be uncomfortable. Indicators are favorable.

4. *Serious.* Vital signs may be unstable, perhaps not within normal limits. Patient apparently is acutely ill. Indicators are questionable.

5. *Critical.* Vital signs are unstable and not within normal limits. Patient may be unconscious. Indicators are unfavorable.

6. *Deceased.* Announcement of death is not made routinely by the hospital. However, news of the death of a patient is public information *after* the family has been notified or after all reasonable efforts to notify the family have been made. The cause of death should not be reported unless it has been entered on the death certificate by the last attending physician or the coroner.

General Nature of Patient's Injuries:

1. Head injuries

   a. A statement that the injuries are of the head may be made.
   b. It may not be stated that the skull is fractured.
   c. No opinion as to the severity of the injury may be given until the condition is definitely determined.
   d. Prognosis is not to be made.

2. Internal injuries

   a. It may be stated that there are internal injuries, but nothing more specific as to the location or the condition of the injuries.
   b. A statement that the condition is good, fair, serious, or critical may be made.

3. Unconsciousness

   a. If a patient is unconscious when brought to the hospital, a statement of this fact may be made.
   b. The cause of the unconsciousness should not be given.

4. Poisoning

a. A statement may be made that the patient is being treated for suspected poisoning.
b. Information as to the trade name of poisoning substances must *not* be given; use generic names only, i.e., caustic, cleaning compound, etc.
c. No statement concerning the possibility of accident or suicide may be made.
d. No prognosis may be given.

5. Intoxication

No statement may be made that the patient is intoxicated or not, or whether the intoxication is by alcohol or other drugs.

6. Burns

a. A statement may be made that the patient is burned and the general location on the body may be given.
b. A statement may be made as to whether the patient has first-, second-, or third-degree burns, but only after diagnosis by a physician.
c. A statement may be made as to how the incident occurred, but only when the absolute facts are known.
d. No prognosis may be given.

7. Sexual assaults

a. Names may not be released.
b. No statement may be made concerning the nature of the incident or injuries.
c. General condition may be released.

8. Battered, neglected or sexually abused (molested) children

No statement may be made that a child's injuries appear to be the result of child abuse, even if an official report has been filed. However, the nature and extent of injuries may be released in accordance with preceding guidelines, including the comments regarding sexual assault.

9. Psychiatric patients or drug- or alcohol-abuse patients

No Information should be given. Federal regulations strictly forbid disclosure of any information about these patients, including information as to whether they are in the hospital or not. While reporters may have information from the police concerning persons who subsequently become mental or drug- or alcohol-abuse patients, it is recommended that all such inquiries be answered, "We cannot, under federal regulations, comment on this case."(Title 42 of the federal regulations, section 2.1)

10. Photographs

When representatives of either news media or law enforcement agencies request the privilege of photographing a patient in the hospital, such permission will be given if:

1) In the opinion of the attending physician the patient's condition will not be jeopardized, and
2) The patient signs a written consent.

Appendix H

Acute Symptoms of Grief

Common Signs and Symptoms of Grief Not Requiring Immediate Action

Physical

Nausea
Upset stomach
Tremors (lips, hands)
Feeling uncoordinated
Profuse sweating
Chills
Diarrhea
Rapid heart rate
Muscle aches
Sleep disturbances
Dry mouth
Shakes
Vision problems
Fatigue

Behavioral

Change in activity
Withdrawal
Suspiciousness
Change in communications
Changes in interactions
Increased/decreased appetite
Increased smoking
Increased alcohol intake
Overly vigilant
Excessive humor
Excessive silence
Unusual behavior

Cognitive

Confusion
Lowered attention span
Calculation difficulties
Memory problems
Poor concentration
Seeing an event over and over
Distressing dreams
Disruption in logical thinking
Blaming others

Emotional

Anticipatory anxiety
Denial
Fear
Uncertainty of feelings
Depression
Grief
Feeling hopeless
Feeling overwhelmed
Feeling lost
Feeling abandoned
Worried
Wishing to hide
Wishing to die
Anger
Feeling numb
Identifying with the victim
Survivor guilt

Common Signs and Symptoms of Distress
Requiring Immediate Corrective Action[83]

Physical

Chest pain*
Difficulty breathing*
Excessive blood pressure*
Collapse from exhaustion*
Cardiac Arrythmias*
Signs of severe shock*
Excessive dehydration*
Dizziness*
Blood in the Stool*
Excessive vomiting*

*Medical evaluation needed.

Cognitive

Marked Withdrawal into self
Difficulties making decisions
Hyper-alertness
Generalized confusion
Disorientation to person, place or time
Seriously slowed thinking
Serious thinking disruption
Suicidal thoughts
Homicidal thoughts
Problems in naming familiar things
Problems with recognizing familiar
    people

Emotional

Panic reactions
Phobic reactions
Inappropriate emotions
General loss of control

Behavioral

Significant change in speech patterns
Shock-like state
Crying spells
Antisocial acts (e.g. violence)
Extreme hyperactivity

---

[83] Material adapted from the UCDMC Critical Incident Stress Debriefing Team Training Manual. Unpublished manuscript, 1990.

Appendix I

Normal Grief Symptoms and How to Cope with Them[84]

Typical Grief Symptoms of the Recently Bereaved

Tension
This includes physical and emotional tension, such as being excessively "hyper" and unable to relax or sit still for very long, and muscle tremors or twitches.

Nausea, vomiting, or other gastrointestinal symptoms
This is especially common early on after a loss.

Body temperature regulation
Includes profuse sweating in cold conditions or chills in warm conditions.

Sleep disturbances
Either the inability to get to sleep, or disruptive dreams or nightmares, or waking up too early (or any combination thereof).

Fatigue
Feeling one can't move without great effort. Enormous weariness, even when there are things you want or need to do.

Crying
Experiencing tears flowing without reasonable personal control. Finding oneself tearful at unexpected moments.

Intrusive thoughts and memories
Thinking about incidents or memories, especially those that are unpleasant, when you don't want to.

---

[84] Material adapted from the UCDMC Critical Incident Stress Debriefing Team Training Manual. Unpublished manuscript, 1990.

Negative feelings
Unpleasant feelings that may come without warning, such as profound sadness, helplessness, fear, anxiety, anger, rage, discouragement, frustration, or depression.

Feelings of vulnerability or lack of control
Feeling exposed to threat or not in control of one's life anymore.

Interpersonal problems
Increased irritability, insensitivity, blaming others, wanting distance instead of closeness.

Increased problems with alcohol or drugs
The desire to "medicate" oneself can be a symptom of stress.

Compulsive behavior
Increased problems such as compulsive eating or other compulsive behaviors.

Vague feelings of self-blame
Usually this feeling identifies some real or imaginary intervention one "should" have made to delay or prevent the loss.

Coping Strategies

Express your feelings

Share your thoughts and feeling with someone you trust, even though it may be painful to do so. Make sure the other person understands you're not asking for a solution to your feelings, just an opportunity to express how you feel.

Pamper yourself

Take time out for something special and indulgent. Healing takes time and works best when it's nurtured.

Pace the pain

Painful and fearful thoughts and memories come back when you don't want them to. That's normal, but our first reaction is to keep this from happening. This procedure says let the memory or thought come back so that some of the release of tension can take place, and then decide when you want to stop it. You can even say to yourself, "Okay, that's enough!" Gradually you will gain more control over these intrusive thoughts and feelings.

Dreams and nightmares

Nightmares are a very common reaction to a traumatic loss, especially when the death was violent in some way. Although they can never be controlled completely, some people have learned to diminish night-mares by deliberately thinking about the trauma sometime before they go to sleep and then saying to themselves, "Okay, that's enough. Now, dream about something else." If you are having trouble sleeping, try reading or watching television. Insomnia will probably resolve itself in a few days.

Recognize self-blame and survivors' guilt

It is normal to feel some blame for just surviving a loss, especially if you were present where other people were killed or severely injured. Recognize this for what it is. It is okay to have survived.

Change the memory

If upsetting memories are troubling you after a particularly traumatic loss, remember that what is upsetting you is the memory itself, interfering with normal grief resolution. In such situations, you can attempt to change what you focus on. Try substituting a memory that has less painful emotions associated with it, one that your loved one would enjoy, too. For example, a memory of positive family interactions or a special vacation may be helpful.

Exercise
Moderate exercise after a loss is very useful, especially if you are already in good physical condition. Don't overdo it, however, and cause more harm than good. Walking is an ideal form of exercise for almost any age.

Get back to work
Return to work when it is realistic, but accept the jitters that you will feel with reminders of the incident. These are normal and will go away in time.

Decrease alcohol consumption
Many people feel a drink eases tension. However, alcohol is actually not useful to the body in coping with the stress of grief and loss.

Accept enjoyment and diversion
It is okay to enjoy yourself. Let your grief work go for a time. You don't have to grieve 24 hours a day, and enjoyable activities can provide welcome relief.

If necessary, ask for professional help
Sometimes grief is so severe that professional help is necessary to work it through. It is a wise person who recognizes the value of help. It takes a great deal of courage to work with a professional to face your own pain and fear. Be proud of yourself and not apologetic.

Don't expect "miracle cures"
Working through grief takes a long time, and it is never really finished, although it becomes much easier with time. Try to accept this part of you and put it in proper perspective with time.

The bottom line
The bottom line in dealing with grief is the requirement to face it. If it can be engaged squarely and dealt with in some constructive way, that is the greatest part of the task.

Appendix J

Resources for Bereavement

General Resources

The following national organizations can assist you in obtaining referrals to bereavement organizations in your area:

American Cancer Society — (800) 227-2345
American Heart Association — (800) 242-8721
American Lung Association — (212) 315-8700
American Red Cross — (202) 737-8300
Easter Seals Society — (202) 347-3066

Specific Resources

American Association of Suicidology: For family and friends of a suicide victim. National headquarters: 2459 South Ash, Denver, CO 80222. For referral to a local chapter, call (303) 692-0985

Sponsoring local suicide hotline services, the association also refers families and friends to local survivor groups. Annual conferences are held at various locations around the country in the fall. Suicide-specific bereavement literature is also available, as well as a quarterly newsletter for members.

Bereavement Publishing, Inc.: *Bereavement,* a monthly bereavement magazine. 8133 Telegraph Dr., Colorado Springs, CO 80920. (719) 282-1948.

The focus of this monthly publication is to provide families and friends with a forum for expressions of loss and coping. The publication also includes numerous referrals and resources. Or send for their 15-page resource guide, available for a nominal fee.

Candlelighters Foundation: Parent support group for those whose children are very sick or dying. 7910 Woodmont Ave., Suite 460, Bethesda, MD 20814. (800) 366-2223.

> A network of peer-support groups primarily dealing with parents who are losing a child to cancer. Many chapters do provide bereavement follow-up groups, literature, and other support.

Compassionate Friends: For parents who have lost a child, and surviving siblings. P.O. Box 3696, Oak Brook, Illinois 60522-3696. Call (708) 990-0010 for referrals to a local chapter.

> Compassionate Friends provides primary bereavement support through self-help groups organized in 675 chapters throughout the United States and the international community. While local chapters provide a variety of resources, membership in the national organization provides a quarterly newsletter, notice of upcoming conferences, and access to bereavement literature. All newly bereaved members will receive a resource packet upon request, listing available resources and a bibliography of applicable literature.

Continental Association of Funeral and Memorial Societies (CAFMS): A nonprofit, educational organization. 6900 Lost Lake Rd., Egg Harbor, WI 54209-9231. To locate the nearest memorial society, call (800) 458-5563 or (414) 868-3136.

> There are more than 150 memorial societies throughout the United States. Dedicated to simple, economical, and dignified funerals, many societies have arrangements with cooperating morticians for low-cost options. "No One Wants to Talk About Death" and nine other pamphlets written for consumers are available from the national office (please include a donation with your SASE). The national office lobbies for consumer protection in funeral matters and serves as an information network for local societies. A quarterly newsletter is available to subscribers.

Family Service America: A bereavement counseling referral network. 11700 West Lake Park Dr., Milwaukee, WI 53224. (800) 221-2681 or (414) 359-1040.

> This agency provides local referrals for counseling, bereavement resources, and literature only.

Fernside: A Center for Grieving Children. P.O. Box 8944, Cincinnati, OH 45208. (513) 321-0282.

> The center provides services primarily to children ages 3-17 who have experienced a loss in the immediate family. In addition to primary local services, the center also provides an international pen-pals forum, bereavement literature, family information packets, school information, etc. Also, notice of regional and national conferences via a newsletter is available.

International Federation of Widows and Widowers (FIAV): For more information, contact Aliette Bellavoine, La Presidente, 10 Rue Cambaceres, 75008 Paris, France.

> An international association to promote greater public understanding of the widowed and their children, and to promote publications and information to benefit them. Implements a conference every three years (1995 to be in the United States). Currently has a project to assist the widowed of Africa providing modest grants to demonstration projects at selected sites.

National AIDS/HIV Foundation Hotline: (800) 342-2437 or 342-AIDS. Spanish-speaking callers, (800) 344-7432. TDD, (800) 243-7889.

> This foundation is administered by the national Center for Disease Control (CDC), and provides 24-hour response. Via the hotline, callers can access a computer bank of information and referral resources, including resources for bereavement support in your area. The focus is, of course, loss due to AIDS and serves families and friends of infected parties both before and after loss.

National Share (Sharing Parents): A support group for those whose babies have died from conception through early infancy. St. Joseph's Health Center, 300 First Capital Dr., St. Charles, MO 63301. For referral to a local chapter, call (314) 947-6164.

> National Share is an organization of 240 local chapters which provide bereavement support to parents and surviving siblings after the prenatal or early postnatal death of an infant. The organization provides bereavement literature; notice of local, regional, and national conferences; and a bimonthly newsletter.

Parents of Murdered Children and Other Survivors: For surviving family and friends of victims of violent crime. 100 East 8th St., Suite B-41, Cincinnati, OH 45202. For local chapter referrals, call (513) 721-5683.

> A support group for survivors, preteen or older who have been intimately affected by the violent death of a loved one at the hands of another person. Service include monthly meetings, education and support in dealing with the grieving process and the criminal justice system, and notice of national and regional conferences. A newsletter is available to subscribing members.

Society of Military Widows: For surviving spouses and family of active duty or retired military persons. 5535 Hempstead, Springfield, VA 22151. (800) 842-3451.

> An organization affiliated with NAUS (National Association of Uniformed Services), dedicated to providing bereavement support to families of military personnel. Largely a social association, they do not sponsor formal support group meetings. Other services include political and legislative involvement, legal resource and benefits information, and referrals. Local chapters may have newsletters for members.

Sudden Infant Death Syndrome (SIDS) Alliance: A support service for parents having lost a child to SIDS, or "cot death." 10500 Little Patuxent Pkwy., Suite 420, Columbia, MD 21004. For referral to a local chapter, call (800) 221-SIDS.

> Services of this organization include bereavement self-help groups; bereavement literature; notification of local, regional, and national conferences; and a newsletter to members. A general information packet is available to bereaved families free of charge, with further information on request.

Widowed Persons Service: A support service for persons who have lost a spouse. 601 -E- St. NW, Washington, DC 20049. For referral to a local chapter, call (202) 434-2277.

> Affiliated with AARP, this agency is an outreach program in which trained widowed volunteers offer support to newly widowed persons of all ages. AARP/WPS identifies community leadership and resources that help persons recover from a spouse's death and to manage the myriad issues arising from that loss. AARP/WPS publishes a newsletter and sponsors regional and national conferences.

Appendix K

Family Funeral Checklist[85]

1. Decide on the time and place of the funeral or memorial service(s).

2. Make a list of immediate family, close friends, and employment or business colleagues. Notify each by phone.

3. If flowers are to be omitted, decide on an appropriate memorial to which gifts may be made. (Such as a church, library, hospital, school, or other charity.)

4. Write the obituary. Include age, place of birth, cause of death, occupation, college degrees, memberships held, military service, outstanding work, and a list of survivors in the immediate family. Give the time and place of the services. Deliver or telephone the information to the appropriate newspapers.

5. Notify insurance companies, including automobile insurance, for immediate cancellation and available refund.

6. Arrange for members of the family or close friends to take turns answering the door and/or phone. Keep a record of these contacts.

7. Make arrangements for visiting relatives and friends, including child care.

10. Coordinate food for the following days.

11. Consider special needs of the household, such as cleaning, which might be done by friends and family.

---

[85] From *Dealing Creatively With Death: A manual of death education and simple burial,* 12th edition, by Ernest Morgan. Barclay House, 35-19 215th Place, Bayside, NY 11361. (1-800-356-9315)

12. Select pall bearers, and notify each. (Avoid men with heart conditions or back difficulties; it may be appropriate to make them honorary pall bearers.)

13. Notify the lawyer and executor. Get several copies of the death certificate.

14. Plan for the disposition of the flowers after the funeral (a hospital or rest home, perhaps).

15. Prepare a list of distant persons to be notified by letter and/or printed notice, and decide which to send each.

16. Prepare the copy for a printed notice, if desired.

17. Prepare a list of persons to receive acknowledgements of flowers, calls, and memorial gifts. Send appropriate acknowledgements. (These can be written notes, printed acknowledgments, or a combination of both.)

18. Check carefully all life and casualty insurance and death benefits, including Social Security, welfare benefits, credit union, trade union, fraternal association, and military. Check also on income for survivors from these sources.

19. Check promptly on all debts and installment payments. Some may carry insurance clauses that will cancel them. If there is to be a delay in meeting payments, consult with the creditors and ask them for additional time before the payments are due.

20. If the deceased was living alone, notify utilities, the landlord, and notify the post office where to forward the mail. Take precaution against thieves at the home.

21. Remember, even though the person is deceased, it will still be necessary to file income taxes. Consult an accountant at some later date.

Bibliography

Bibliography

Aitken-Swan, J. & E. C. Easson. "Reactions of Cancer Patients on Being Told Their Diagnosis." *British Medical Journal*, 1959, vol. 1, pp. 783-799.

Albery, N., G. Eliot, & J. Eliot (Editors). *The Natural Death Handbook*, 1993. London: Virgin Books.

Anonymous physician. "Doctor, Watch Your Words." *Australian Family Physician*, 1991, vol. 20, no. 10, pg. 1481.

Aries, P. *Western Attitudes Toward Death: From the middle ages to the present*, 1974. Baltimore, MD: Johns Hopkins University Press.

Beis, E. B. *Mental Health and the Law*, 1984. Rockville, MD: Aspen Systems Corp.

Bergman, A. S. "Emergency Room: A role for social workers." *Health and Social Work*, 1976, vol. 1, no. 1, pp. 33-43.

Blumenfield, M., N. B. Levy, & D. Kaufman. "The Wish to Be Informed of a Fatal Illness." *Omega*, 1979, vol 9., no. 4, pp. 323-326.

Bowlby, J. "Separation & Attachment in Grief and Mourning." In *American Handbook of Psychiatry: New Psychiatric Frontiers*, by D. A. Hamburg and H. K. Brodie, 1975, vol. 6., chapter 14, pp. 292-309. New York, NY: Basic Books.

Bowlby, J. "The Making and Breaking of Affectional Bonds." *British Journal of Psychiatry*, 1977, vol. 130, pp. 201-210.

Brewin, T. B. "Three Ways of Giving Bad News." *The Lancet*, 1991, vol. 337, pp. 1207-1209.

Brieland, D. & J. A. Lemmon. *Social Work and the Law*, 2nd Ed., 1985. St. Paul, MN: West Publishing.

Buckman, R. *How to Break Bad News*, 1992. Baltimore, MD: Johns Hopkins University Press.

Burrows, A. "The Man Who Didn't Know He Had Cancer." *Journal of the American Medical Association*, 1991, vol. 266, no. 18, pg. 2550.

Capone, R. A. "Truth Telling: a cultural or individual choice?" *Journal of the American Medical Association*, 1993, vol. 269, no. 8, pp. 988-989.

Carey, R. G. "Weathering Widowhood: problems and adjustment of the widowed during the first year." *Omega*, 1979, vol. 10, no. 2, pp. 163-174.

Carlson, L. *Caring For Your Own Dead: A final act of love*, 1987. Hinesburg, VT: Upper Access, Inc.

Chandler, N. J. "How to Make a Lonely Place a Little Less Lonely: the ICU waiting room." *Nursing,* October 1982, pp. 47-50.

Charlton, R. C. "Breaking Bad News." *Medical Journal of Australia,* 1992, vol. 157, pp. 615-621.

Charmaz, K. C. "The Coroner's Strategies for Announcing Death." In L. H. Lofland (Ed.), *Toward a Sociology of Death and Dying,* 1976. Beverly Hills/London: Sage Publications.

Clark, D. "A Death in the Family: providing consultation to the police on the psychological aspects of suicide and accidental death." *Death Education,* 1981, vol. 5, pp. 143-155.

Clark, R. E. & E. E. LaBeff. "Death Telling: managing the delivery of bad news." *Journal of Health and Social Behavior,* 1982, vol. 23, pp. 366-380.

Clement, J. & K. S. Klingbeil. "The Emergency Room." *Health and Social Work,* 1981, pp. 83-90.

Collins, S. "Sudden Death Counseling Protocol." *Dimensions of Critical Care Nursing,* Nov-Dec 1989, pp. 375-385. Lakewood, CO: Hall Johnson Communications, Inc.

Cotsonas, C. E. "Informed Consent: Law, clinical reality, and the role of the physician." *Journal of the American Board of Family Practice,* 1992, vol. 5, no. 2, pp. 207-214.

Crase, D. & D. Crase. "Helping Children Understand Death." *Young Children,* 1976, vol. 32. no. 1, pp. 21-25.

Davidowitz, M., and R. D. Myrick. "Responding to the Bereaved: an analysis of helping statements." *Death Education,* 1984, vol. 8, no. 1, pp. 1-10.

Davis, J. "Soloing: breaking the news." *American Journal of Nursing,* 1983, vol. 83, no. 10, pp. 1457-1458.

Davis, J. M. "Hope or Hopelessness?" *Postgraduate Medicine,* 1990, vol. 87, no. 8, pp. 22-26.

Davis-Barron, S. "Cold Hard Death, Cold Hard Doctors." *Canadian Medical Association Journal,* 1992, no. 146(4), pp. 560-563

Dunkel, J., & S. Eisendrath. "Families in the Intensive Care Unit: their effect on staff." *Heart & Lung,* 1983, vol. 12, no. 3, pp. 258-261.

Engel, G. L. "Sudden and Rapid Death During Psychological Stress." *Annual of Intern Medicine,* 1971, vol. 74, pp. 771-782.

Epperson, M. M. "Families in Sudden Crisis: process and intervention in a critical care center." *Social Work in Health Care,* 1977, vol. 2, no. 3, pp. 265-273.

Fallowfield, L. "Giving Sad and Bad News." *The Lancet,* 1993, vol. 341, pp. 476-478.

Farber, J. M. "Emergency Department Social Work: a program description and analysis." *Social Work in Health Care,* 1978, vol. 4, no. 1, pp. 7-18.

Fins, J. "The Patient Self-determination Act and Patient-physician Collaboration in New York State." *New York State Journal of Medicine,* 1992, vol. 92, no. 11, pp. 489-493.

Fletcher, W. S. "Doctor, Am I Terminal?" *The American Journal of Surgery,* 1992, vol. 163, pp. 460-462.

Freedman, B. "The Validity of Ignorant Consent to Medical Research." *IRB Review of Human Subjects Research*, 1982, vol. 4, no. 2, pp. 1-5.

Freedman, B. "Offering Truth." *Archives of Internal Medicine*, 1993, vol. 153, pp. 572-575.

Gardner, D., & N. Stewart. "Staff Involvement with Families of Patients in Critical-care Units." *Heart & Lung*, 1978, vol. 7, no. 1, pp. 105-110.

Glick, I., R. Weiss, & C. Parkes. *The First Year of Bereavement*, 1974. New York, NY: John Wiley and Sons.

Golan, N. "Crisis Theory." In *Social Work Treatment*, 2nd Ed., Francis J. Turner (Ed.), 1979. London: Free Press.

Goldberg, R. J. "Disclosure of Information to Adult Cancer Patients and Issues and Updates." *Journal of Clinical Oncology*, 1984, vol. 2, pp. 948-955.

Goss, E. "Religious Views on Organ Donation and Transplantation." *Life Cycles*, Summer 1987, p. 17.

Graham, N. K. "Psychotraumatology: crisis therapy in the trauma room." *The Digest of Emergency Medical Care*, 1981, vol. 1, no. 5.

Greenberg, L. I. "Therapeutic Grief Work with Children." *Social Casework*, July 1975, pp. 396-403.

Greenlaw, J. "Talk About Not Talking." *Archives of Internal Medicine*, 1993, vol. 153, pp. 557-558.

Grollman, E. A. *Talking About Death: a dialogue between parent and child*, 1990. Boston, MA: Beacon Press.

Grollman, E. A. (Ed.) *Concerning Death: A practical guide for the living*, 1974. Boston, MA: Beacon Press.

Grollman, E. A. *Talking About Death*, 1976. Boston, MA: Beacon Press.

Groner, E. "Delivery of Clinical Social Work Services in the Emergency Room: a description of an existing program." *Social Work in Health Care*, 1978, vol. 4, no. 1, p. 1929.

Gwinn, M. E. "On Call Is Not Enough: social workers in the ER." *Hospitals*, December 1979, pp. 73-75.

Hall, J. "Remembering Philip: a mother's story of stillbirth." *Good Housekeeping Magazine*, March 1982, pp. 58-62.

Hall, M. N. "Law Enforcement Officers and Death Notification: a plea for relevant education." *Journal of Police Science and Administration*, 1982, vol. 10, no. 2, pp. 189-193.

Hansen, Y. F. "Development of the Concept of Death: cognitive aspects." (Doctoral dissertation, California School of Professional Psychology, Los Angeles, 1972). *Dissertation Abstracts International*, vol. 34, no. 2, pp. 853-854.

Hardt, D. V. *Death: The final frontier*, 1979. New Jersey: Prentice-Hall.

Harris, J. S. "Stressors and Stress in Critical Care." *Critical Care Nurse*, Jan-Feb 1984, pp. 84-97.

Healy, J. "Emergency Rooms and Psychosocial Services." *Health and Social Work*, 1981, pp. 36-43.

Helm, A. & D. J. Mazur. "Death Notification: legal and ethical issues." *Dimensions of Critical Care Nursing*, Nov-Dec 1989, pp. 382-385.

Hendricks, J. E. "Death Notification: the theory and practice of informing the survivors." *Journal of Police Science and Administration,* 1984, vol. 12, no. 1, pp. 109-116.

Herring, M. E. "Humor in the Management of Serious Medical Disorders." *Trends in Health Care, Law & Ethics,* 1993, vol. 8, no. 1, pp. 80-82.

Higgs, R. "On Telling Patients the Truth." In *Moral Dilemmas in Modern Medicine,* Lockwood, M. (Ed.), 1985. Oxford: Oxford University Press.

Hinchliffe, P. "Keeping Hope Alive." *Nursing Times,* 1991, vol. 87, no. 12, pp. 28-29

Hodovanic, B. H., D. Reardon, W. Reese, & B. Hedges. "Family Crisis Intervention Program in the Medical Intensive Care Unit." *Heart & Lung,* 1984, vol. 13, no. 3, pp. 243-249.

Holland, L. & L. E. Rogich. "Dealing with Grief in the Emergency Room." *Health and Social Work,* 1980, pp. 12-17.

Hollingsworth, C. E., & R. O. Pasnau. *The Family in Mourning: A guide for health professionals,* 1977. New York: Grune & Stratton.

Holmes, T. H., & R. H. Rahe. "The Social Readjustment Scale." *Journal of Psychosomatic Research,* 1967, vol. 11, no. 213.

Jackson, E. N. *Telling a Child About Death,* 1965. New York: Hawthorn Books.

Jackson, J. "Telling the Truth." *Journal of Medical Ethics,* 1991, vol. 17, pp. 5-9.

Jensen, A. H. *Healing Grief,* 1980. Redmond, WA: Medic Publishing Co.

Johnson, S. "Giving Emotional Support to Families after a Patient Dies." *NursingLife,* 1983, vol. 1, pp. 35-36.

Jones, W., & M. Buttery. "Sudden Death: survivors' perceptions of their emergency department experience." *Journal of Emergency Nursing,* 1981, vol. 7, pp. 14-17.

Kelly, D. F. "Religious Symbolism of Organ Transplants." *Health Progress,* 1987, vol. 11, pp. 52-57.

Krahn, G. L., et al. "Are There Good Ways to Give 'Bad News'?" *Pediatrics,* 1993, vol. 91, no. 3, pp. 578-582.

Kübler-Ross, E. *On Death and Dying,* 1970. New York: Macmillan.

Langlands, A. (1991). "Doctor, What Are My Chances?" *Australian Family Physician,* vol. 20, no. 10, pp. 1426-1430.

Laurent, C. "Finding the Right Person for the Job." *Nursing Times,* 1991, vol. 20, no. 12, pp. 27-28.

Lester, D. & A. T. Beck. "Early Loss as a Possible 'Sensitizer' to Later Loss in Attempted Suicides." *Psychological Reports,* 1976, vol. 39, pp. 121-122.

Lehman, D. R., C. B. Wortman, & A. F. Williams. "Long-term Effects of Losing a Spouse or Child in a Motor Vehicle Crash." *Journal of Personality and Social Psychology,* 1987, vol. 52, no. 1, pp. 218-231.

Leliaert, R. M. "Spiritual Side of Good Grief: what happened to holy saturday." *Death Studies,* 1989, vol. 13, pp. 103-117.

Lindemann, E. *Beyond Grief: Studies in crisis intervention,* 1979. New York: Jason Aronson.

Linn, E. *I Know Just How You Feel . . . avoiding the cliches of grief,* 1986. Cary, IL: Publishers Mark.

Lloyd, A. "Stop, Look and Listen." *Nursing Times,* 1991, vol. 87, no. 12, pp. 30-32.

Malamud, B. *The Stories of Bernard Malamud,* 1983. New York: Farrar, Strauss, Giroux.

Manning, H. "Sudden Death." *Nursing Mirror,* 1985, vol. 160, no. 18, pp. 19-21.

Matter, D. E. & R. M. Matter. "Developmental Sequences in Children's Understanding of Death with Implications for Counselors." *Elementary School Guidance and Counseling,* December 1982, pp. 112-118.

McFadden, S. D. "On Withholding Information from Patients" [Letter]. *The Pharos,* Summer 1991.

Merz, J. F., M. J. Druzdzel, & D. J. Mazur. "Verbal Expressions of Probability in Informed Consent Litigation." *Medical Decision Making,* 1991, vol. 11, pp. 273-281.

Merz, J. F. & B. Fischhoff. "Informed Consent Does Not Mean Rational Consent: cognitive limitations on decision-making." *The Journal of Legal Medicine,* 1990, vol. 11, pp. 321-350.

Michaels, E. "Doctors Can Improve on the Way They Deliver Bad News, MD Maintains." *Canadian Medical Association Journal,* 1992, no. 146(4), pp. 564-566.

Michalowski, R. J., Jr. "The Social Meanings of Violent Death." *Omega,* 1976, vol. 7, no. 1, pp. 83-93.

Miles, M., & K. Perry. "Parental Responses to Sudden Accidental Death of a Child." *Critical Care Quarterly,* 1985, vol. 8, no. 1, pp. 73-84.

Miyaji, N. T. "The Power of Compassion: Truth-telling among American doctors in the care of dying patients." *Social Science and Medicine,* 1993, vol. 36, pp. 249-264.

Monat, A., and R. S. Lazarus. *Stress and Coping: An Anthology,* 1977. New York; Columbia University Press.

Moonilal, J. M. "Trauma Centers: a new dimension for hospital social work." *Social Work in Health Care,* 1982, vol. 7, no. 4, pp. 15-25.

Montgomery, B. J. "Emergency Medical Services: a new phase of development," *Journal of the American Medical Association,* 1980, vol. 24, no. 10.

Morgan, E. *Dealing Creatively With Death: A manual of death education and simple burial,* 12th Edition, 1990. Barclay House Books. 35-19 215th Place, Bayside, NY. 11361 (1-800-356-9315).

Neils, R. "How People Grieve," 1976. Unpublished manuscript, Montana State University, Cooperative Extension Service.

Noyes, R. Jr., & D. J. Slymen. "The Subjective Response to Life-threatening Danger." *Omega,* 1979, vol. 9, no. 4, pp. 313-321.

Nursey, A. D., J. R. Rohde, & R. D. T. Farmer. "Ways of Telling New Parents about Their Child and His or Her Mental Handicap: a comparison of doctors' and parents' views." *Journal of Mental Deficiency Research*, 1991, vol. 35, pp. 48-57.

Papenbrock, P. L. & R. F. Voss. *Loss: How children and teenagers can cope with death and other kinds of loss,* 1990. Medic Publishing Co. P.O. Box 89, Redmond, Washington 98073.

Pellegrino, E. "Is Truth Telling to the Patient a Cultural Artifact?" *Journal of the American Medical Association*, 1992, vol. 268, no. 13, pp. 1734-1735.

Pennebaker, J. W. & R. C. O'Heeron. "Confiding in Others and Illness Rate Among Spouses of Suicide and Accidental-death Victims." *Journal of Abnormal Psychology,* 1984, vol. 93, no. 4, pp. 473-476.

Peppers, L. G. & R. J. Knapp. "Maternal Reactions to Involuntary Fetal/Infant Death." *Psychiatry,* 1980, vol. 43, pp. 155-159.

Persaud, R. "Breaking Bad News—comment on." *The Lancet,* 1993, vol. 341, pp. 832-833.

Peteet, J. R., et al. "Presenting a Diagnosis of Cancer: patients' views." *Journal of Family Practice,* 1991, vol. 32, no. 6, pp. 577-581.

Poster, E., & C. Betz. "When the Patient Dies: dealing with the family's anger." *Dimensions of Critical Care Nursing,* 1984, vol. 3, no. 6, pp. 372-377.

Quentmeyer, C. A. & J. B. Quentmeyer. "Social Work in Trauma Care," 1983. Unpublished master's thesis, California State University, Sacramento, CA.

Quill, T. E. & P. Townsend. "Bad News: delivery, dialogue, and dilemmas." *Archives of Internal Medicine,* 1991, vol. 151, pp. 463-68.

Rando, T. A. "Bereaved Parents: particular difficulties, unique factors, and treatment issues." *Social Worker,* 1985, vol. 30, no. 1, pp. 19-23.

Raphael, B. "A Primary Prevention Action Programme: psychiatric involvement following a major rail disaster." *Omega,* 1979, vol. 10, no. 3, pp. 211-226.

Resnik, H. L. P. & H. L. Ruben. *Emergency Psychiatric Care,* 1975. Bowie, MD: Charles Press Publishers, Inc.

Robinson, M. "Informing the Family of Sudden Death." *American Family Physician,* 1981, vol. 23, no. 4, pp. 115-118.

Robinson, M. "Telephone Notification of Relatives of Emergency and Critical Care Patients." *Annals of Emergency Medicine,* November 1982, pp. 37-39.

Sanders, C. M. "A Comparison of Adult Bereavement in the Death of a Spouse, Child and Parent." *Omega,* 1980, vol. 10, no. 4, pp. 303-322.

Sanders, C. M. "Effects of Sudden vs. Chronic Illness Death on Bereavement Outcome." *Omega,* 1982, vol. 13, no. 3, pp. 227-241.

Schonfeld, D. J. "Crisis Intervention for Bereavement Support: a model of intervention in the children's school." *Clinical Pediatrics,* Jan. 1989, pp. 27-33.

Schultz, C. A. "Sudden Death Crisis: pre-hospital and in the emergency department." *Journal of Emergency Nursing,* 1980, vol.6, pp. 46-50.

Shanfield, S. B. & B. J. Swain. "Death of Adult Children in Traffic Accidents." *Journal of Nervous and Mental Disease,* 1984, vol. 172, no. 9, pp. 533-538.

Sheskin, A. & S. E. Wallace. "Differing Bereavements: suicide, natural and accidental death." *Omega,* 1976, vol. 7, no. 3, pp. 229-242.

Silverman, E. "The Social Worker's Role in Shock-trauma Units." *Social Work,* July-August 1986, pp. 311-313.

Simpson, M. A. "Brought in Dead." *Omega,* 1976, vol. 7, no. 3, pp. 243-248.

Sinacore, J. M. "Avoiding the Humanistic Aspect of Death: an outcome from the implicit elements of health professions education." *Death Education,* 1981, vol. 5, pp. 121-133.

Slavin, L. A. "Communication of the Cancer Diagnosis to Pediatric Patients: impact in long-term adjustment." *American Journal of Psychology,* 1982, vol. 139, pp. 179-183.

Spencer, E., et al. "Death Notification." *Bulletin Amer. Acad. Psychiatry Law,* 1987, vol. 15, no. 3, pp. 275-281.

Staff. "Caring for Surviving Children." *Compassionate Friends Newsletter,* 1982, p. 1.

Stott, M. *Forgetting's No Excuse,* 1973, London: Faber and Faber.

Surbone, A., "Truth Telling to the Patient." *Journal of the American Medical Association,* 1992, vol. 268, no. 13, pp. 1661-1662.

Thomasma, D. C. "The Quest for Organ Donors: a theological response." *Health Progress,* 1988, vol. 9, pp. 22-28.

Thornton, G., K. D. Whittemore, & D. U. Robertson. "Evaluation of People Bereaved by Suicide." *Death Studies,* 1989, vol. 13, pp. 119-126.

Turner, J. T. *Violence in the Medical Care Setting: A survival guide,* 1984. Rockville, MD: Aspen Publications.

Ward, C. G. "The Die is Cast: telling patients they are going to die." *Journal of Burn Care and Rehabilitation,* 1992, vol. 13, pp. 272-274.

Weinberg, N. "The Health Care Social Worker's Role in Facilitating Grief Work: an empirical study." *Social Work in Health Care,* 1985, vol. 10, no. 3, pp. 107-117.

Wells, P. "Preparing for Sudden Death: social work in the emergency room." *Social Work,* 1993, vol. 38, no. 3, pp. 340-342.

White, M. L., & J. C. Fletcher. "The Story of Mr. and Mrs. Doe: 'You can't tell my husband he's dying; it will kill him'." *The Journal of Clinical Ethics,* 1990, vol. 1, pp. 59-62.

Whittaker, J. K. *Social Treatment,* 1974. Hawthorne, NY: Aldine Publishing.

Williams, W. V., J. Lee, & P. R. Polak. "Crisis Intervention: effects of crisis intervention on family survivors of sudden death situations." *Community Mental Health Journal,* 1976, vol. 12, no. 2, pp. 128-136.

Wofford, J. L. "Ways of Giving Good News—comment on." *The Lancet,* 1993, vol. 338, pp. 453.

Woodard, L. J., & R. J. Pamies. "The Disclosure of the Diagnosis of Cancer." *Primary Care,* 1992, vol. 19, pp. 657-663.

Worden, W. *Grief Counseling and Grief Therapy,* 1982. New York: Springer Publishing Co.

Zastrow, C. *The Practice of Social Work,* 2nd Ed., 1985. Chicago, IL: Dorsey Press.

Index

Index

*Upper Access publishes nonfiction books
to improve the quality of life and death.
Please call or write for our catalog.*

**Upper Access Books
One Upper Access Road
P.O. Box 457
Hinesburg, Vermont 05461**

For book orders from the U.S. and Canada
1-800-356-9315 (voice) or 1-800-242-0036 (fax)

All other calls
802-482-2988 (voice) or 802-482-3125 (fax)